NASTAWG.

The Canadian North by Canoe & Snowshoe

A Collection of Historical Essays

Edited by Bruce W. Hodgins
and Margaret Hobbs

'Nastawgan' is an Anishinabai word meaning
'the way or the route one must take to get
through the country.'

Betelgeuse Books
Toronto, Canada

Nastawgan is used with the consent of the Wilderness Canoe Association which publishes a quarterly journal of the same name.

Wilderness Canoe Association
PO Box 496
Station K
Toronto, Ontario
Canada M4P 2G9

Published by Betelgeuse Books
in co-operation with the
Ontario Recreational Canoeing Association
1220 Sheppard Avenue East
Willowdale, Ontario
Canada M2K 2X1

First Edition 1985 (hardcover) ISBN: 0-9690783-3-1
Second Printing 1987 (paperback) ISBN: 0-9690783-4-X

Betelgeuse Books
PO Box 1334
Station B
Weston, Ontario
Canada M9L 2W9

Canadian Cataloguing in Publication Data

Main entry under title:
Nastawgan : the Canadian north by canoe & snowshoe

Bibliography: p.
Includes index.

1. Canada, Northern - Description and travel -
Addresses, essays, lectures. 2. Canoes and
canoeing - Canada, Northern - History - Addresses,
essays, lectures. I. Hodgins, Bruce W., 1931-
II. Hobbs, Margaret.

FC70.N37 1985   917.1'04   C85-098989-2
F1012.N37 1985

Printed in Canada

Typeset and assembled by Directart Inc., Hamilton, Ontario

This volume is an acclamation of
the northern wilderness. Let us
strive for its survival.

The publisher gratefully acknowledges the contribution of Ria Harting who provided all the sketches for this book.

NASTAWGAN
The Canadian North by Canoe & Snowshoe

Edited by Bruce W. Hodgins and Margaret Hobbs

Foreword: Eric W. Morse

Foreword

Change in Wilderness Canoeing in Canada During the Past 65 Years

*From an address to the A.G.M. of
the Wilderness Canoe Association, March, 1984 by*

Eric W. Morse

I made my first wilderness canoe trip in 1918, just over sixty-five years ago. My memories of that trip are still vivid. The equipment was, of course, different from today's. The earliest maps, for instance, were less accurate as to rivers and lakes, in those days before aeroplanes and pilots had been released from World War I to start our first aerial mapping. Portages, on the other hand, were most faithfully portrayed, so that the map as a whole rather resembled a picture of an old fishnet hung up to dry. Dehydrated foods were practically non-existent till well after the war, making provisioning more difficult, and food a lot heavier to portage. Our mattresses consisted merely of bracken, and hemlock or balsam branches, spread under waterproof sheets. Light mountain tents were unavailable; our tents were large and heavy, if they were taken at all. Often we slept simply with heads under a mosquito bar, sometimes two beneath an overturned canoe. A candle in a can served as a flashlight. A copper trolling line was always out when crossing lakes, for we counted on any fish we could catch. Berries, too, were picked with a sense of purpose.

But beyond such matters of equipment was the difference in the sense of wilderness. In fact a canoe trip was a total wilderness experience. I cannot recall encountering other canoe parties until the early thirties. My most vivid wilderness image is the bird chorus, mostly warblers and thrushes, whose insect diet was soon to be killed off by sprayed insecticides. From five in the morning or earlier, every diminutive male was voicing, clamorously and rapturously, his own particular version of the territorial imperative, in chorus so loud that few could sleep through it. The ugly prophecy implicit in Rachel Carson's *Silent Spring* has since, tragically, been fulfilled.

Canoeing traffic increased appreciably after 1918 and again after 1945. I was slowly becoming aware that, at least in the pressure zones of Montreal and Toronto, we were unlikely again to experience the wilderness I had once been lucky enough to know.

Provincial Parks such as Algonquin and Killarney, designed to fence out developing interests such as mining and lumbering, for a time provided good canoe country free of developers, but even in that they failed: paradoxically, the Parks began attracting canoeists in such numbers as to defeat their end. A friend of mine, in one Park encountered no fewer than 300, not canoeists, but canoes— in a single day.

Trying to stem what was happening, Park authorities began to stipulate "designated campsites only," which only made these into dusty pockets. Canoe parties of as many as forty were admitted to Parks. On the more popular routes, often the portage path became marked out, like some sordid paper chase, by gum wrappers and orange peel. The business of loading and unloading at portage landings—even the simple matter of two parties passing on a narrow portage path—became seriously impeded.

This was change—not individual, trivial changes, but one big, almost revolutionary change. For the wilderness canoeist, at least in the east, could no longer find readily accessible canoe country. Not canoeing as such, but its essential milieu, had retreated.

In 1951 I joined a group of canoeing friends. Though a little long in the tooth, we were a strong if not yet fully experienced party, choosing to learn skills such as whitewater as we went along. There were no "schools" as yet set up for learning canoeing techniques—and we certainly did not want to take along guides, who already were becoming more proficient at fixing outboard motors than in adopting the strenuous regimen of an amateur canoe party.

In 1952 we decided to look at the Quetico region. From a camp that we made near the shore of Lake Superior we portaged the nine miles of the Grand Portage and paddled along the beautiful Border Lakes canoe route as far as Fort Frances at the west end of Rainy Lake. Here we were entertained by the local Chamber of Commerce, as being the first canoeing group that had paddled from Lake Superior to Fort Frances in recent years. In 1953 and 1954 we made two more exploratory trips in Quetico, during one of which we came upon a large sign erected by the Minnesota Historical Society, on the Grand Portage. The sign informed us that the portage path we were on had first been trodden by La Vérendrye in 1732, and had carried those voyageurs of the Northwest Company who were bearing trade goods from Montreal to Fort Chipewyan on Lake Athabasca, and fur pelts back. Every Canadian explorer of the west (Mackenzie, Fraser, David Thompson, and others)—in an age when there was no rail, nor air, nor motor means of travel, and when the only "highways" were rivers and lakes—had used this path. Running beside the Pigeon River, it ascended the thousand-foot rise from Lake Superior to reach the plateau on top where the continental divide lay, and whence the waters flowed west. This was their very path.

We were impressed by the reading of the sign and all were inspired, for our next year's trip, to attack the other end of this celebrated fur trade route, but without the labour of going over the thirteen-mile Methye Portage. That route headed east down the Churchill and Saskatchewan, and crossed Lake Winnipeg to pick up the Winnipeg River, connected to the Grand Portage by the water route we were already on.

In 1955 we therefore flew out to Ile à la Crosse near the source area of the Churchill River in northern Saskatchewan. In the next three weeks we descended the Churchill, Sturgeon-weir, and Saskatchewan Rivers for 500 miles, to take out at The Pas, Manitoba. We had seen so few other canoeists as to confirm our feeling that we did not really require wilderness by legislation: difficulty, danger, and occasional discomfort took care of its protection. Sigurd Olson, the most experienced of our party, said after the Churchill River trip that this was as good canoe country as he had ever paddled.

In 1957, looking for another route in the same general area, we scanned early journals during the winter months and planned next summer's route. Nearly 200 years earlier the Northwest Company had found that canoes sent up the Churchill and across the Methye Portage were likely to be blocked by ice in the higher lakes. The Company ordered David Thompson to explore a back route, whereby these lakes and the long thirteen-mile portage itself could be avoided. In 1796 therefore Thompson went up the Reindeer River, lying 20 miles east of Frog Portage, and continued northward for another 100 miles on Reindeer Lake. From its northern end he headed west then north via Swan Lake and the Blondeau River, which he ascended as far as possible, then portaged over to Wollaston Lake. The Fond du Lac River then led him into the east end of Lake Athabasca, not far from Fort Chipewyan. We followed Thompson's route, enjoying good canoeing with beautiful, wild scenery.

Over the next decade we canoed waterways along Superior's rugged north shore, across the top of Manitoba and Saskatchewan, and through the Territories, amounting in the end to a transcontinental paddle from Montreal to Alaska.

All this was mostly in Pre-Cambrian terrain, the Churchill and Fond du Lac so beautiful that we wondered why they had not been set aside as national parks.

And so the quest for good canoe country led on, shifting further north to the great rivers of the arctic and sub-arctic, where primitive wilderness still existed.

A less purely personal account would say, more succinctly, that change in wilderness canoeing in Canada during the past sixty-five years has been twofold: the retreat of wilderness in the eastern canoe country (Haliburton, Muskoka, the shore of Georgian Bay, Algonquin Park, and Temagami), which was more vulnerable to the population pressure from the large eastern cities—this was a qualitative change affecting only the wilderness environment once offered; and a quantitative change, extending the concept of canoe country into the areas of the Shield in the northern parts of the three prairie provinces, and eventually to the arctic and subarctic portions of the mainland.

E. W. M.
"Wildwood"
March, 1985

Introduction

Bruce W. Hodgins and Margaret Hobbs

The canoe, the snowshoe, the wilderness and the North are inextricably entwined with each other and with our Canadian heritage. This volume of essays explores this historic matrix. For generations the northern landscape has gripped the popular imagination, luring thousands of men and women from North America and abroad, to experience first hand its hardships and rewards. By canoe and by snowshoe, these adventurers have traced the routes of fur traders and prospectors, and followed the ancient portage trails and complex waterways of the native people, their *nastawgan*.[1] Their attraction to the North and their modes of travel have simultaneously reflected and inspired this country's northern tradition—a tradition which the late W. L. Morton argued lends itself indispensably to the uniqueness of Canadian history.[2] The North, the Shield, the Barrens, and the bush—these are all words which have influenced the collective psyche of Canadians, enhancing our cultural distinctiveness.

* * *

In this volume, we define the North in its broadest sense. Rather than restricting it geographically to the Northwest Territories and the Yukon, we consider the North as a territorially shifting entity and an imaginative construct. In our view, the historic North moves southward as one moves backward in time. We follow the North as it shifts through time and place. When the fur traders of the North-West Company assembled their great brigades with their long Montreal canoes to voyage into the interior, the *pays d'en haut*, or north country, began just above Lachine. Thus we include not only the region north of latitude 60, but also the northern portions of most of the provinces, and some areas even farther south. One of the articles, for instance, discusses an expedition in the 1830s from Georgian Bay to the Ottawa through present-day Muskoka, Haliburton, and Algonquin Park—hardly part of the North of the 1980s.

The concept of *nordicity*, as a scale for measuring "northness," was recently developed by Louis-Edmond Hamelin.[3] Based on such factors as climate, geography, vegetation, remoteness, economic activity, and population density, it provides a valid and innovative approach for identifying northern areas. We would add to Hamelin's index a psychological component for throughout this book the term North denotes a state of mind as well as certain material conditions.[4] Central to this revised notion of *nordicity* is the concept of wilderness. Indeed, as wilderness has shrunk and remoteness declined over time, so too have Canada's various Norths. The North is not a frontier. It is the wilderness beyond the interrupted agrarian frontier and the urban islands of mid-Canada. The North is not found along a line. It is a space with depth, a land full of lakes, rivers,

creeks, swamps, rocks and wildlife, a land of beauty ever threatened with extinction.

This study focuses primarily on travel in the northern wilderness, from
the perspective of the recreationalist, who canoed and snowshoed for pleasure,
and the professional—including the surveyor, scientist, and law enforcer—whose
career involved extensive movement about the North. Because of their apparently differing emphases on work and play, these two groups might at first seem
incongruous within the same cover. Yet we suggest that their motives and experiences were not so dissimilar. Whether one travelled as a recreationalist or in a
professional capacity, one could expect a good deal of arduous work to accompany
the peaceful pleasures of viewing nature or the thrills of running dangerous
whitewater. Moreover, the *choice* to participate was not simply the preserve of the
recreationalist. Indeed, most children were initially *sent* on recreational canoe
trips, while many professionals, such as J. B. Tyrrell and George Douglas, actively
pursued the opportunity to go North. With the notable exception of the elderly
David Thompson, whose 1837 travels were accomplished reluctantly, the scientists and other professionals examined here were lured North by hopes and dreams
similar to those of the recreationalist; only they relied on their careers rather than
on private money to facilitate their journeys.

Another important group of individuals, whose work also bound them
closely to the North were the voyageurs, chief factors, trappers, and clerks of the
fur trade. These people are beyond the immediate scope of our study, but they
nevertheless hover about in the background, along with the northern natives and
Métis. Such northern veterans proved invaluable to the success of many of the
wilderness trips we examine. While the white men stationed at Hudson's Bay
Company posts provided the travellers with companionship and supplies, the
Indians, Métis, and Inuit usually played crucial roles as guides, teachers, hunters,
and labourers. In some cases, as a few of our authors suggest, the northern natives
were further depended upon to steer the travellers safely through life threatening
rapids. In other cases, however, the whitewater skills of the adventurous southerners were clearly remarkable.

The earliest expedition discussed in this volume is David Thompson's
1837 survey undertaken for the British government. As the century wore on,
public servants with refined wilderness skills (and varying whitewater skills) were
increasingly roaming the North, charged with the tasks of exploring, surveying,
and mapping the land. Of particular note were the employees of the Geological
Survey of Canada, who, from about the 1870s through the early years of the
twentieth century, commonly canoed and snowshoed about the near, middle, and
far North in voyages of staggering lengths and incredible difficulty. They were
joined around the turn of the century by a number of Mounted Policemen, who
left their horses behind on the prairies, learned to canoe, snowshoe, and manage
a dog team, to venture far into the Northwest. With some earlier exceptions,
canoe tripping in the North for purely recreational purposes began in the 1870s,
becoming a popular and significant summer pastime well before World War I.

This volume ends, somewhat arbitrarily and not too precisely, at 1950. Exceptions will be noted in the pieces by Bruce Hodgins and William James, which dip into a later period for certain selective purposes, and in John Wadland's article, which is theoretical and not bound by periodization. Otherwise, the historical descriptions and analyses stop at 1950, since the decade of the fifties represents a watershed in the history of recreational canoeing. It was in the late 1920s that the volume of canoe trips undertaken by adults peaked, and it was largely children at summer camps who sustained the activity throughout the 1940s and 1950s. During these later years, wilderness tripping was at a low point, having been seriously curtailed by numerous phenomena, including the Second World War. Despite the appearance late in the fifties of an important group of reflective northern canoeists that included Eric Morse and Pierre Elliott Trudeau, it was not until the 1960s and especially the 1970s, that the quantum leaps in recreational wilderness canoeing involving all generations of Canadians occurred. The ebb and flow in the volume of recreational canoeing prior to this enormous growth is, in fact, a topic which some of our authors examine and attempt to explain.[5] Snowshoeing almost ceased as a recreational activity by the 1940s. In the late sixties, its cousin cross-country skiing underwent a surge in popularity and by the 1980s there was even a modest revival in snowshoeing.

When wilderness canoeing experienced its resurrection in the sixties and seventies, its nature was altered by postwar advances in transportation, communication facilities, and southern technology, all of which inevitably hastened the erosion of the northern solitude. It was only after 1950, for instance, that airplanes played any central role in the entry and egress of northern expeditions. During the later decades of the period we examine, bush planes were sometimes used for canoe trips in the far North, but were rarely associated with tripping in the near North. Moreover, during the 1930s and 1940s nearly all canoeists paddled in canvas-covered wooden canoes of between 15 and 17 feet in length. Most of these vessels were manufactured in Ontario's Peterborough county, New Brunswick's Fredericton (home of the Chestnut), Quebec's Loretteville, or Maine's Old Town. Grumman aluminums were only just appearing, while fiberglass, ABS, and Kevlar canoes had yet to become significant, if they existed at all.

We therefore leave our readers at a juncture of northern recreational history, as well as in the midst of a period of rapid change in the North. Following the northern defense controversies of the Second World War and the Cold War, Diefenbaker's northern vision and Richard Rhomer's plan for a mid-Canada development corridor enjoyed a certain popularity but did not signify any real change in lifestyles and thought processes. But somewhat later, the 1968-70 sovereignty crisis triggered by the discovery of oil in Alaska was one of several manifestations of a dramatic reawakening of Canadian interest in the North. Ironically, the surging number of northern canoeists and wilderness preservationists were confronted with a nation intensifying its commitment to northern resource development.

*   *   *

The contributors to this book sought to rescue from the footnotes of history the stories of numerous generations of wilderness travellers. Where did they go? Perhaps more significantly, *why* did they go? While the tracing of routes has proven generally straight- forward, the uncovering of motives has not. Hence answers to the second question are diverse and often impressionistic; they may emerge subjectively for each reader by the end of the volume. In their search for understanding, several authors reveal a complexity of meanings and motives, related to the search for adventure, the pursuit of pleasure, the need for challenge, the yearning for escape from the concrete of urbanism to a more natural environment, the spiritual and mythical quest, and the Herculean-like voyage of personal testing into the unknown.

Many of the notable northern adventurers of the decades before World War I, such as David Hanbury and Warburton Pike, came from abroad. Intending to explore a far-off exotic place, they could expect to later write about their expeditions for a growing and eager world-wide English-speaking audience. The Thelon and the Porcupine in Canada's far Northwest were, in their minds, similar to the Khyber Pass in India's Northwest Frontier or the Upper Nile of Uganda in "darkest Africa." Such places were just beyond the outposts of the Empire, at a time when imperialism was still a good word. The canoe and the dog team were thus analogous to the camel and the yak. Later it would be different; the market for colourful accounts of wilderness travel would be less extensive. Yet the actual voyages into the personal unknown continued and even expanded in number and diversity.

Herein lies the mystery. Somehow the wilderness, made experiential by the canoe and the snowshoe, became and remains, as John Wadland suggests in his article, an ironic but essential part of Canada's urban-centred way of life. Certainly, it is no accident that recreational canoe tripping was initially an urban, upper middle-class and later a broad (though often professional) middle-class phenomenon. Canoe tripping was never a majority recreation, rarely a significant spectator sport, always a participatory activity. The recreational exploration of the wilderness logically grew alongside the growth of cities. Urbanism, even metropolitanism, and wilderness travel expanded together. And in recent decades, the increase in wilderness activities and the struggle for wilderness preservation have developed a symbiotic relationship. Especially in the early 1970s, the rapid expansion of environmental movements and of remote, extensive adult canoe tripping converged. Urban sophisticates were involved in both activities, and frequently their leaders were post-war immigrants from Britain and the continent.

Not surprisingly then, the wilderness traveller of the past and present frequently displays an inner tension resulting from a simultaneous commitment, both personal and political, to the "natural" and to the urban world. This tension was acknowledged by many of the wilderness seekers discussed in this volume and is examined by some of the authors. Struggling to reconcile two such antithetical states of existence, a compromise was, and still is, found by many to exist in the various conservation and environmental movements. Although the term "conservation" was not coined until 1902, earlier adventurers like Caspar Whitney and Warburton Pike played an important part in its evolution as a concept and a movement. Conservation, preservation, and ecology, though not identical, are concepts united by their implicit condemnation of the raw and limitless exploitation of nature.[6] While conservationists fight for controls on the extent and pace of development and against waste, preservationists go further in demanding that certain wilderness areas be exempt entirely from the ethos of progress. Some would also restrict access to these designated preserves to those willing to accept nature entirely on its own terms. In contrast, an ecological perspective demands much more radical restructuring of our values and priorities, a total rejection of the anthropocentric world view which lies at the heart of urban industrialism. While the philosophical and political positions of our contributors vary on these issues, the travellers under study generally ascribed to the more moderate views.

*   *   *

Some of the travellers described in this book voyaged through the rough country of the southern reaches of the Shield. Others wandered with a purpose through the treeless Barrens, north to the Arctic Ocean and east to the remote sounds of northern Hudson Bay. Because of the special interests of the authors, the book highlights specific geographic areas. These include in the far North the huge Thelon watershed emptying into Baker Lake and Chesterfield Inlet, and in the near North the headwaters country of Ontario's Temagami Forest. Historically, major expeditions in the Barrens attracted considerable public attention. Of no less importance, however, were the thousands of personally memorable but frequently unsung voyages of personal discovery by youth campers or adult vacationists on the Temagami waterways. In addition, the Peterborough-Kawartha area is featured as an early centre of both canoe building and canoe racing. We also follow travels through the James Bay watershed and down the remote Coppermine and Porcupine Rivers.

In the first essay of this collection, William James addresses some fundamental questions concerning the nature and meaning of the wilderness canoeing experience. Through application of the heroic quest pattern featured in classical mythology, the canoe trip is revealed as a voyage of personal, as well as territorial, discovery; the canoe becomes a vehicle for exploring the landscape of the mind. The author leaves us pondering both the positive and negative implications of the questing process and the spiritual transformation it involves. The quest theme is an integral one in this volume, often echoed in other authors' accounts of specific travellers.

The second article, by Ned Franks, follows David Thompson in 1837 on his last major canoe expedition through the precambrian bush country in what is now the middle latitudes of Ontario. Thompson, one of the earliest and most skilled public servants to survey the wilderness by canoe, was by this time an older man with serious misgivings about the task that lay ahead. In examining the records he left, Franks reveals the suffering and discouragement Thompson endured, the magnitude of his accomplishment, and the character of the North he traversed.

Four authors next look at specific travellers voyaging mainly in the Barren Lands. George Luste provides an historical survey of travel throughout this awesome region and a thoughtful consideration of its appeal. Margaret Hobbs examines the sudden surge of recreational, scientific, and government interest in the Barrens beginning on the eve of the 1890s. John Jennings highlights the Mounties' use of the canoe and their role in the far North by recounting the little known voyage of Inspector Ephrem Pelletier, who crossed the Barrens via the Hanbury–Thelon route in 1908. The next article features a somewhat more familiar name in northern history, George Mellis Douglas. Removing Douglas from the shadow of the nortorious John Hornby, Shelagh Grant explores his background and personality, his draw to the Coppermine River, and suggests his significance as a veteran traveller in the North.

The roster of names usually associated with northern exploration reads like a membership list to an exclusive all-male club. Yet in the next essay, Gwyneth Hoyle samples the part that women have played in roaming the northern wilderness. Defying the conventions of their time, the women she describes canoed, snowshoed, or walked about the North, sometimes in the company of men, other times with a female friend, and in one instance, unaccompanied.

We then turn to several considerations of recreational canoe tripping, its sustained attraction for a variety of individuals and organizations, its assorted purposes and its varying techniques. Bruce Hodgins examines several decades of canoe manuals in an effort to determine and analyze the advice people received about how to canoe, where to canoe, what types of canoes to use and whether to fear and avoid or confront and enjoy whitewater. Linking the manuals to the expansion of youth camping, he considers the philosophic rationale underlying the adult-led canoe trips for boys, and somewhat later, for girls. Why, he wonders was it frequently perceived as important and healthy for young people to escape into a cleaner, more natural environment? And how did the powerful Euro-Canadian idea of progress fit into the scheme? Was the youth supposed to experience the unspoiled wilderness in order to encourage him or her to help preserve it, or was the youth expected to play a future part in taming, subduing, or exploiting the North?

In Jamie Benidickson's article, further insight is provided into these and other questions, with an examination of the nature and extent of recreational canoeing's popularity during the years between the two World Wars. The essay which follows, by Bruce Hodgins, discusses the role of the Temagami area, including its summer youth camps, in sustaining the tradition of wilderness canoeing over many decades.

In Craig Macdonald's article, the focus on recreational canoeing in the Temagami area is continued, but from a very different perspective. This essay explains the contributions of Temagami's native people in establishing the ancient *bon-ka-nah* and *onigum*, the winter and summer trails and portages, *nas-tawgan* now used by recreationalists.

John Marsh then discusses the importance of Peterborough, Ontario, as a major centre for canoe building, especially in the nineteenth and early twentieth centuries. Of particular interest is the information he provides about the famous "Peterborough canoe." This craft was popular among recreationalists locally and preferred by many travellers for far northern expeditions. Recreational canoeing of a different sort than the wilderness tripping featured elsewhere in this volume is highlighted in Jean Murray Cole's article. Focusing primarily on the 1883 canoe regatta on Stoney Lake near Peterborough, the author introduces us to an aspect of the time when the Kawartha Lakes were still considered by some to be the North.

In the closing article, John Wadland addresses some of the broad issues related to the wilderness canoeing tradition in Canada. While exposing the ironies inherent in that tradition, the author nonetheless constructs an argument affirming the centrality of wilderness, of the North, within our culture.

*   *   *

We hope that this book will interest at least two categories of readers, though we anticipate that many people will locate themselves in both camps, as do most of the authors. The authors write for the wilderness traveller with a reflective bent, including the winter and summer day-tripper, the northern canoeist, and the armchair adventurer. In addition, they write for the scholar interested in the broad field of Canadian social and intellectual history. The relatively new study of recreational history is already making serious and valuable contributions to an understanding of the social and intellectual framework within which Canadians of all classes and backgrounds lived their lives. It is our hope that this study, through its focus on recreational wilderness travel will suggest certain insights into the values, myths, and aspirations of a significant, if generally small, segment of society at particular times in history. Moreover, the articles should testify to the power and importance of a well-entrenched idea in Canadian history—the idea of the North.

Many questions have been posed by this volume, and many answers provided. These answers, however, are often speculative and certainly not definitive. Indeed, we hope to some extent that for our readers this book will end with a question mark, inspiring further enquiries into the role of the canoe, the snow-shoe, and the North within the Canadian culture and heritage.

ENDNOTES

1. See Craig Macdonald, "Nastawgan: Traditional Routes of Travel in the Temagami District" appearing in this volume.

2. W. L. Morton, "The 'North' in Canadian Historiography", *Transactions of the Royal Society of Canada* Series IV, 8 (1970); "The Relevance of Canadian History", *The Canadian Identity* (Toronto 1975).

3. Louis-Edmond Hamelin, *Canadian Nordicity: It's Your North, Too* (Montreal 1978).

4. See Bruce Hodgins and Jamie Benidickson, "The Meaning of the North in Canada," *Alternatives* (Spring 1973).

5. See the articles in this volume by Bruce Hodgins entitled "The Written Word on Canoeing and Canoe Tripping Before 1960" and "The Lure of the Temagami-Based Canoe Trip", and also Jamie Benidickson's "Idleness, Water and a Canoe: Canadian Recreational Paddling Between the Wars". Also see the latter's "Paddling for Pleasure: Recreational Canoeing as a Canadian Way of Life" in John Marsh and Geoffrey Wall, eds. *Recreational Land Use: Perspectives on its Evolution and Management* (Ottawa 1982) and "Recreational Canoeing in Ontario Before the First World War", *Canadian Journal of the History of Sport and Physical Education*, IX (Dec. 1978). For a somewhat differing view see C. E. S. Franks, *The Canoe and White Water: From Essential to Sport* (Toronto 1978) pp. 53-68.

6. Note especially John Wadland, *Ernest Thompson Seton: Man in Nature and the Progressive Era, 1880-1915* (New York 1978).

The Quest Pattern and the Canoe Trip*

William C. James

> What sets a canoeing expedition apart is that it purifies you more rapidly and inescapably than any other. Travel a thousand miles by train and you are a brute; pedal five hundred on a bicycle and you remain a bourgeois; paddle a hundred in a canoe and you are already a child of nature.[1]
>
> *Pierre Elliott Trudeau.*

In the summer of 1975, our party took a wrong turn and lost the main channel while paddling up the labyrinthine meanderings of a creek in Algonquin Park. When the tributary finally became impassable a stranger who had been foolishly following our canoes for more than an hour, but who to that point had not spoken a word, asked, "Have any of you read *The Lord of the Rings?*" The sympathy was immediate. Like Frodo and his questing companions we had lost our way, been deflected from our goal, expended much time and energy uselessly, and now had to go back and begin again.

That episode was the beginning of my conscious reflection on the similarities between the quest, as I had become acquainted with that theme in literature, and my experience of the canoe trip. All of the ingredients were there: the departure from the known, the voyage into the unknown, and the return to civilization; the obstacles of high winds, rough waters, brutal portages, dissension, and long dreary rainy days; the unexpected pleasures of new vistas, of wildlife seen, of achievements and minor triumphs, and the joy of one's companions; the sense of participation in a primitive reality, or the re-enactment of an archetypal event, the sloughing off of the inessential and the experience of renewal.

My argument, briefly, is this: the primary fact of the Canadian experience is a geographical one, whose major ingredient is the presence of the Canadian Shield, which dominates our country, comprises most of its wilderness and, in some respects at least, is still best explored by canoe. An encounter with that wilderness by means of a canoe trip is a repetition of the quest pattern as described in its most familiar form by Joseph Campbell. But I want also to suggest that this particular version of the quest has its perils too, so that it can be misapplied or misunderstood with results that are often unfortunate and sometimes disastrous.

---

* This chapter is a revised version of an essay first published under the title "The Canoe Trip as Religious Quest," in *Studies in Religion/Sciences religieuses* 10/2 (Spring 1981): 151-66. It is reprinted here with the permission of the author and publisher.

In his book *The Hero with a Thousand Faces* Campbell draws upon the stories of such figures as Prometheus, Jason, Aeneas, Mohammed, the Buddha, Jesus, and Moses to set forth the 'monomyth' of his composite hero: "A hero ventures forth from the world of common day into a region of supernatural wonder: fabulous forces are there encountered and a decisive victory is won: the hero comes back from this mysterious adventure with the power to bestow boons on his fellow man."[2] The career of the hero has three main stages: separation or departure; the trials and victories of initiation; and the return and re-integration into society. Within each of these stages Campbell and others have further delineated additional elements or episodes exhibited in the lives of the heroes of folklore or legend. But the three main stages of the quest will be a sufficient basis for consideration, and for the most part I will refrain from too specific an analysis of details. There will be no attempt, for instance, to show that within the first stage (Departure) one might find parallels in the canoe trip to "The Call to Adventure," "Refusal of the Call," or "The Crossing of the First Threshold" (to cite some of Campbell's section headings).

Although the hero of myth achieves a "world-historical, macrocosmic triumph," the canoeist's triumph is more domestic and 'microcosmic' like that of the fairy-tale hero. Campbell argues in his concluding chapter, "The Hero Today," that the modern hero's quest is more personal and internal than it is social. Thus, the mythologies which were formerly societally based and visibly expressed through various rites are now seen by Campbell to have their modern counterpart *within* the individual, as expressed through dreams. But since in the canoe trip there is still visible an "objective correlative" (to use T.S. Eliot's phrase) of the monomythic quest, this comparison will draw upon external resemblances with the original quests at some points (for example, the canoeist makes an actual journey), while at other points finding an internal or spiritual significance in the canoeist's quest (for example, there is no literal counterpart to the boon which the returning mythic hero bears with him). Throughout I have concentrated on writings of two main kinds: first, literary art of this century and of the last in which canoeing is featured; and, second, recent texts on wilderness canoeing or magazine articles on particular canoe trips.

The journey, with its image of the road, is a familiar analogue closely corresponding to our subjective experience of life as historical. Most of us are familiar with journeys, though perhaps not in a very simplified or 'pure' form. In the era of the jumbo jet few aspects remain of travel from a pre-industrial age, when travel was by boat or foot or horse, each day's destination was variable, and one's food and lodging were either carried along or were uncertain. While a canoe trip is in some respects similar to a trip by bicycle, a back-packing expedition, or a cross-country ski tour, by virtue of the traveller being self-propelled and travelling light, it has several unique features too, notably in being ideally adapted to Canadian conditions, in its historical significance, and in the fact that to travel by water rather than by land is a more radical departure from the known into the unknown.

In *The Canadian Identity* W. L. Morton speaks of how central is the Canadian Shield—that grim precambrian horseshoe—to Canadian geography and history and, indeed, "to all understanding of Canada." He points out that whereas the heartland of the United States is one of the world's most fertile regions, the heartland of Canada is one of the world's most forbidding wildernesses, a waste of rocks and lakes and bush comprising one-half of this country's area. In days gone by it was traversed by fur traders, lumberjacks, prospectors, and miners who "wrested from it the staples by which Canada has lived," though they had always to return to their home base in southern Ontario, or in the St. Lawrence valley, or in the prairies, for that was where their food came from. Morton claims that "this alternate penetration of the wilderness and return to civilization is the basic rhythm of Canadian life."[3] This rhythm, of course, is parallel to the rites of passage in the nuclear unit of Campbell's monomyth (separation—initiation—return). It remains to consider the canoe trip as an exemplification of this general movement outlined by Campbell and given a specifically Canadian context by Morton. Then I will examine two different kinds of canoe trip to see which is more appropriate to the Canadian setting and to contemporary needs.

A canoe trip remains the best means of penetrating the wilderness of the Shield, even considering that it is now accessible by bush plane as well. If one wants to take a wilderness canoe trip, even some Americans concede that Canada may be the only place where that can be accomplished. Two students from New England begin a book on canoeing with a chapter entitled "Finding a Wilderness." They describe the situation this way: "We rolled a big map and took a good look at the U.S.A. (that is, the lower forty-eight). And couldn't find a self-respecting wilderness anywhere. Unless you have a better eye than we do, you'll get pretty discouraged about the U.S.A. and turn to Canada and Alaska."[4]

*   *   *

The first main stage of the quest is separation or departure and includes the whole business of preparation: not only poring over maps, but also perusing catalogues from outfitters, reading books and brochures describing various routes, discussing plans with the rest of the party, making lists of food and equipment, and so on. The significance of such preparation should not be missed or minimized. The careful selection of food and clothing of a kind not associated with the profane routines of ordinary life suggests a break with the usual and the familiar, like the irruption into everyday life occasioned by the sacred festivals of less secular cultures than our own. The very necessity of reducing one's baggage to a minimum demands an awareness of essentials not common in our cluttered world. When at last the cars are loaded, the canoeist proceeds to the "threshold of adventure." John and Janet Foster describe that initial occasion each spring when this threshold is crossed and the journey into the other world begins:

Every year it is just as cold. But there is pure magic in that first moment as you push away from shore. The canoe seems to hang suspended above the dark water, momentarily floating in space, quietly separating from the land that has held you throughout the winter months. And now the noise and tumult and vibrations of the city 200 miles away begin to fade.[5]

The Fosters go on to stress, as do so many accounts of canoe trips, the therapeutic benefits of exposure to the wilderness, its ability to release one's tensions, and the healing effects of solitude. This emphasis is not just the reaction of modern conservationists, for similar effects are remarked upon in nineteenth-century writings too. Susanna Moodie says that in leisure hours spent upon the water in their canoe she and her husband experienced "a magic spell upon our spirits" and "began to feel charmed with the freedom and solitude around us."

The language used by Mrs. Moodie suggests an Edenic experience: "Every object was new to us. We felt as if we were the first discoverers of every beautiful flower and stately tree that attracted our attention, and we gave names to fantastic rocks and fairy isles."[6]

Anna Jameson, who in the summer of 1837 made a "wild expedition" from Toronto to Sault Ste. Marie and back, a large part of it by canoe, reports her experience in the form of a travel-diary. Her writing bears a strongly romantic tinge: "I cannot, I dare not, attempt to describe to you the strange sensations one has, thus thrown for a time beyond the bounds of civilized humanity, or indeed any humanity; nor the wild yet solemn reveries which come over one in the midst of this wilderness of woods and waters." Her comments upon the effects of "solitude" and of "nature unviolated" parallel Mrs. Moodie's in their suggestion of a return to paradisal innocence: "we its inmates . . . might have fancied ourselves alone in a newborn world."[7] And, at about the turn of the century, Egerton Young relates his travels by birchbark canoe with an emphasis upon the necessity of travelling with an outfit "as light as possible." He continues: "There is something glorious and exhilarating in getting away from civilization for a time, and living close to the heart of nature in some of her wildest domains. Then, when it is possible to throw them off, we get some ideas of the despotism of many of the customs of civlization."[8] For one modern couple, throwing off the customs of civilization meant an escape from the tyranny of the watch and calendar, as they paddled down the Yukon River without keeping track of the time and without adhering to a fixed schedule: "It was a pleasure: My watch was now my prisoner, confined to the depths of a waterproof bag. Eating, sleeping, starting and stopping whenever we felt like it—there was a freedom that we wouldn't have again for years."[9] In such accounts as these there is a surprising degree of consistency in the portrayal of the canoe trip as an experience of separation from civilization and a departure from the known world.

While such descriptions stress the great gulf between the world of adventure and the ordinary world, it would be a mistake to see the canoe trip as nothing more than an idyllic retreat from civilization to nature. The integration with nature must be achieved through a series of trials and ordeals in a genuine quest, or else there remains the suspicion that the initial sense of harmony with the natural world is something precarious, illusory, or easily lost. Most canoeists, therefore, make reference to the trials and ordeals which occur subsequent to the separation from civilization and which are central to the initiation into the wilderness. And so it should be if Campbell's scheme is applicable. In Algonquin Park, in order to escape the crowded Highway 60 corridor, to get away from the busy access points at Canoe and Opeongo Lakes, and to reach the interior, it is necessary to traverse at least one major portage of several thousand yards to achieve something like the solitude sought. The Fosters' experience is typical of that of many canoeists:

> In the fall of 1970 we chose one of those canoe routes that you can't get to from here,' and battled in through a dozen overgrown portages, an endless series of beaver dams and uncounted fallen trees to the shallow end of the Nipissing River. There the river was nothing more than a stream, the water was low and the mud deep, and much of the time we were pulling or pushing the canoe through a soggy jungle of tag alders. But every obstacle passed was another psychological barrier between us and the city we had left behind, and the photographic and spiritual rewards were remarkable.[10]

Canoeing literature is filled with tales of hardships endured, especially on an initial journey: the first lengthy portage over rough terrain; an upset which soaks all of the gear; a miscalculation resulting in a shortage of provisions or losing one's way; the impossibility of starting a fire to cook supper; the interruption of a journey by winds or rain. Such difficulties are significant chiefly as ordeals demanding a re-orientation of the self or of one's values. The kinds of skills cherished and fostered in the classroom, office, or marketplace are often worthless under these conditions, and that realization is itself a humiliating experience. Thus the perilous journey may lead to a purification of the self, or the dissolution of past images of the self.

The notion of an ordeal undergone in order to penetrate into the wilderness is epitomized in the writings of Grey Owl who in his characteristically colourful style writes of "The Trail," where "the soul of man is stripped bare and naked, exposed for all to see, and [where] his true nature will come out, let him dissemble never so wisely."[11] The wilderness is presided over, according to Grey Owl, by the "brooding relentless evil spirit of the Northland" who haunts the "fastnesses, with a view to the destruction of all travellers."[12] On The Trail, proceeding by snowshoes in the winter and canoe in summer, "newcomers must undergo the severe scrutiny of the presiding powers, and all who enter are subjected to trial by ordeal, from which only the chosen few emerge unscathed."[13] Or, again: "Day by day, he penetrates deeper and deeper into the Kingdom of the Spirit of the North, where, jealous of such encroachment on his domain, with a thousand imps of mischief to do his bidding, master of all the powers of evil, the brooding Killer grimly bides his time; nor does he always wait in vain."[14]

Grey Owl, perhaps deliberately and for rhetorical effect, overstates the evil character of this "spirit of the Northland." He must have known, from his acquaintance with the Indians of the Biscotasing area, that the Ojibway god of the water (Misshipeshu or the Great Lynx), though possessed of great power, knew both good and evil and always brought luck to those who respected him. Similarly, the "imps" or Maymaygwaysiwuk who were water-dwellers residing especially near rapids, were likewise powerful, but more mischievous than malevolent, and were met as friends by the Indians who bestowed gifts of tobacco at the appropriate sites. Sigurd Olson learned that these spirits inhabiting rapids along the Churchill River system delighted in tipping over the canoe passing through, but at the same time ensured that the canoe did not smash itself to pieces.[15]

In any event, many canoeists testify that the real difficulties result from friction among the members of the party, when a small, isolated group is thrown together in close quarters. As John McPhee notes: "When trouble comes on a canoe trip, it comes from the inside, from the fast-growing hatreds among the friends who started."[16]

This possibility was one factor which convinced Kamil Pecher to make his journey alone by kayak along the fur-trade rivers of northern Saskatchewan. However, Pecher fell prey to "The Enemy Within" (to use one of the chapter titles of his book, *Lonely Voyage*), and became ill from stress which he attributed to the tension of loneliness. At least in a group there is always someone else to care for or to compete with, and one's own weaknesses can be covered up through comparison with others'.

One must not lay too much stress on the physical hardships of the canoe trip alone. Whatever form the ordeal of the adventure takes—whether physical obstacles and hardships, the spirits of the wilderness, relationships among the party, or the inner enemy—the trial should culminate in some kind of victory, or perhaps insight, being won by the canoeist. A. Y. Jackson describes the difficulties of his initial canoe trip, especially overturning the canoe in a strong current, and learning how to portage properly. At the end of his brief account Jackson comments laconically: "By the end of that trip we had learned a lot about getting around by canoe, how to choose a campsite, how to make fires in the rain, and how to adapt ourselves philosophically to whatever transpired."[17] And, Grey Owl speaks of "the spiritual satisfaction, the intellectual pleasure, and the knowledge of power that comes with a victory over the valiant but ruthless adversary . . . ."[18] Probably more common than either statements of increased competence or of victory over a ruthless enemy (although strongly implied by both A. Y. Jackson and Grey Owl) is the change wrought within the individual in response to the trials of the journey. A typical example is found in the foreword to *Still Waters, White Waters*: "Canoeing inspires humility: We were always the lowest object on the landscape, often vulnerable to water and weather, and, at the beginning, badly in need of guides. But at the end, alone at night on a corner of the Arctic Ocean, we had confidence in our canoes and ourselves."[19]

Of course, such achievements must be assessed in terms of their continuing effects in the ordinary world, which brings us to a consideration of the third stage of the monomyth when the hero re-emerges from "the kingdom of dread" bringing the boon that restores the world. As would be expected, with the internalization of the quest and the resulting emphasis on inner transformation, the return to domesticity is necessarily more prosaic. Whereas the mythic adventurer brings back the runes of wisdom, the sleeping princess, or the Golden Fleece, Campbell suggests that such tangible boons are symbolic of spiritual vision, perhaps amounting to a glimpse of the secret of the cosmos which the returned hero bears with him. The adventurer has gone through a death and self-annihilation which is prerequisite to rebirth in the realization of truth—that is, a religious transformation has been effected in the other world. The problem frequently arises of applying those insights to the ordinary world. Thus, the crossing of the return threshold is supremely difficult (a well-known instance is provided by Lemuel Gulliver). Campbell cites the story of Rip van Winkle as typical of the returning hero who (perhaps like the canoeist) has nothing to show for the experience but his whiskers.

The returning canoeist often has an experience of what G.K. Chesterton called *mooreeffoc*—the queerness of ordinary things when seen or experienced from a new angle (and which may be necessary for a sense of wonder). Even today it is not uncommon for canoeists to spend a week in an interior wilderness without seeing a building, hearing an engine, or getting any news of the 'outside.' The return in such cases is often dramatic. Davidson and Rugge recommend that "your expedition, if you run it according to the Ideal, should end with a final bursting out of the pristine wilderness back to the world of man and machines."[20] Mrs. Jameson provides a good example of the problems of returning to civilization at the end of her "summer rambles." She had looked forward to sleeping "once more on a Christian bed" at the inn at Penetanguishene ("not the worst of Canadian inns"): "But nine nights passed in the open air, or on the rocks, and on boards, had spoiled me for the comforts of civilization, and to sleep *on a bed* was impossible: I was smothered, I was suffocated, and altogether wretched and fevered;—I sighed for my rock on Lake Huron."[21]

Modern accounts of canoe trips are almost unanimous in their testimony that the major change experienced by the canoeist is an inner one, the exploration of the wilderness becoming a voyage into the interior of the self. A book on canoeing written for children and published by the Canadian Red Cross Society strikes the right note: "Like the voyageurs of the past three centuries, you'll find that the path of discovery leads, in the end, to learning about . . . yourself."[22] Even the magazine *Outdoor Life*, that formulaic celebration of aggressive masculinity, concludes an account of a 700-mile journey down the Back River in the Northwest Territories with the remark that the two voyagers in their three months of paddling had "certainly made marks of their own. Not on the land. But in the frontiers of their minds."[23] The editor of *A Book of Canada*[24] wisely includes as one of three short pieces comprising his Epilogue the poem "Canoe-Trip" by Douglas LePan in which the poet, having returned from the wilderness with its limitless "pinelands," "the millions of lakes," "the clearings enamelled with blueberries," and "the flames of sunset," asks:

> Now what shall be our word as we return,
> What word of this curious country?

And, the answer, in part, is that "it is a good stock to own though it seldom pays dividends," that there are holes here and there for a hydro plant or a gold mine, but that "whoever comes to tame this land, beware," for there is "no hope to harness the energy here." Though "the map suggested a wealth of cloudy escapes," the canoeist must circle back from the maze to "face again the complex task" and to convert "the dream to act":

> . . . here are the crooked nerves made straight.
> The fracture cured no doctor could correct.
> The hand and mind, reknit, stand whole for work.

The entire poem is pertinent to our considerations here in its expression of the theme of return, the superiority of spiritual wisdom to material boon, and the relationship between the change effected in the course of the adventure and the demands of the ordinary world to which the canoeist returns.

Another poem by LePan, "Coureur de Bois," continues the motif of inner transformation, but whereas in "Canoe-Trip" this change occurs in the absence of any permanent alteration of the landscape, in "Coureur de Bois" the idea is advanced that once the forests are cut down and the rivers charted, then one's travel must be "through the desperate wilderness behind your eyes, /So full of falls and glooms and desolations." In the final line of the poem LePan describes the modern *coureur de bois* as "Wild Hamlet with the features of Horatio."

"Never," claims Robertson Davies, "did anyone pack so much insight into the Canadian character into a single phrase," our climate having made us a combination of moody introspection and roaring extroversion. Having established the applicability of Campbell's monomyth as a scheme by means of which the canoe trip may be comprehended, it follows to investigate further the content and nature of the transformation which the canoe trip facilitates, in its relationship to the Canadian character (or what *ought* to be, in my view, the Canadian character).

*   *   *

W. L. Morton argues that the rhythm of penetration into the wilderness and return to civilization "form the basic elements of Canadian character": "the violence necessary to contend with the wilderness, the restraint necessary to preserve civilization from the wilderness violence, and the puritanism which is offspring of the wedding of violence to restraint."[25] Yet such an analysis is bound to leave one with a feeling of discomfort in an age when we perceive all too readily the effects of our having contended violently with the wilderness. The discomfort increases when we are told that 'questing' is an essentially male activity, requiring that the quester leave home, and that its female counterpart is the 'nesting' activity, the cosmicization of the home and the creation there of a sacred space.[26]

Even from nineteenth-century accounts, the testimony of female as well as male canoeists abounds. In addition to Anna Jameson and Susanna Moodie and Catharine Parr Traill, Lady Dufferin has left in My *Canadian Journal* a narration of incidents of canoeing when her husband was Governor General of Canada. We have as well the story of the journey by canoe of four Grey Nuns from Montreal to the Red River in 1844. Among the Indians, canoes seem as often to have been paddled by women as by men. Of a dozen poets cited by the author of *The Romance of the Canadian Canoe* as having celebrated the canoe in poetry, half are women, the most notable being Pauline Johnson. Among artists who used the canoe to gain access to their subject, or else painted the canoe as their subject, one thinks of Paul Kane and Tom Thomson, but also of Frances Hopkins and Emily Carr. The photographs in a recent book, *Canoeing and Kayaking*, show a woman demonstrating methods of paddling and portaging. There is something important in these facts, something which ought to make it possible for women to develop the ramifications of thisparticular quest story, rather than prematurely abandoning it an exclusively male preserve in preference for the relatively underdeveloped area of nesting stories.*

Margaret Atwood, in *Survival*, tells us that the attempt to dominate and order nature through the imposition of straight lines (walls and roads and fences) upon the curvature of nature results as often in defeat as in victory (tumbledown barns and fallen fences). Indeed, if we are to believe Atwood, it seems that in Canada defeat results more often than victory. Religious feminists have urged us to balance the male or rationalistic dominance of the religion of the Sky Father by the cultivation of a more naturalistic religion, one of the Earth Mother or of animism, or through ecstasy and wonder—the religion of Dionysus as well as of Apollo. Two of the most remarkable works of recent Canadian fiction, Margaret Atwood's *Surfacing* and Marion Engel's *Bear*, tell of the penetration of the wilderness by a female protagonist, who there becomes integrated with nature through adaptation rather than aggression before making the return to civilization—a marked contrast, to be sure, with the male hunters of the fictional worlds of Faulkner and Hemingway. Such seems to be the trend as well in many of the writings stressing a new ethic of conservation: an adaptation to, rather than a hostility towards, nature.

---

*See, for example, Annis Pratt, "*Surfacing* and the Rebirth Journey", in *The Art of Margaret Atwood: Essays in Criticism*, ed. Arnold E. Davidson and Cathy N. Davidson (Toronto: Anansi, 1981), pp. 139-56, and Carol Pearson and Katherine Pope, *The Female Hero in American and British Literature* (New York and London: R.R. Bowker Co., 1981).

Northrop Frye, in an essay on Canadian poetry, characterizes the European settlers as having seen nature in Canada as hostile, as monster or leviathan.[27]

This "immigrant mentality" understands man's essential power to be rational, derives from a Cartesian egocentric consciousness, and results in a turning away from nature. But in some Canadian poetry, Frye states, Indians come to symbolize a primitive mythological imagination which may be reborn in us, resulting in the "immigrant mentality" being replaced by an "indigenous mentality." If we are to be no longer immigrants and to make of this territory a home, there is the necessity to form attitudes appropriate to those who really do belong here, to descend into the self and be reborn. Significantly, in both *Surfacing* and *Bear*, it is in large measure through the legacy or tutelage of native peoples (our true ancestors), and in the context of a setting in the wilderness, that the transformations of the female protagonists are brought about.

Something like this, it seems to me, is one significance of the canoe trip seen as a transformative quest. In enabling us to encounter our geographical uniqueness, in making possible a completion of that circuit of separation, initiation, and return, and bequeathed to us by those peoples who were here before we were, the canoe may well be an effective vehicle, not only for the exploration of the wilderness of the Shield, but also for exploring that inner frontier, and perhaps for effecting an appropriate transformation of attitudes through a kind of indigenization. C. E. S. Franks at the end of his magnificent book, *The Canoe and White Water*, quotes Father Brébeuf's reflection that although on his journeys by canoe he was "sometimes so weary that the body could do no more," he nonetheless experienced a deep peace in his soul, "considering that I was suffering for God." Professor Franks concludes: "A modern canoeist can also experience a deep peace in the midst of fatigue. It comes to him for the same reason that it came to Father Brébeuf. He also is converting the savage, only now we know that the savage who needs converting is the man from civilization, including the canoeist himself."[28]

The questing pattern of departure, initiation, and return best describes the type of trip which begins and ends at the same place. This circular quest in which the quester returns to his starting point inwardly changed recalls the familiar words from Eliot's 'Little Gidding':

> We shall not cease from exploration
> And the end of all our exploring
> Will be to arrive where we started
> And know the place for the first time.

But what about a different kind of canoe trip—one which is linear, rather than circular? To avoid retracing their steps or because of the impossibility of planning a circular route, many canoeists arrange to be delivered to their point of departure or picked up at their destination, either by car or plane or train. Thus, the internal combustion engine makes easier, for example, a long trip down a river. At first it seemed to me that a linear canoe trip as contrasted with a circular one might be similar to downhill skiing as contrasted with cross-country skiing: a mechanical conveyance becomes necessary and thereby destroys the 'purity' of the original activity. I wondered as well whether the linear trip was not more likely to become an aggressive assault upon the wilderness. Consider, for instance, the situation in which would-be whitewater enthusiasts set out to conquer a river, as in James Dickey's *Deliverance*. Thus, the circular canoe trip would be preferred by the environmentalist and the purist as obviously more natural, harmonious, and adaptive.

However, this simple dichotomy will not do: there are examples of down-river linear quests of a gentle and adaptive kind just as there are vigorous and assaultive circular canoe trips. For example, in the instructional film *Doubles Whitewater* in "The Path of the Paddle" series by the National Film Board, Bill Mason, accompanied by his son Paul, combines expertise in the demonstration of paddling strokes, the ability to read rapids, and the exhilaration of challenge and achievement with the exploration of rivers as "a spiritual link with the natural world." For, as Mason states at the film's end, the white man's way of living left little time for learning from nature, whereas the Indians experienced a harmony with the natural world which we have been slow to discover. Further, the relationship between father and son as portrayed in the film depends upon mutual respect, constant consultation, and Paul's learning to make judgements about the wisdom of attempting to shoot particular rapids without pressure or intimidation from his father. This was an adaptive, harmonious yet linear trip.

By way of contrast, another NFB film, *The New Boys*, depicts a circular trip of three hundred miles from the St. John's School at Selkirk, Manitoba in 1973. This trip is set up at the beginning of the school year to function as an initiation rite, a kind of trial by ordeal, and a demonstration of the school's credo that "only by confronting the wilderness does a boy become a man." Once the trip is begun the boys stop only to eat and sleep, the object being to get back to the school as quickly as possible. Here canoeing provides a mock battleground on which the adolescent boys test themselves and toughen up their moral fibre through meeting a challenge and hard work. Most viewers wince as they watch the boys become increasingly wet, cold, and exhausted. Especially in one sequence in which the boys cross a large lake in heavy winds, their canoes shipping water, the film takes on a sinister and foreboding aspect in the light of the Lake Temiskaming tragedy experienced five years later by a group from the sister school at Claremont, Ontario. And, in sharp contrast with the relationship between the two Masons, here the adult leaders function more as 'demon-masters' presiding over a cruel rite as they spur their young charges to stretch themselves to the limits of their endurance. The trial by ordeal is given religious sanction as the trip begins and ends with a chapel service in which the muscular Christianity common to Anglican boys' boarding schools provides the explicit framework of the rite. It might be suggested that if the adaptive 'feminine' quest errs in too quickly forcing a false harmony with nature, while avoiding the agony of spiritual growth, the assaultive 'masculine' quest errs in overstressing the trials and ordeals of initiation as ends in themselves.

*   *   *

Undergirded by the same principles and objectives displayed in *The New Boys*, the fatal expedition which on the first day out resulted in death for thirteen young canoeists on Lake Temiskaming in June 1978 was criticized by the Quebec coroner as "an exaggerated and pointless challenge."[29] It is difficult to escape the conclusion that the tragedy was at least in part a consequence of the St. John's School philosophy which encouraged not only confrontation with difficulty and danger, but at times deliberate risk-taking and even foolhardiness.

In *The New Boys* the headmaster exhorts the boys to learn to look after themselves. He tells them that "Mommy won't be there" if they forget their raincoats or if their sleeping bags get wet. Here, as in many initiation rites for male adolescents, the exclusion of the female is a prominent aspect. The St. John's Schools, founded as "a reaction against a permissive and increasingly godless society," might be successful in producing aggressive self-starters. It is questionable whether their formula for manhood can foster in boys passivity as well as aggression, vulnerability and dependence as well as self-assertion, kindess as well as courage.

The St. John's philosophy, then, celebrates values aimed at producing male achievers. The exclusively masculine orientation of the initiatory canoe trips suggests this conclusion. In addition, the St. John's expeditions illustrate what Frye has termed the "immigrant" mentality towards the Canadian wilderness, cultivating rather than subjugating the ego. Joseph Campbell describes the model of what the returned adventurer ought to be: "His personal ambitions being totally dissolved, he no longer tries to live but willingly relaxes to whatever may come to pass in him; he becomes, that is to say, an anonymity."[30]

Kamil Pecher, in the account of his lengthy journey by kayak in northern Saskatchewan, continually contrasts the white man's approach and the Indian's: "The Indian way is to yield to the natural forces and live in harmony with them... The white man's way is to conquer or be conquered."[31] Pecher, an immigrant to Canada, had been sent off by his Indian mentor with the warning not to "hurry like a white man," but to "feel the country." Before his integration with nature can be fulfilled, Pecher develops a duodenal ulcer, that classic affliction of the overworked executive and the result of his taking his "city rush and white man's ways" with him – he has to be air-lifted out of the bush. When he resumes his journey, it is with a new attitude of patience: "No longer need I strive for achievement. . . . From the point of view of white people I had probably become bushed; to the Indians this was harmony with nature. Here I was, returning not as a conqueror, but as a humble pilgrim."[32] This 600-mile journey by kayak is a remarkable instance of an immigrant to this country acquiring the indigenous mentality which stands in stark opposition to the St. John's School philosophy.

*   *   *

The application of Joseph Campbell's scheme of the heroic journey-quest to the recreational canoe trip may seem at first to be a frivolous and pointless exercise. What could be called "mythomania" – searching for metaphors, finding parallels, looking for resemblances and synchronicities – is fraught with pitfalls. The search for the figure in the carpet can become a bit ridiculous: Are you re-enacting the *Odyssey* when you go for a leisurely paddle at the cottage? There is always the danger of straining to find superficial parallels when using any typological approach – the tendency is to overlook the differences and to stress similarities, to neglect the historical realities of time and place when one searches for mythic patterns underlying everyday reality.

Perhaps as Canadians we are never more nostalgic, never more atavistic, than when we get in a canoe. But it is well to be cautious before we begin too uncritically to rhapsodize about the transformative possibilities inherent in canoe trips seen as mythic quests. The canoe has no magical properties enabling people to be purged of their vices, frogs to be changed into princes, or even anxieties to be laid to rest. It is easy to be romantic and sentimental about the restorative properties of the wilderness. But Canadians also seem singularly possessed of a healthy suspicion of anything that appears easy, whether it be harmony with the natural world or the making of boys into men.

At the very least, then, there can be adaptive linear quests as well as assaultive circular ones. And some quests which set out with the intention of being transformative sometimes end disastrously (the old stories tell us too that sometimes bad things change into worse things). One of the tests of a model such as Joesph Campbell's quest pattern when applied to something like a canoe trip is to see if it can take account of a problematic realtity. Has it anything instructive or relevant to say about a canoeing tragedy? We should be prompted to ask questions about the *kinds* of transformations canoe trips have been used to inculcate. Indeed, the true "wilderness" may be discovered to lie behind our own eyes, within rather than without, in the city rather than in the bush.

What we normally think of as leisure activities have important implications, implications whose importance may grow even as the time available for leisure grows. At the furthest extreme, they may become as great as matters of life and death. The application of Joseph Campbell's quest pattern to the canoe trip can illuminate the significance and gravity of canoeing, enrich our appreciation as we become aware of some of its hidden meanings; but such an application should also warn us of perils even as it holds out promise, all the while unveiling some of the ways in which our deepest concerns and most fundamental humanity display themselves.

ENDNOTES

1. "Exhaustion and Fulfilment: The Ascetic in a Canoe," in Borden Spears (ed.), *Wilderness Canada* (Toronto 1970), p. 4. This remarkable essay was first published in French in *Jeunesse etudiante catholique* in 1944.

2. Joseph Campbell, *The Hero with a Thousand Faces* (New York 1956), p. 30. Cf. pp. 36 and 245-46.

3. W.L. Morton, *The Canadian Identity* (Toronto 1961), p. 5.

4. James West Davidson and John Rugge, *The Complete Wilderness Paddler* (New York 1976), p. 5.

5. John and Janet Foster, *To the Wild Country* (Toronto 1975), p. 88.

6. Susanna Moodie, *Roughing it in the Bush: Or Forest Life in Canada* (Toronto 1962), p. 155.

7. Anna Brownell Jameson, *Winter Studies and Summer Rambles in Canada (Selections)* (Toronto 1965), pp. 124-25.

8. Egerton R. Young, *The Battle of the Bears: Life in the North Land* (Boston and Chicago 1907), p. 191.

9. Tim Palmer, "Teslin Experience," *North/Nord* (May-June 1977), p. 51.

10. Foster and Foster, *Wild Country*, p. 89.

11. Grey Owl, *The Men of the Last Frontier* (Toronto 1976), p. 49.

12. Ibid., p. 76n.

13. Ibid., p. 51.

14. Ibid., p. 64.

15. Sigurd Olsen, *The Lonely Land* (Toronto 1974), p. 206.

16. John McPhee, *The Survival of the Bark Canoe* (New York 1975), p. 68.

17. A. Y. Jackson, *A Painter's Country: The Autobiography of A. Y. Jackson* (Toronto 1964), p. 85.

18. Grey Owl, *Last Frontier*, pp. 51-52.

19. Sam Abell, "Foreword," in Ron Fisher, *Still Waters, White Waters: Exploring America's Rivers and Lakes* (Washington 1977), p. 5.

20. Davidson and Rugge, *Wilderness Paddler*, p. 239.

21. Jameson, *Summer Rambles*, p. 165.

22. *Canoeing: The Adventures of Lester and Linda on Top of the Water World* (n.p. 1975), p. 5. The ellipses appear in the text itself.

23. Pat Smith, "The River that Calls to the Bold," *Outdoor Life* (August 1977), p. 107.

24. See William Toyes ed, *A Book of Canada* (London 1962), pp. 409-10.

25. Morton, *Canadian Identity*, p. 5.

26. From a paper entitled "The Feminine and the Sacred," read by Kathryn Allen Rabuzzi at the Eastern-International Region Meeting of the American Academy of Religion in Rochester, 14 April 1978.

27. Northrop Frye, "Haunted by Lack of Ghosts: Some Patterns in the Imagery of Canadian Poetry," in David Staines (ed.), *The Canadian Imagination: Dimensions of a Literary Culture* (Cambridge: Havard University Press, 1977), pp. 24-25.

28. C.E.S. Franks, *The Canoe and White Water: From Essential to Sport* (Toronto: University of Toronto Press, 1977), p. 205.

29. The details of the Lake Temiskaming disaster are dealt with at greater length by the author in the earlier version of this essay published in *Studies in Religion*. See also Robert Collins, "God Can Bring Good Out of It," *Reader's Digest* 144 (February 1979), 183-210 and articles appearing the Toronto daily newspapers in June and July of 1978.

30. Campbell, *Thousand Faces*, p. 237.

31. Kamil Pecher, *Lonely Voyage: By Kayak to Adventure and Discovery* Saskatoon 1978), p. 161.

32. Ibid., p. 172.

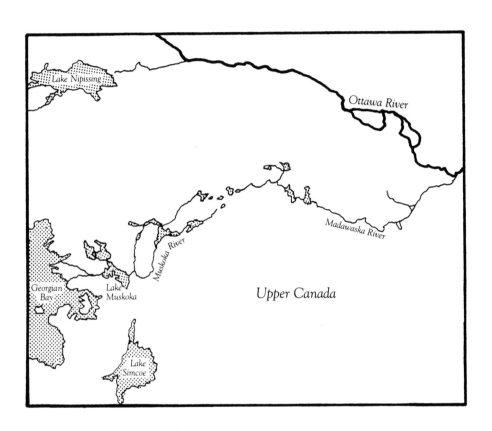

Lake Nipissing

Ottawa River

Madawaska River

Georgian
Bay

Lake
Muskoka

Muskoka River

Upper Canada

Lake
Simcoe

David Thompson's Explorations of the Muskoka and Madawaska Rivers

C. E. S. Franks

In 1837 David Thompson, noted explorer and map-maker of the Canadian West, surveyed the Muskoka-Madawaska River route from Georgian Bay to the Ottawa River. He was 67 years old at the time. The survey itself was not an important achievement. It is remarkable only as an episode in the later life of one of Canada's great men. However, during the survey Thompson continued his life-long habit of keeping a detailed journal, amounting to more than 100 pages,[1] which together with his maps and ancillary records are of great historical value.

Those documents illustrate the skills and resources that were needed for wilderness travel and exploration and which form a part of the web of human experience which has shaped our existence as Canadians. They show to what a degree this region was then a northern wilderness. Since then the southern boundary of the part of Canada which can be considered as the North has shifted hundreds of miles to the north. The wilderness Thompson travelled is now the heart of the vacation land of southern Ontario. The Madawaska River is now highly regarded as a white water canoeing river, and the rapids which were difficult obstacles to Thompson are sources of delight to modern canoeists.

David Thompson was not the first to explore the Muskoka and Madawaska Rivers. After the war of 1812-14, the British Imperial Government had launched several explorations for canal routes linking the Ottawa River and Lake Huron. Many of the ambitious entrepreneurs among the pioneers of the Ottawa valley saw a canal as a path to increased settlement and prosperity. These earlier surveys were marked by poor navigation and cartography. A present-day examiner of the maps and reports feels that not only he, but the exploration parties as well, were equally uncertain about where they had actually gone and what they had discovered.*

The official reaction, however, accepted the surveys' credibility in concluding that a canal was impractical:

> . . . From the concurring testimony of Captn. Catty [1819], of Lieut. Briscoe [1826] and of Lt. Walpole [1827] who have each, at different periods, explored the country between Lake Simcoe and the Ottawa there can be very little doubt but that a water

---

*Some documentation of the early surveys, by Lieutenants Catty, Briscoe, and Walpole, along with a response to the first two issued by the Duke of Wellington in 1827, can be found in Florence B. Murray, ed. *Muskoka and Haliburton, 1615-1875: A Collection of Documents*. The Champlain Society for the Government of Ontario (Toronto 1963), pp. 31,32,44,58.

communication can never be established by the Madawasca — The Madawasca which is about 130 miles in length seems to offer a series of rapids and waterfalls; and the River itself to be of too impetuous a character to make it an eligible navigation.[2]

Nevertheless, in 1829 Charles Shirreff, an Ottawa valley entrepreneur, again proposed a canal. He claimed that there were millions of acres of habitable country waiting for settlement, needing only access by canal. In 1834 the Muskoka Region was explored on order of Lieutenant Governor Colborne. Then in 1837 the Legislative Assembly of Upper Canada authorized an expenditure of three thousand pounds "to be applied in the employing of a Surveyor and Engineer, to ascertain the nature of the country lying between the River Ottawa and Lake Huron, and to report the practicability of establishing a communication by Water between the same." Three surveys were ordered: one of the Sturgeon-Temagami-Temiskaming and French Rivers; one of the Magnetawan-Petawawa and Mattawa; and one, which David Thompson was appointed to make, of the Muskoka-Madawaska route.[3] Thompson completed the survey between August and December of that year, not without hardship, difficulty, and displays of resourcefulness and ingenuity that modern canoe trips cannot match.

*　　*　　*

By 1837 David Thompson had enough experience behind him to fill the lifetimes of several men. Born in England in 1770, and apprenticed to the Hudson's Bay Company when he was 15, Thompson learned the techniques of surveying from Philip Turner at Cumberland House on the Saskatchewan in 1789-90, while he was recovering from a broken leg. In 1797 he left the Hudson's Bay Company to become a full partner in the North-West Company. He stayed with them in the west until 1812, when he retired to Montreal, as a man of some means.

During his years in the west Thompson surveyed more than 2 million square miles. He travelled over 50,000 miles on foot, by canoe, and on horseback. He was the first white man to explore and map the length of the Columbia River, and many other parts of the west. He was of firm Christian character, and refused, unlike most Nor-Westers, to trade liquor for fur with the Indians. While in the West, he married a part-Indian woman, and again unlike most of his contemporaries, when he retired to Montreal, he brought his Indian wife and children with him. One of the first acts after reaching Montreal was to have the marriage solemnized.

Thompson might well have lived in comfort for the rest of his life, but he lost much of his money in bad investments and paying off the debts of his children. To avoid poverty, he used his map-making skills and became a surveyor. Between 1816 and 1826 he served as "Astronomer and Surveyor to the British Boundary Commission" on behalf of the British Government, and mapped the Canada-U.S. border from St. Regis in Quebec to the northwest angle of Lake of the Woods. Later he surveyed much of the eastern townships in Quebec, and conducted hydro- graphic surveys of the St. Lawrence. His 1837 survey of the Muskoka and Madawaska Rivers was one of these late-in-life, money-earning tasks which altogether added another 30,000 miles to his travels, making a lifetime total of over 80,000 miles.

Thompson died in 1857 in abject poverty, almost forgotten. The magnificent maps which he had made were not credited to him, and the narrative of his travels was left incomplete and unpublished. He might well have remained in obscurity if J. B. Tyrrell, a geologist with the Geological Survey of Canada and himself a remarkable explorer, had not, during his surveys of the Canadian West in the 1880s, been surprised by the accuracy and the detail of the then existing maps. After lengthy enquiries, Tyrrell found a yellowing map and notebooks of Thompson's in the records of the Government of Ontario. These and other discoveries proved that the unacknowledged source of later maps was David Thompson. After Tyrrell published an article describing Thompson's achievements, he was offered, and purchased, the manuscript of David Thompson's narrative, which was later published by the Champlain Society. Tyrrell commented in his preface:

> Between the years 1883 and 1898, when engaged on the staff of the Geological Survey of Canada, it fell to my lot to carry on exploration in canoes, on horseback and on foot, over many of the routes which had been surveyed and explored by David Thompson a century before, to survey the rivers that he had walked, to cross the plains and mountains on the trails which he had travelled, to camp in his old camping grounds, and to take astronomical observations on the same places where he had taken them. Everywhere his work was found to be of the highest order, considering the means and facilities at his disposal . . .[4]

Tyrrell concluded that David Thompson's achievements in exploration and surveying on land were as remarkable as those of Captain Cook on the oceans.

Thompson's *Travels* is a remarkable document, as Thompson was a remarkable man. A recent editor of the *Travels* says:

> The special excitement of Thompson is to be with him as mapmaker and historian, feeling history almost transformed into myth. Thompson is the mapmaker of the Canadian half-continent. But he is more than that, he is the foundation mythmaker of the Canadian West. He is one of the mapmakers of the Canadian mind.[5]

Thompson's journal of his 1837 survey is in no way comparable to his great *Travels*. It is the working record of a difficult task undertaken by an old man. It does not have the depth of observation, or the insights into geography and Indian culture that give quality to the *Travels*. Nevertheless, the 1837 journal gives the clearest impression of the difficulties of travel, and the character of the country in a part of southern Ontario which was then untracked and hostile northern wilderness.

*   *   *

Ever since he left the Hudson's Bay Company, Thompson had been subject to some calumny, and his character was not without blemishes. It is still surprising, however, to find Captain Baddely, one of the three-man commission established to oversee the surveys of 1837, writing to the Surveyor General in May of that year:

> Mr. Thompson dined with me yesterday . . . he is highly qualified for the duty in point of scientific and professional requirements, and with a young man like Mr. Hawkins, who from personal knowledge I can strongly recommend, much may be done. I think it is necessary, however, from the confidence which has been placed in me, and my desire to see the service properly conducted, to acquaint you that there are rumours abroad that Mr. T. is not trustworthy as to reporting of facts. This I mention without knowing what degree of credit to attach, although I must confess that there is something in his conversation which I do not like and which makes me suspect his candour . . . .[6]

Later surveys of Thompson's routes have shown that he was more trustworthy, as to reporting facts, than most of his contemporaries and successors, although his qualities were not appreciated at the time, nor for many years after. In spite of these doubts, Thompson was engaged to make the survey. Preparations were made during May and June. One issue that arose was whether to have wooden or tin canoes. Capt. Baddely preferred tin, but Thompson had his way — a cedar canoe was made at Holland Landing on Lake Simcoe and shipped to Georgian Bay to await the survey party. Cedar canoes were better: one voyageur recounted about a metal canoe of the period that he had "several excursions up Lake Huron in it. It was rigged for sailing, but was not good in a storm, as it cut through the waves and was a danger of filling, while the bark canoe bounded over them."[7] Tin canoes would also have been far too heavy and awkward for the numerous portages, rapids, and small streams the party encountered. Birch bark canoes would not have been satisfactory. At one point in the survey the crew came across a deserted Indian camp with "many rolls of very good Birch Rind for canoes." Thompson asked his men "if they would have a Birch Rind Canoe made. They said not as it would not stand the required rough usage which our business must have.""[8]

Thompson's crew began the survey from Penetanguishene on Georgian Bay on August 1, 1837. There were five men in one canoe, about 25 feet long, the size of a *canot du nord*. The party reached the Ottawa on October 23, after completing a difficult survey of more than 300 miles. The day-to-day narrative in Thompson's journal describes an arduous trip through barren and hostile land, where the weather was foul, with excessive rainfall, an early winter, and a cold October. There was little game or fish for provisions and the party encountered no Indians from whom to purchase food until they reached the Madawaska River in October. Their canoe was far too big for the rivers and terrain they encountered. They were often cold, wet and hungry. In spite of this Thompson's maps are extraordinarily accurate. Each day, weather permitting, he would take sun and star sights for latitude, and often the much more difficult sights for longitude as well. His four maps and 30,000-word journal together form the most accurate record from the early nineteenth century of the Muskoka-Madawaska river route.

*   *   *

From the vantage point of the present day it is hard to appreciate how difficult Thompson's survey was: he had no maps, the countryside was unknown and practically uninhabited, his canoe was heavy and cumbersome, his tents leaked in the rain, food was in short supply, and the route had not only to be discovered but also made passable and mapped. For the three months of the journey they were out of touch with civilization, and had to rely on their own equipment and skills for survival. Even in the far northern wilderness a modern canoeist has no comparable problems. His equipment is light, waterproof and durable. His maps and river guides are accurate, detailed, and up-to-date. He is only gone for a few weeks or a month, and is rarely more than a few days away from contact with civilization. He is not usually burdened with the tasks of finding and clearing portages, or of mapping his route. Travel is much easier and more pleasant for us today.

It took nearly two days for Thompson to find the mouth of the Muskoka River. On August 1 his party was camped on one of the Christian Islands about five miles from Penetanguishene, and on August 5, when their preparations were complete, they set off: "On coming to the great island [Bone Island] at the north end of which we were led to believe we should find the Southern Branch of the Muskoka River I soon found from the appearance of all about us that we had to find the Main Land, as all before us were rocky granite Islands, in order to be sure to find the River we were in search of. We had much difficulty in getting to the Main Land, and in following it, in hopes of finding Rivers, etc. we were led into Channels and Bays, later Rivers, from which we had to return.""[9]

By August 7 they were well up the river, and had reached the first fall (now Three Rock Falls), about 15 feet high. Here Thompson made his first comments on engineering the proposed canal: "Where the 1st Measurements are of a Canal, it is not wide enough but will come part of it on the path we carry a rise of about 6 to 8 ft. say for 25 ft. width, on a supposition of a Lock of 50 ft. width. MM the 1st CP [carrying place] is a rude Islet Rock, and only to be done anything with on the L Chan. and for 50 ft. width some high Rock say 15 ft. to [be] blasted. This 2nd Fall has a descent of 12 ft. & 3 ft. more may be added for Rapids can be dammed up at the lower narrow of it. The 1st may require a Wall on the R of Canal where it spreads on the Island."[10] This canal building approach of damming a river to create a series of lakes connected by short stretches of locks had been used by Colonel By very successfully on the Rideau Canal connecting Ottawa with Kingston.

The main emphasis of the survey was, however, mapping, and as the voyage progressed Thompson kept detailed notes of the route and of the geographical and other features. He was an observant traveller: animals, trees, geological features, signs of men, weather, and incidents along the route all find their place in his journal. There was a piece of conventional wisdom at the time that where hardwoods grew the land was good for agriculture; hence there are frequent journal entries such as: "Examined the Land in the interior found after going back about 300 yd. on both sides, apparently extensive level land of good hard Wood of Maple, Elm, Basswood, Oak, Birch, etc. Bored the Soil for 2 feet a good dark grey loam, with about 2 or 3 In. of rich vegetable Mould on the top. appears very good for Agriculture."[11] These spots were the exception, however, and a much more common sort of entry is: "The whole of the Country we have come over these 3 days, from the time we came to the main Shore is a very rude Country of Quartz and Sienite Granite with small scanty woods mostly of Firs, Canadian Pines some Red Oak and Aspens in old sheltered Spots. no Birds or any thing, all is desolation, and very little frequented by the Indians."[12] Thompson's perception of the barrenness of the land was not inaccurate. This is one of the least fertile parts of Ontario, far less fertile than the forests of northern Saskatchewan and Manitoba where Thompson had traded earlier. It was partly this lack of fertility which later led the Government of Ontario to create Algonquin Park as protection for the headwaters of the Muskoka, Madawaska, and many other rivers.

The weather was not benign. A constantly recurring refrain in the journal is the difficulties of rainy weather, and the efforts to dry things. On August 7 they "spread out all our wet things to dry which are getting bad with being long wet and hot weather." On August 13, when they were at what is now Bala, "Rain in Showers again came on — but our Things were Tolerably dry and we examined the Provisions and put all in the best order we could. The Tent is all mildewed, getting full of small holes and will soon be useless." The next day "At 3-1/2 PM the Rain ceased but the weather cloudy and threatening — by 4-1/4 PM got to writing up my Journal — everything again wet and my Papers for drawing wet." On September 2, "At 3-1/2 AM steady heavy Rain came on, and continued, it passed thro' my Tent like thick Mist so that every thing is wet . . . ." It wasn't until the improvements in tent and clothing materials and design in the 1960s that wet weather changed from being a severe problem to a minor obstacle for canoeists.

The party met few signs of Indians. On August 14 they camped where Indians had been, and the next day found a deserted Indian lodge. On August 25, just before they reached what is now Bracebridge, they met two Indians, a very old man and a sick boy. Signs of white men were even fewer. They found a piece of birch bark with names and the date 1831 on August 16, a blazed line on August 26 (above Bracebridge) with a post inscribed "William Hawkins D.S. . . . 20th August 1835 God save the King — and a line, not readable. . . . 23 Miles NE corner of Mara." This is less evidence of humans than a modern canoeist would find even along some rivers in the barren grounds of the Northwest Territories. Not until they were well down the Madawaska River did they find evidence of lumbering, and settlement.

As they progressed up the Muskoka and the river got smaller and the portages more difficult, the party found their canoe too large and cumbersome. Often they had to clear a path. On August 31 (near Baysville on the Lake of Bays) Thompson noted they had to stop "to dry again our Canoe, for it has suffered much on the Rocks and Stones coming up the Fall and Rapids and is now rather leaky." On September 9, on the Oxtongue River, they "set to work to clear a way to get the Canoe over this CP. which we effected by 5 of us dragging and pushing the Canoe up on its bottom and myself with a double Line round a tree holding what we gained — and carried the Canoe the latter part." Every half hour they had to stop and haul the canoe up on steep rocks to bail it, and were being further delayed by the frequent need to gum the canoe. By then they had been on the survey for a month and a half. They had met only the two Indians, had killed no game except a few birds and fish, and were still less than half way along their journey. The difficult traverse from the headwaters of the Oxtongue to the Madawaska still had to be made. By September 13 they were at what is now South Tea Lake in Algonquin Park. Thompson recorded:

> As we are now at the 1st Lake at the height of Land, I resolved to do what I have long seen necessary from the shoal water, Rapids, etc. The necessity [for] exploring the Country to know what it is according to my Instructions etc. — and our large Canoe being too heavy for shoal Water, and also that with one Canoe we cannot separate ourselves to examine two Rivers at the same time, etc. etc. I determined to make two small Canoes which should be able to take all our Provisions, Baggage, etc. — for this purpose we crossed to the north side where we had seen Cedar trees, and examined the Ground and in a deep sandy Bay, Thank God, we found on a bank of about 25 feet high, sufficient good Cedar for our purpose.[13]

The canoes they built were not birch bark, but were clinker built out of split cedar. Thompson's own words best describe this experience:

Sept. 14, "dense fog — visited the Net, nothing in it All hands at work. 3 Men knifing Timbers, 2 Men with myself split out the Gunwales for the Canoes to be 19 ft in length. brought them to the Camp. split out 40 more Timbers. Set the net in another place."

Sept. 15, "cool clear morning . . . visited the Net. nothing. let it stand. all hands at work. by noon with two Men split out 33 Boards for the Canoe . . . For want of something fresh find myself weak. Took chocolate for Dinner with Crackers and much better. In the afternoon with 2 Men split out 53 Boards for the Canoe, in all 88 Boards. Tho' some not good, which I think will be enough. Split out the Bars, etc. so that we have nearly completed splitting out all that is required for 2 Canoes of 19 ft. length on the Gunwale or abt. 18 ft. length direct. very fine day. . . ."

Sept. 16, ". . . Knifing Boards etc. — all the timbers of the Canoe are turned and drying etc. — Sent Baptiste to look for 2 young Trees with curved Roots for stern, which he brought."

Sept. 18, "SE Gale with steady rain, working hard to get all ready to begin a Canoe, when the weather permits, as we have no shelter from the Rain, etc. everything is wet. Knifing Boards for the Bottom, Sides, etc. etc. cleared a place for the building of the Canoes. I put the Bars in the Gunwales. got the stern partly ready. etc. etc. . . ."

Sept. 19, " . . . put the bottom and Stern on the Canoe Bed by 1 PM got in the necessary Timbers, put one round of Boards along the Gunwales. cut logs for the Canoe to rest on, & put one round on each side of the bottom."

Sept. 20, "Ice about 1/10 of an in. thick in a kettle about 4 yds from the Fire. . . ' Early all at work. 2 Men collecting Gum for the Canoes. put all the Boards abt. the Canoe & took it off the Bed & gave it to Baptiste to finish. Cut down two Cedars and split out 14 Boards. We have employed more time for want of Nails. The Canoe is 19 ft on the Gunwales by 42 in width and 20 in depth . . ."

Sept. 21, "All hands at work on the Canoes . . . put the 2d Canoe on the bed . . ."

Sept. 23, " . . . Early get the Canoe finally boarded in, & set to work on getting the rest of the Timber in, etc. etc. which occupied all day, with the two canoes. pegs instead of Nails, we have not one third enough Nails. picked an old piece of Line into Oakum to help the stopping the seams of the Canoes etc. . . ."

Sept. 24, "Men employed on the Canoes, running gum into the seams, caulking slightly etc. etc."

Sept. 25, "Sent all the Men to gather Gum, for it is a very scarce Article, & is what details us here. by 2 PM each returned with a little, altho' they have searched round this Lake, as there are few Pines, boiled it, & got it ready for the Canoes. but at 3 PM, Rain came on, & soon became very heavy. so that we could do nothing. The season getting late.

Sept. 26, "Steady small Rain & a Gale of Wind, bad weather. The Canoes wet, cannot gum them. sent the Men across the Lake to look for Gum. They returned by 2 PM. The Clouds broke away, & the afternoon, fine, put the Canoes near the fire to dry, and began gumming late, but it will break off with the first shoal, or Rapid, as the Canoes are not dry enough. . . ."

Sept. 27, ". . . Finished the Gum we have on the Canoe, which is by no means enough, but no more can be procured at this place . . . In the 14 days for making the Canoes we had 6 fine days — 6 days of Rain and 2 days of half Rain & half dry cloudy weather. . . ."

*   *   *

On September 29 Thompson's party, in their two smaller canoes, left the building site on South Tea Lake and began their journey across the south end of the present Algonquin Park to the headwaters of the Madawaska. They reached to where Whitney on the Madawaska now stands on October 12, after taking fourteen days to make a trip the modern canoeists can complete in two. Although some of the difficulties Thompson found were caused by the constant and time consuming search for gum to waterproof the canoes, the bulk of the time was spent in searching for the route, and in clearing out portages from lake to lake. There were no marked portages, they had no maps, and the route, as canoeists know, is a maze of small lakes, marshes, and wooded slopes, without rivers or streams to guide travellers.

On October 7, after leaving Phipps Lake, Thompson noted: "These Lakes are small but deep, and by damming up at a small expence, make excellent reservoirs of Water for Locks & fine Steam Boat navigation. plenty of good materials at hand, except Lime. The Lands are generally good, mingled Woods but near the Lakes & Brooks too strong, tho' in my opinion not more so than

many parts of Up [per] Canada, especially the Eastern District."[14] This optimism
is belied, however, in the day-by-day chronicle of his arduous journey across these
headwaters, and it seems to be a perfunctory afterthought placed in the journal to
please his patrons—the kind of thing a politician could quote to justify spending
money on public works. On October the tenth, at Rock Lake, above Whitney,
they came across an Indian camp:

> . . . here we found an old Indian of the name Cha un d e and enquiring what River we
> were on, he told us, we were on the middle Branch, or the proper Madawaska River, that
> no white man had been on it, that it was the shortest, best, and had the greatest Water of
> the 3 Branches which form the main Stream. had fewer Rapids, and was by far the most
> navigable & that we had been fortunate in finding it. I wanted him to give me a Sketch
> of the North Branch [Opeongo River], which he declined, but procured from him a
> sketch of the River Lakes and [carrying] Places for some distance. he advised us to be
> careful on the Rapids, adding that when you are below them all, there will be no more
> danger. he gave us two Joints of Deer for all of which I paid him 6/3 and some Salt and
> Pepper.[15]

This was their second encounter with other people since Georgian Bay in early
August, and the first adequate supply of fresh meat in the same two months.
    From this point on, the rapids they ran and portaged are ones familiar to
modern whitewater canoeists. Thompson's journey, rapid by rapid, can be compared with the present day river. Much of it is unchanged. But Thompson's river
running was vastly different. His canoes were inferior: "Early set to work to
strengthen the Canoes, as the rough hard usage they have had among the
Embarras & Rapids has almost torn the Gunwales from the Canoe, for want of
Nails etc. They are no longer able to stand a Gale of Wind, or heavy Rapids,
undid all the Boxes for Nails, except Two."[16] He portaged many of the rapids
modern canoeists run. His concerns were surveying and survival, not pleasure.
    Below Whitney they met another party of Indians in canoes on the river,
and engaged one of them to serve as guide. In spite of this help, their canoes were
damaged and their belongings wet by the time they reached Bark Lake. But here
the journey took on a different aspect. Though the rapids were still difficult, the
shanties of lumberjacks appeared on the banks, and at Lake Kamineskeg on
October 15 they met their first white man, a Mr. McCrae, who gave them a bushel
of potatoes, and sold them some flour. Here their Indian guide left them. The rest
of the journey, though still difficult, was in territory where settlement had begun.
They were able to get supplies from farmers, and the lumberjacks had cleared
portages and made the river more passable.
    Thompson marvelled, at Bell's Rapids where the Madawaska Kanu Camp
now is, that "the sides of these Falls and Rapids like all others are wholly of
Boulders heaped on these two Shores. Some weigh 5 to 7 Tons, how they got
there, and formed the sides & shores of the Falls & Rapids hitherto, is the
question, perhaps by the agency of the Ice.""[17] They ran these rapids with empty
canoes. At the bottom of the Slate Falls portage, above Griffith, Thompson
noted, as modern canoeists do, "at this lower end and on the left the Rock in

Strata and placed almost vertically and much dislocated."[18] There were log booms, gates, and a timber slide at this fall.

On October 24, the party reached Arnprior. Thompson stated categorically in his journal the day before that "All of the lower part of this River may be pronounced impracticable to improvement."[19] Any lingering illusion that the route was feasible for a canal had vanished.

Thompson's survey was not completed, however. After reaching Bytown (Ottawa) on October 26, he began a further survey up the Ottawa River to the mouth of the Petawawa, which was not finished until late December, and Thompson himself did not reach his home in Montreal until December 30. The last entry in his journal reads:

> December 31st. A fine mild Sunday. Cloudy. here is an end of my engagement with the Commissioners as Civil Engineer.
> Ther 36 Easterly & Cloudy.[20]

*   *   *

Thompson's journal is not the diary of a happy man. He found the weather unpleasant. He feared the rapids, and the pages of the journal contain many expressions of "Thank God" at the fact that his party successfully surmounted yet another arduous challenge. Rations were meagre, the barrenness of the land made food-gathering difficult, and they were often hungry. Although Thompson frequently recorded his delight in nature and the unexpected—the leaves turning in the fall, a butterfly in November, the pattern of frost—his journal is more the record of an old man making a difficult voyage he would rather not have done, than the narrative of an interested and happy explorer. That he could overcome the obstacles of old age, weather, and terrain, and produce such excellent maps and journal, is testimony to his strength and abilities.

His conclusion that the Muskoka-Madawaska route was not a feasible path for a canal still stands. The results of the other surveys suggested that if a canal were to be built between the upper Ottawa and Lake Huron, the most sensible route would be the Mattawa-Lake Nippissing-French River track. This canal, however, was never built. Instead, years later, the Trent canal was built to connect the Bay of Quinte with Lake Simcoe and Georgian Bay.

Thompson's reports and maps were submitted to the government, ignored and then forgotten. It was not until 1854-62 that further surveys were made of the Muskoka region, and these later surveyors appear neither to have known that Thompson made his 1837 survey, nor to have seen his maps. Hence, apart from any immediate impression created when Thompson submitted his report, his efforts had no impact. They remain today largely as an historical curiosity, and as a footnote to the unhappy old age of one of Canada's neglected great men.

One reason for the lack of impact can be found in the last pages of Thompson's 1837 journal. On December 26, while he was in Ottawa, he noted:

> . . . Capt[n] Baker arrived yesterday. Waited on him and settled Accts with him and drew 16.4 to make the sum of 180. He gave me a Letter from the Commissioners dated the 14 Nov[r] which puts an end to my employment on the last day of this month. Mr. Cartwright, with whom I hoped to settle accts at Kingston I learn has gone to Toronto, my only way is to get to Montreal, but by what road is not easy to determine on acct of the Civil War, but go I must some way or the other.

And on December 27:

> . . . can find no conveyance to Montreal on account of the disturbed state of the Country. at length Francois La Riviere undertook to get me a conveyance, that is a Horse and Train for the morrow morning. for 3.15. a high price, but no alternative.

Then on December 30:

> . . . came to the Grande Brule stopped to feed the Horse. here is a sad view of the effects of unnatural Rebellion the Church, Mill & many houses burnt. At 2 PM came to St Eustache here is a sadder spectacle the Church and perhaps 40 or more Houses burnt. . .
> . . . Thank God, arrived in Montreal & at my lodging at 8 PM.

The rebellions, in both Upper and Lower Canada, set politicians' minds to work on more important things than improbable canals through the barren northern wilderness. The next few years were occupied with the struggle for responsible government, not with canals and exploration. Here, probably, is the reason for the total oblivion into which Thompson's survey fell.

Today the Muskoka and Madawaska Rivers and Algonquin Park are prime vacation country. The few sections of rapids along the rivers as yet unaltered by dams also permit excellent whitewater canoeing, within easy reach of the metropolitan centres of southern Ontario. One especially interesting whitewater stretch of the Madawaska River, from Palmer Rapids to Griffith, is in the process of being made into a provincial park. There could be no more fitting memorial in Ontario for David Thompson than to consolidate this new park and the other crown land along the Muskoka and Madawaska Rivers into a David Thompson River Park, reaching from Algonquin Park east to the Ottawa River, and west to Georgian Bay. This would preserve the rivers and rapids, which Thompson found so difficult, as a playground for those who have followed him, and would create, along the route he explored, a recreation resource for the present and future with roots extending deep into Canada's history. This historical and geographical link between the nineteenth century's North and the twentieth century's South would then be a living part of Canadian experience.

ENDNOTES

1. David Thompson's "Journal of Occurrences from Lake Huron to the Ottawa River." Public Archives of Ontario, David Thompson Papers, v. 28, no. 66. Hereafter referred to as: Thompson, *Journal*.

2. Quoted in Florence B. Murray, ed., *Muskoka and Haliburton, 1615-1875: A Collection of Documents*. The Champlain Society for the Government of Ontario (Toronto 1963), p. 58.

3. Upper Canada, House of Assembly, *Appendix to Journals*, 1839, 4th Session, 13th Parliament, "Report of the Commission on the Survey of the Ottawa River etc." The portion of Thompson's survey not covered in this paper, of the Ottawa River, is included in this appendix.

4. J. B. Tyrrell, ed., *David Thompson's Narrative of his Explorations in Western America, 1784-1812* (Toronto: Champlain Society, 1912), p. iv.

5. Victor G. Hopwood, ed., *David Thompson: Travels in Western North America, 1784-1812* (Toronto: Macmillan, 1971), p. 34.

6. Quoted in Murray, *Muskoka and Haliburton.*, p. 84.

7. Quoted in Edwin E. Guillet, *Pioneer Travel in Upper Canada* (Reprinted Toronto: University of Toronto Press, 1963), pp. 30-31.

8. Thompson, *Journal*, Aug. 15. I am very grateful to Mrs. Eleanor Gunn for putting Thompson's *Journal* into typescript from holograph.

9. Ibid., Aug. 5.

10. Ibid., Aug. 7.

11. Ibid., Aug. 10.

12. Ibid., Aug. 7.

13. Ibid., Sept. 13.

14. Ibid., Oct. 7.

15. Ibid., Oct. 10.

16. Ibid., Oct. 11.

17. Ibid., Oct. 15.

18. Ibid., Oct. 17.

19. Ibid., Oct. 23.

20. Ibid., Dec. 31.

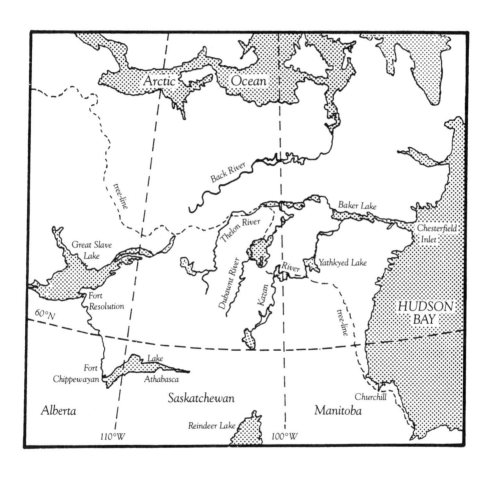

History, Travel and Canoeing in the Barrens

George J. Luste

My father, you have spoken well; you have told me that heaven is very beautiful;
tell me now one thing more. Is it more beautiful than the country of the muskox
in summer, when sometimes the mist blows over the lakes, and sometimes the
water is blue, and the loons cry very often?

Saltatha, a Yellow Knife Indian.[1]

But in my opinion, there cannot exist a stronger proof that mankind was not
created to enjoy happiness in this world, than the conduct of the miserable
beings who inhabit this wretched part of it.

Samuel Hearne, a European explorer.[2]

Saltatha was responding to a missionary priest of the late nineteenth century who
had offered his biblical description of heaven. A hundred years earlier, on his
punishing journey across northern North America Samuel Hearne perceived
little aesthetic beauty in the same landscape.

It is hard to believe that these two quotes depict the same country — the
Barren Lands of northern Canada. The two points of view betray the differing
backgrounds and world view of the individuals who are expressing them. While
Saltatha's words are those of a native inhabitant describing his beloved home,
Hearne's reflect the view of a fearful and foreign intruder from a totally different
landscape and culture. Hearne was committed to a struggle for survival in what he
clearly viewed as a strange, inhospitable and harsh environment. His accounts, as
well as those of many other early white explorers caught in similar struggles, often
reflect this grim, stark view.

The Barren Lands occupy those lands west of Hudson Bay, north of the
spruce forests up to the arctic coastline. They reach from north of Great Bear Lake
in a sweeping arc down to Churchill on Hudson Bay. Very few Canadians have
experienced first hand this inaccessible region, walked on its rich summer mantle
of flora, or observed its nesting bird life and migrating herds of caribou. Except for
isolated pockets in scattered river valleys, no trees grow in the Barrens. Technically it is a desert. But the frozen permafrost layer underground acts as a sealing
membrane and no water escapes except along the surface. Thus innumerable
glistening ponds, lakes, rivers and streams thread this desert. A canoeists' paradise!

Today, two hundred years after Hearne stumbled across his "wretched"
Barren Lands, modern travellers who canoe and trek this vast northern tundra are
much more apt to agree with Saltatha than with Hearne. Perhaps this also reflects
on the individuals who choose to go north today, who in all likelihood already
possess a strong affinity for the natural environment. What is this affinity and

why do individuals go out of their way to experience the isolation and difficulty of primitive travel in remote corners of the world? For the moment suffice it to suggest that perhaps it is a yearning for kinship with the past and the natural forces of our existence. Another reason for our positive view today may be that we have the security of accurate maps, stronger equipment, ample provisions and the luxury of a much shorter stay. In other words, we do not suffer much, if at all. It is easier for us to perceive Saltatha's beauty in the Barrens, a beauty that escaped Hearne.

Saltatha's words were recorded by Warburton Pike. Unfortunately, because these native people had an oral culture, rather than written, we cannot read their words first hand but must do so indirectly through the ears and writings of those whites who, like Pike, travelled and lived with them. Two such interpreters of the native culture stand out amongst their contemporaries in terms of accuracy and genuine experience. One is David Thompson who, from 1784 to 1812, travelled and mapped much of Western Canada while employed by the Hudson's Bay and North-West Companies.[3] His most northern travels took him near Lake Athabasca, in the land of the Chipewyan Indians but not out into the open Barren Lands themselves. The second is Knud Rasmussen, who was part Eskimo, spoke the Eskimo language as his native tongue and in 1902 began a lifelong pursuit of ethnographical studies of the Eskimos. In the early 1920s Rasmussen travelled by dog sledge, with two Eskimo companions, across the northern continent from Greenland to the Bering Sea.[4] His travels included a trip south, up the Kazan River to Lake Yathkyed where he met the Padlermiut, the Willow-Folk — a tribe of the Caribou Eskimo. The writings of both these authors are among the most intimate and perceptive statements regarding our northern native cultures.

The naturalist C. H. D. Clarke, who in 1937 canoed the Hanbury-Thelon Rivers to Baker Lake, describes the attraction of the North for all of us:

> The northern barrens have a beauty of their own. There is something in the boundlessness of the rolling plains that is even more humbling than mountains and the monotony disappears completely on close inspection.[5]

Hearne and Clarke reflect the two extreme relationships of white culture with the northern environment. The evolution of this relationship over time, the change from fear and hate to respect and appreciation can be observed as one reads the writing of the early northern travellers. One could argue that this dichotomy of love and fear for our wilderness surroundings is still with us, that it is part of the Canadian psyche. Today Canada is still predominantly a wilderness land mass. Almost all of the Canadian population inhabits less than ten percent of the landscape, primarily along a narrow ribbon hugging the southern border. As yet no roads penetrate the Barren Lands from the south. Except for the float plane, canoeing is still the only practical form of summer travel. However, there is little in common between observing the northern landscape seated in a plane several hundred feet above it, and paddling slowly, yard by yard, mile after mile across it. This simple exertion of muscle and body against the yielding canoe paddle bonds a relationship with the northern lakes, rivers and land that travel by car or plane never can. During four separate summers over the last twelve years I have canoed almost three thousand miles in the Barrens. In the winters and the intervening years down south this joy has been repeatedly rekindled by reading and rereading the history and literature of this northern region. The combination has given an historical perspective to my experiences of canoe travel in the Barrens.

There is a prevailing view among the northern old timers that after five years in the north every new visitor is an expert but after ten years a novice. Unfortunately this humbling logic places me somewhere near the cradle.

*　　*　　*

Is it not odd to describe the exploration of land that was already populated by an indigenous native people? Yet most of our history and discovery texts do just that. Because they did not leave a written record to make it official, or have access to the prestigious London publishing houses, the native Indians and Eskimos of northern Canada, who undoubtedly were the original explorers of our North, have simply faded without distinction or credit into a nameless historical mist. This understanding is implicit in the following discussion of the recorded discoverers of the North. Most of these early discoverers represented either the Hudson's Bay Company or the Royal Navy. Later, not necessarily in order, came the Catholic Church, the Canadian Geological Survey, the Royal Northwest Mounted Police, the trophy hunters, scientists, naturalists, and northern adventurers. The most frequently used access route into the Barrens was from the west via Fort Resolution on Great Slave Lake, but some did come from the east via Churchill or Chesterfield Inlet on Hudson Bay and still others came from the south via Lake Athabasca or Reindeer Lake. For obvious reasons no white traveller started in the high arctic and came south into the Barrens.

Samuel Hearne was the first white traveller to cross the Barrens. In his third attempt, starting in December of 1770 and concluding in June 1772, he succeeded in a truly remarkable journey from Churchill (then Fort Prince of Wales) on Hudson Bay northwest to the mouth of the Coppermine River on the Arctic Ocean and back again to Churchill. Hearne's accomplishment is even more astonishing when one realizes that not only was he the first white man into the Barrens but his travels covered far more distance than did later travellers. He was the true Marco Polo of the sub-arctic and the phrase "Barren Lands" originates from his narrative, which is one of the classics of the North. The next to travel into the Barrens, to experience its harsh reality, was the first Franklin expedition in 1820 and 1821.[6] Franklin came back to the arctic for two subsequent trips, finally to die there in 1847. His two ships and all the crew members disappeared with him. In the 1830s George Back, who had assisted Franklin on two earlier expeditions, travelled down the Great Fish River that now bears his name, in search of the lost arctic expedition of Captain John Ross. The same route was retraced twenty years later by Chief Factor Anderson and his party, who this time were searching for the missing arctic expedition of the elderly Sir John Franklin.[7] It would appear that a considerable amount of "exploration" in the arctic took place while searching for other lost explorers. This is particularly true of the many Naval sea searches for Franklin which started in 1847 and continued for thirty years. While these Naval narratives provide interesting reading about the arctic they deal primarily with life on the ships and with the difficulties of battling sea ice. They say little about the native Indians or Eskimos who routinely travelled vast distances in the Barrens and who the later explorers used as guides whenever possible. But the more typical early Naval attitude was to ignore the natives and the possibility that one might learn about travel on land and ice from the Indians and Eskimos.

Few early missionaries ventured into the Barrens but two exceptions stand out. One was the Oblate Father Alphonse Gasté who in April 1868 left his Reindeer Lake mission and travelled north into the Barrens in the company of Chipewyan Indians.[8] It was seven months before he returned. In his travels he made contact with the Caribou Eskimos and reached Tuantue Lake, now known as Dubawnt Lake. To the Chipewyans "Tuantue" meant "the lake with water on the edges" because the centre ice did not melt. My 1969 canoeing experience on Dubawnt Lake in the last week of July attests to the appropriateness of this name. We encountered considerable solid ice that year, noted for late ice throughout the North. Judging from earlier writings it does seem that on the average more summer ice and snow was encountered in the past than in the present. This would support the generally accepted hypothesis that today we are in the midst of a warming cycle in global weather. In 1893, twenty five years after Gasté, the Tyrrell brothers, J. B. and James, also found Dubawnt Lake full of ice in August. James Tyrrell makes the droll comment in his book: "it was a point of discussion with us whether the season of this land was spring or autumn"[9], the point being that summer is so very brief in the far north, it can be missed altogether. Fall freeze up in the Barrens can start before the end of September, which leaves a narrow window of six to eight weeks for reasonably reliable summer conditions and canoe travel on the bigger lakes. Eric Morse, the pioneer of the modern canoeing interest in the sub-arctic, emphasizes this important point.[10]

A second missionary, Father Emile Petitot, made numerous exploratory trips into the western Barrens from 1864 to 1872[11]. He was stationed at Resolution on Great Slave Lake and later at Fort Good Hope on the Mackenzie River. It is interesting to note in passing the nature of the names selected for the early northern outposts — Resolution, Good Hope, Reliance, Enterprise and Providence; clearly the theme was one of optimism. But the true basis for this positive emphasis on hope must have been an underlying fear, unease and a sense of isolation in a hostile environment.

The frequency of travellers into the Barrens increased dramatically in the 1890s.* In 1890 Warburton Pike, an explorer and musk-ox hunter, together with James Mackinley, the Hudson's Bay Company manager from Fort Resolution, travelled by canoe from Great Slave Lake northeast to Beechey Lake on the Back River[12]. Three years later the Candian Geological Survey sent the Tyrrells on two epic south-to-north traverses of the Barrens, first in 1893 via the Dubawnt River and in 1894 via the Kazan and Ferguson Rivers[13]. In his official report, J. B. Tyrrell explains the prior lack of information on the Barrens:

> Since a large portion of this region lies north of the country where fur-trading animals are abundant, it had not been traveled over by fur-traders, or even by voyageurs or Indians in search of furs, and the character of the lakes and streams were, therefore, unknown to any but the few Indian and Eskimo deer-hunters who live on their banks, and who come south once or twice a year to trade wolf or fox skins for ammunition and tobacco.[14]

Tyrrell's Geological Survey report for 1896, which describes both trips, represented all the information available on this vast area of Canada until aerial surveying started nearly fifty years later. In the 1890s other brief expeditions into the Barrens followed in rapid succession, namely Russell, Whitney, Munn, and Jones[15]. All these expeditions originated from Great Slave Lake and were primarily winter musk-ox hunting adventures in the company of the local Indians. The numerous accounts written by these men, describing their hunting exploits, must have caused genuine concern for the musk-ox who like the buffalo of the prairies, were in danger of extermination. The killing was substantial. It has been estimated that the Peary expeditions alone, in their quests for the north pole, killed six hundred musk-oxen. In Hanbury's book[16] there is a picture, c.1900, taken at Fort Churchill showing hundreds of musk-ox robes hanging out to dry. The accounts of all these expeditions describe the frightful vulnerability of the musk-oxen who, when confronted by the hunters, formed a stationary circle and defended their young in the centre to the last animal or the last bullet. Eventually, in 1927, the Thelon Game Sanctuary was established in the very centre of the Barrens. So today one of the highlights of canoeing the Thelon River is the sight of the musk-oxen in this region. The 1898 winter trip of Charles Jesse Jones into the central Barrens is generally not well known. His journey is of special interest because he travelled from Great Slave Lake as far east as Dubawnt Lake and tried, although unsuccessfully, to bring back live musk-oxen[17].

Two other travellers of this decade might be mentioned since they penetrated the Barrens from the east, contrary to convention. Talbot Clifton, another English gentleman and world traveller, made a brief winter trip west from Chesterfield Inlet into the Barrens in the 1890s.[18] It was not a particularly successful or noteworthy venture. Then in July 1899 David Hanbury began the first complete east-to-west traverse of the Barrens by canoe from Chesterfield Inlet.[19] He travelled up the Thelon River to Great Slave Lake and reached Fort Resolution three months later in late September. In the summer of 1901 he repeated his trek in the

*See Margaret Hobbs "Purposeful Wanderers: Late Nineteenth Century Travellers to the Barrens" elsewhere in this volume.

opposite direction from west to east. Hanbury then spent the winter of 1901-02 travelling north and west in the company of Eskimos. By spring his party was at the mouth of the Coppermine River, which they ascended, and heading south via Great Bear Lake reached Edmonton in the fall of 1902. All told Hanbury had successfully accomplished three impressive and complete traverses of the Barrens.

Other expeditions continued to explore the various corners of Barrens. In 1900 J. M. Bell surveyed Great Bear Lake area and went northeast to the Coppermine River[20]. That same spring and summer James Tyrrell explored the height of land area east of Great Slave Lake[21]. In 1903 E.A. Preble led a biological study of the Great Bear Lake area and four years later he and Seton canoed northeast of Great Slave Lake to Aylmer Lake.[22] The following year, in 1908, the Royal North West Mounted Police entered the Barren Lands with a canoe patrol from Great Slave Lake via the Thelon River to Hudson Bay.[23] Inspector E.A. Pelletier* commanded this patrol, which took two months from their departure at Fort Resolution to reach Hudson Bay to the east. It is noteworthy that this party of four officers in two canoes was not accompanied by any native guides on the Barren Lands portion of their journey, a sign perhaps that sufficient information was available by 1908 for unguided summer travel by white visitors to the Barrens. Three years later, in 1911, the same Thelon River route from Great Slave Lake to Baker Lake was followed by H. V. Radford and T. G. Street who were on a zoological expedition for American museums. That winter they travelled north of Bathurst Inlet and the following June they were killed by local Eskimos. This triggered another arduous winter patrol by the RCMP in 1917 from Baker Lake to Bernard Harbour in search of the Eskimos responsible for the killings.[24] In total the patrol accomplished 4000 km of winter travel — an impressive achievement which no doubt helped foster the RCMP legend that they always get their man.

The Baker Lake area is significant in a discussion of the Barren Lands. It penetrates 250 km into the Barrens from Hudson Bay and is accessible by ship from the Bay. Today it is unique as a major inland Eskimo settlement. In 1915 a temporary RCMP base was established at the east end of Baker Lake. A year later, in 1916, the Hudson's Bay Company established a trading post at the mouth of the Kazan River, on Okpiktuyuk Island. In 1924, Revillon Frères, a competing fur trading company set up its operation at the present site of the settlement near the west end of Baker Lake. Knud Rasmussen, Kaj Birket-Smith and the 5th Thule Expedition passed this way in 1922.[25] In 1927 two competing missions, Anglican and Roman Catholic, were established in the small community. At about this time the wonders of air travel came to the Barrens. But the early airplanes, like the early white explorers, encountered harrowing experiences when they first ventured out to the vastness of the empty Barrens. In the autumn of 1929, Colonel C. D. H. McAlpine and his party disappeared while flying over the

---

*See John Jennings "The Mounted Police in the Barren Lands: The Pelletier Expedition of 1908" elsewhere in this volume.

Barrens.[26] The subsequent search made headline news across the country and the Colonel himself was 50 lbs. lighter when finally rescued. This familiar refrain of near starvation and hardship sounds all too similar to the earlier days of Hearne and Franklin.

In the western Barrens, between 1908 and 1912, individuals like Hornby, Stefansson, and Douglas were actively travelling and exploring in the vicinity of, and north of, Great Bear Lake.[27] Of the three, Hornby is unique. His habit, perhaps crazy, of tempting fate year after year out on the land, and finally losing to fate in the central Barrens on the Thelon River is now part of Barren Land legend. For Hornby the northern tundra embodied a seductive enticement, a profound isolation and a final recompense for being careless. This is still part of the mystique and attraction of going into the Barrens today.

Guy Blanchet and Thierry Mallet travelled in the Barrens during the mid-1920s.[28] Blanchet, while working for the Government, mapped the area north and east of Great Slave Lake as far as the Back River and the region between Lake Athabasca and Great Slave Lake. Mallet, an officer of the Revillon Frères fur trading company, entered the Barrens from the south, following the Chipewyan route to the Kazan River used thirty years earlier by J. B. Tyrrell. Solid ice on Yathkyed Lake in mid-July forced him to turn back south and return to Reindeer Lake rather than continue north to Baker Lake. Mallet was a sensitive and observant traveller who wrote movingly about his experiences in the land of the Caribou Eskimo.

To conclude this selective history of Barren Land travel prior to 1940, one final individual should be mentioned. In 1939 P. G. Downes canoed north from Reindeer Lake to Nueltin Lake and the Hudson's Bay post at Windy Lake on the edge of the Barrens.[29] Downes travelled extensively in the North from 1935 to 1951 and in 1940 attempted to reach Kasba Lake on the Kazan River. He failed, primarily because he had neither accurate map nor guide to assist him. Downes was the first northern canoeist of the contemporary period, when flying to the North is an easy option. Downes, however, chose to canoe his way to the Barrens. He prefered to experience the North by the more demanding, traditional mode of travel. Judging by the lack of written accounts it appears that few recreationalists travelled the far northern rivers immediately following Downes. However, since 1960 there has been a tremendous awakening of interest in northern canoeing. The unique combinations of challenge, beauty, isolation and self discovery in the wilderness of northern Canada has captured the imagination of many.

*   *   *

J. B. Tyrrell claimed that his travels through the Barrens taught him that there are really only two essentials in life — food and warmth. He went on to say it was nice to have both but, of the two, food was the more important. The importance of food is a recurring theme in all Barren Land narratives, both ancient and recent. Souci, Guy Blanchet's travelling companion during his 1923 trip into the Barrens, echoed a similar opinion: "To me a fire is like a father, but the caribou of the Barren Grounds, she is my mother."[30] The prophetic John Hornby described the Barren Lands as the "land of feast and famine." It was his intention to write a book with this title but ironically a winter caught him in the middle of the Barrens with insufficient food; famine followed and he starved to death on April 16th 1927. His two companions died soon after. Winter is particularly cruel in the Barrens if one has to attempt living off the land. The days are short, the cold is intense, fishing is very difficult and almost all the caribou have gone south to the tree line. All this changes in the summer when the days are long, the sun shines warmly, the lakes and rivers are full of trout, and the caribou are wandering throughout the Barrens.

The Eskimos, who adapted amazingly to what perhaps is the harshest environment that any race has to face on this earth, are universally described as a happy, gregarious people. At first reflection this may seem surprising. Knud Rasmussen, in his travels among them during the 1920s, heard an Eskimo give the following simple explanation for this love of life:

> Oh! You strangers only see us happy and free of care. But if you knew the horrors we often have to live through, you would understand too why we are so fond of laughing, why we love food and song and dancing. There is not one among us but has experienced a winter of bad hunting, when many people starved to death around us and we ourselves only pulled through by accident.[31]

The continued exposure of the native digestive system to the vagaries of the hunt and the resulting extremes of feast and famine appear to have provided these people with a special physiology. The early explorers were often amazed at the huge quantities they could consume in times of plenty. Warburton Pike, when in the Barrens with his Indian companion King Beaulieu, reproached him for his wasteful eating. The old native replied angrily:

> 'What is this improvidence? I do not like that word. When we have meat why should we not eat [well] to make up for the time when we are sure to starve again?[32]

And who are we today to judge otherwise? In the journals of Tyrrell and others who had the memorable experience of running out of food, invariably it was the native companion who could draw on some mysterious source of reserve or courage and go ahead, hunting game or seeking help, after the white explorers had given up, exhausted. To Hearne's great credit, he must have realized that his one chance for survival over a prolonged period in the Barrens was to join a band of native Indians and rely on their knowledge and inherited instincts. Pike had a similar view: "My best chance seemed to be to follow Hearne's example and trust to the local knowledge of Indians to help me".[33] J. B. Tyrrell on the other hand did not trust himself to the local Indians on his first trip in 1893. Perhaps as a result of this decision they suffered unnecessary hardships. Tyrrell had hired six canoemen, three of whom were Iroquois Indians from Caughnawaga near Montreal, but they had never been in the Barrens. It was two of his "western half-breeds" who, in the desperate last days of their frightful canoe race with winter on the frozen shores of Hudson Bay, had enough energy to save the party by walking the last fifty miles to Fort Churchill to bring back help.

During Tyrrell's long sojourn down the Dubawnt River two important incidents regarding their food supply stand out. By the end of July in 1893 Tyrrell had reached Barlow Lake in the Barrens, was running low on food and still had a long way to go. James Tyrrell in his book writes: "if game should not be found within a week or ten days, we would have to return or else proceed with the probability before us of starvation." Within a few days, however, their luck changed: they fell in with a vast herd of migrating caribou. Tyrrell observes:

> The valleys and hillsides for miles appeared to be moving masses of carribou. To estimate their number would be impossible. They could only be reckoned in acres or square miles.[34]

They easily killed all they needed and preserved the meat from twenty carcasses. No doubt this good fortune and their satiated appetites influenced Tyrrell's decision to continue paddling farther north into the unknown. Five weeks later, again short of provisions, they reached Baker Lake. It was early September. With another 1200 km to Churchill to the south and with winter almost upon them, they were in a desperate situation, forced to gamble. J. B. writes:

> hunting was not allowed to interfere with the greatest possible expedition in travel. It had become evident that it would be possible to reach Churchill before winter only by travelling with the utmost speed. In order to gain this speed and avoid the delay from the long portages which we expected still to reach, very little fresh meat was taken into the canoes at a time, and thus we assumed the risk of a shortness of provisions.[35]

And shortness of provisions they did experience. Survival was uncertain. In J. W. Tyrrell's book, the chapter describing this experience has the apt title of "Life or Death". It really was with some luck, and more important with the absence of bad luck, that they reached Churchill alive on October 19th, 1893. It is said that J. B. Tyrrell weighed 145 pounds when he reached civilization instead of his usual 200. It was a telling statement of J. B. Tyrrell's character that at this point, half starved, even before he had returned from this first difficult venture, he was already planning another expedition into the Barrens for 1894.

Could the Tyrrells have been more self-sufficient by bringing a larger quantity of provisions? The Tyrrell party of eight left Fort Chipewyan on Lake Athabasca the 21st of June in three canoes and it took them 120 days to reach Churchill. It is difficult to estimate how much food each man required per day back then. Today, with freeze dry technology and plastic packaging, about 2½ pounds of concentrated, processed food per day per individual is adequate for a four to seven week canoe trip in the warm summer months. Even this average number, however, which probably is on the low side for Tyrrell's day, would have required 300 pounds of provisions for each man in order that their expedition be self-sufficient for four months. Of course, the more food one brings, the more trips are required on the portages, the slower the travel rate becomes, the longer it takes to cover a fixed distance and this in turn then requires even more provisions in order to be self-sufficient. The early travellers into the Barrens, whether they came by canoe in the summer or by snowshoe in the winter, simply could not afford to carry enough food to be totally self-sufficient on trips that took three, four or more months.

The total weight of the Tyrrell outfit, leaving Fort Chipewyan at the start of their 1893 venture, was the incredible sum of 4000 pounds. It took their five packers (the sixth was injured) eight trips each with a load of 100 pounds per carry to transport everything across a portage at the beginning. The first two portages out of Lake Athabasca were three miles each. These two portages represent a staggering ninety miles of walking for each packer over rough country to portage the six miles. By way of comparison, most canoe trips in the North today are down to two carries per portage. This means one fifth the walking distance per carry that Tyrrell initially required. Even with this awesome amount of supplies, five weeks later the Tyrrell party was already concerned about a shortage of provisions. One cannot help but conclude that Tyrrell brought a considerable amount of heavy gear and one wonders whether it was not excessive. James Tyrrell gives the following brief list of their outfit:

> tea . . . bacon, axes, flour, matches, oatmeal, alcohol, tin kettles, evaporated apples, apricots, salt, sugar, frying-pans, dutch oven, rice, pepper, mustard, files, jam, tobacco, hard tack, candles, geological hammers, baking powder, pain killer, knives, forks, canned beef, . . . tin dishes, tarpaulins and waterproof sacks. Besides the above there were our tents, bags of dunnage, mathematical instruments, rifles and a box of ammunition.[36]

It would be interesting to do a careful comparison between this first trip into the Barrens and the following one in 1894. One just might discover that Tyrrell's outfit and his travel had become much more efficient after this difficult 1893 experience. In contrast to Tyrrell, Hearne, during the eighteen months he accompanied Matonabbee and his band, personally carried his minimal belongings on his back.

Meeting with Indians on north shore of Lake Athabasca – the Tyrrell expedition.

The Barrens at Bloody Falls on the Coppermine River.

While a large, heavy outfit may appear to provide some security, it can also act as a heavy anchor, diminishing mobility, slowing progress and thus increasing one's already uncertain dependence on local hunting. When starvation is at hand, searching for game quickly over a wide area is absolutely essential.

What quantities of provisions did these early Barren Land travellers carry with them? Tyrrell does not say. Hanbury in his book obliges us by providing a list of food and tobacco supplies he had sent to him via Hudson Bay[37]. The list is interesting because it is so short and shows clearly what was available, what lasted and what was important.

Tobacco plug for self	50 lbs.
Tobacco plug for natives	24 lbs.
Oatmeal (coarse)	100 lbs.
Sugar in whiskey barrel	330 lbs.
Hard tack biscuit	600 lbs.
Salt	30 lbs.
Pepper	15 lbs.
Pork (clear)	1 barrel
Tea (best)	10 lbs.
Cocoa, Van Houtens	25 lbs.
Coffee (ground)	25 lbs.

Hanbury does not say if he carried all 1200 pounds with him in his travels. It is a rather sparse list but it was assumed that caribou and to a lesser extent musk-ox or fish would provide a far greater amount of appetizing fare as well as the necessary protein and fat.

As both Tyrrell and old Souci noted earlier, survival in the Barrens not only required food but also warmth. Given the absence of trees in the Barrens, a fire was not always available. What heat a body could generate internally from its fat had to be protected from exposure to the numbing wind and cold of winter. Caribou skins are acclaimed as the best there is for severe cold. The fur is strong, light, and warm. Because each caribou hair has an air-filled cavity, it provides exceptional insulation against the severe cold of the far north and all the early winter travellers outfitted themselves with caribou skin clothing made by the local Indians and Eskimos.

One difference between the inland Caribou Eskimo and the coastal Eskimo is that the latter used a blubber lamp for light and warmth inside their snow igloos while the Barren Land Eskimo did not have easy access to blubber. They used moss and willow fires for cooking but these could not be used inside snow dwellings. Consequently they lived in very cold conditions with outside temperatures between −35°C and −50°C in winter. Without caribou meat for food and caribou clothing for warmth they could not have survived.

Because there is no wood for a drying fire, body moisture can be a serious danger during winter travel in the Barrens. For the Eskimo this was not a great problem, for they apparently did not perspire like their white companions.

Inspector Pelletier in his official report of their sled trip down the coast of Hudson Bay emphasized this discomfort.

> It will be noted that at no time on the journey were we in a precarious position: the longest period the dogs went without food was four days. These dogs can stand ten or twelve days of starvation and still work, but it is very hard on them . . . .
> As to ourselves we never suffered from privation, we had at all times a good supply of meat. We ran short of sugar and coffee, these two were very much missed. We had hoped to meet natives on the way and procure a new outfit of shoes and deer skin (caribou) socks, but as we did not, we employed those days when stormbound to patch and mend what we had and make the clothing last as long as it would. The worst feature of a long journey like this (we were 43 days) in a country where no fuel is to be procured, is the absolute impossibility of drying clothing, bedding, etc.. The moisture from the body accumulates, and there are no means to dry clothing to get rid of it in any way, and every day sees it harder to put on in the morning, and the bed harder to get into at night, until both clothing and bedding become stiff as a board from the ice. It is a very uninviting task and disagreeable procedure getting into an icy bed at night, and the same thing in the morning getting into icy clothes. Sleeping with one's clothes on only makes matters worse. There is no fuel to be procured all the way between Fullerton and Driftwood point near Churchill, and even there it is only by chance that a stray piece is picked up.[38]

In the warm summer months of June to September, while there may be brief periods of near freezing or raw, wet days, cold temperatures are not a serious problem to the summer canoeist. But a harsh wind, the frigid water, and hypothermia can be fatal in the large lakes should one swamp a canoe some distance from shore. In the far North this danger is much more serious than in the warmer waters of the south. Perhaps it can be debated which is more dangerous to the northern canoeist, rapids or large lakes. For me it is the latter. While rapids can be very hazardous to the inexperienced, they can always be scouted from shore and portages are relatively easy in the treeless tundra. A careful, experienced canoeist should not encounter surprises running a rapid that has been scouted, but even if he should do so and go for a swim in the rapid cold water, shore is much closer than it is from the middle of a large lake. The lake looms as a far less forgiving danger.

In addition to food and warmth, a visitor in the Barren Lands also requires information on the route. All of the nineteenth century travellers relied on Indian or Eskimo assistance, either directly as guides or indirectly as a source of map sketches. Today, with detailed aerial photographs and accurate topographical maps, following a route is relatively easy. Without maps, following the current in a stream or river is trivial, finding the exit of a large lake can be extremely time consuming, but going across the country or changing watersheds without a map or a guide is difficult or nearly impossible. The Barren Lands are a maze of water and land. Most modern voyageurs would be helpless if they lost their maps while in the midst of this maze.

It is significant that in his 1894 travels Tyrrell had local guides almost continuously and his progress across the Barrens was rapid and efficient. But during the earlier 1893 Dubawnt trip he had no local native guides for most of his route. He describes the consequent frustration:

> In searching our way through the irregular lakes, we were obliged to climb all the hills from which extensive views might be obtained, and to explore many deep bays which were found to have no other outlet than the one by which we had entered. In this way a considerable tract of country came under observation, but progress was correspondingly slow.[39]

P. G. Downes, in his book *Sleeping Island*, describes in vivid detail the difficulties of travelling alone in the northern forest with only crude instructions as a guide. In his journey from Reindeer Lake to Nueltin Lake he experienced constant anxiety and uncertainty, because he had no clear map or native guide. His notes read:

> Lakes, lakes, lakes innumerable. Some seem interlocking, some do not. This is all a crazy jigsaw puzzle of sand and water, dry potholes, coulees, kettle holes. God help the man who gets off the route in this country! Nothing — nothing to go by, just up and down, around sandhills and dry washes, and thousands and thousands of caribou trails"[40].

Today, with our maps, we no longer have to face this uncertainty.

*   *   *

Why did the early Barren Land travellers willingly come to this harsh, isolated wilderness region? Why did they suffer starvation and cold, yet willingly return to experience the Barrens again? Why do they still come today? In almost every traveller's writings there is some suggestion that these men were seeking something that they could not find in the hustle of civilized life. J. B. Tyrrell in a letter prior to his Dubawnt adventure wrote: "A crowd of people in a city wearies me beyond endurance, and though the northern life is very lonely, there are none but the powers of Nature to struggle against."[41] Tyrrell rarely allowed personal sentiment to enter his official reports, but we do catch a glimpse of it in the following description from his 1894 travels down the Kazan:

> The whole landscape, seen in the early morning light, presented such a picture of wild but quiet beauty, as I have seldom had the good fortune to enjoy."[43]

In later life Tyrrell, who lived to be 99, would recollect his Barren Land travels and their quiet beauty with tears glistening in his eyes. The Barren Lands affect those that make a special effort to experience them. After my own hard trip on the Dubawnt in 1969, I was keen to come back and experience more, and so I did in 1974, in 1979 and again in 1981. Warburton Pike in writing the concluding chapter to his Barren Lands book, while surrounded by "all the luxuries that only ultra-civilization can give", sums it up appropriately:

> On looking back one remembers only the good times, when meat was plentiful and a huge fire lit up the snow on the spruce trees; misery and starvation are forgotten as soon as they are over, and even now, in the midst of the luxury of civilization, at times I have a longing to pitch my lodge once more on the edge of the Barren Ground, . . . to hear the ptarmigan crowing among the little pines as the sun goes down over a frozen lake and the glory of the Arctic night commences.[43]

What prompts this unrequited yearning to experience the primitive, to live with Nature in all her moods and to observe her harmony and beauty in the tranquility and isolation of the wilderness? Books have been written on this question. My brief answer is that this is simply part of our heritage. Man, who evolved over the millenia from the wilderness and this natural harmony, today still longs for those primitive experiences, to hear the "Voices of Earth" which, in Canada, call out so clearly from the North.

> To him who hears them grief beyond control,
> Or joy inscrutable without a name,
> Wakes in his heart thoughts bedded there, impearled
> Before the birth and making of the world.
>
> *Voices of Earth*, Archibald Lampman

ENDNOTES

1. Quoted in Warburton Pike, *The Barren Ground of Northern Canada*. (London 1892) p. 302.

2. Samuel Hearne, *A Journey From Prince of Wales Fort in Hudson's Bay to the Northern Ocean in the Years 1769-70-71-71*. (London 1795) p. 81.

3. David Thompson, *David Thompson's Narrative* edited by J. B. Tyrrell. (Toronto 1916).

4. Knud Rasmussen, *Across Arctic America*. (New York 1927)

5. C. H. Clarke, *A Biological Investigation of the Thelon Game Sancturary*. Natural Museum of Canada Bulletin No. 96. (Ottawa 1940) p.

6. John Franklin, *Narrative of a Journey to the Shores of the Polar Sea in the Years 1819-20-21-22*. (London 1823).

7. J. Anderson, *Back River Journal of 1855* (Ottawa 1940).

8. Alphonse Gasté, "Father Alphonse Gasté", *Eskimo Magazine* (1960).

9. J. W. Tyrrell, *Across the Sub Arctics of Canada* (London 1897) p. 97.

10. Eric Morse, "Fresh Water Northwest Passage," *Canadian Geographical Journal* (June 1965); "Summer Travel in the Canadian Barrens," *Canadian Geographical Journal* (May 1967).

11. Emile Petitot, *Les Grands Esquimoux* (Paris 1887).

12. See Pike, *The Barren Ground*.

13. J. B. Tyrrell, "Report on the Doobaunt, Kazan and Ferguson Rivers and the Coast of Hudson Bay," Geographical Survey of Canada, *Report* for 1896, vol. IX (Ottawa 1897); J.W. Tyrell, *Across the Sub Arctics of Canada*.

14. J. B. Tyrell, "Report," p. 5f.

15. Frank Russell, *Explorations in the Far North* (Iowa 1898); Caspar Whitney, *On Snow Shoes to the Barren Grounds* (New York 1896); Henry Toke Munn, *Prairie Trails and Arctic By-Ways* (London 1932); H. Inman, *Buffalo Jones' Forty Years of Adventure* (London 1899).

16. David T. Hanbury, *Sport and Travel in the Northland of Canada* (London 1904).

17. Inman, *Buffalo Jones' Forty Years of Adventure*.

18. V. Clifton, *The Book of Talbot* (London 1933).

19. Hanbury, *Sport and Travel*.

20. J. M. Bell, "Report on Great Bear Lake," Geological Survey of Canada, *Summary Report* (Ottawa 1901).

21. J. W. Tyrrell, "Exploratory Survey Between Great Slave Lake and Hudson Bay," Dept. of Interior, *Annual Report* (Ottawa 1902).

22. E. A. Preble, "A Biological Investigation of the AthabaskaMackenzie Region," U.S. Dept. of Agriculture. *N. A. Fauna* 27, 1908; E.T. Seton, *The Arctic Prairies* (London 1912).

23. Royal Northwest Mounted Police, Report of 1909 by Inspector Pelletier.

24. Royal Northwest Mounted Police, Report of 1917-18, the Bathurst Inlet Patrol (Ottawa 1919).

25. Rasmussen, *Across Arctic America*; Kaj Birket-Smith, *The Eskimo* (London 1959).

26. G. H. Blanchet, *Search in the North* (Toronto 1960).

27. On Hornby see Edgar Christian, *Unflinching: A Diary of Tragic Adventure* (London 1937); M. Waldron, *Plain Tales of the North* (New York 1925); George Whalley, *The Legend of John Hornby* (London 1962). On Stefansson and Douglas see V. Stefansson, *My Life with the Eskimos* (New York 1913) and George M. Douglas, *Lands Forlorn* (New York 1914) respectively.

28. Guy H. Blanchet, "Caribou of the Barren Ground," *Beaver Magazine* (Sept. 1930) and "Into

Unknown Country," *Beaver Magazine* (June 1950); Thierry Mallet, *Plain Tales of the North* (New York 1925) and *Glimpses of the Barren Lands* (New York 1930).

29. P. G. Downes, *Sleeping Island* (New York 1943).

30. Blanchet, "Caribou of the Barren Ground," p. 66.

31. Quoted in F. Bruenner, *Seasons of the Eskimo* (1971).

32. Pike, *The Barren Ground*.

33. Ibid., pp. vi-vii.

34. J. W. Tyrrell, *Across the Sub Arctics of Canada*, pp. 76-7; 77.

35. J. B. Tyrell, "Report," p. 12f.

36. J. W. Tyrell, *Across the Sub Arctics of Canada*, p. 48.

37. Hanbury, *Sport and Travel*, p. 290.

38. Pelletier, "Report."

39. J. B. Tyrrell, "Report," p. 10f.

40. P. G. Downes, *Sleeping Island*, p. 136.

41. Edith Tyrrell, *I Was There* (Toronto 1938), p. 52

42. J. B. Tyrrell, "Report," p. 131f.

43. Pike, *The Barren Ground*, pp. 301-2.

J. B. Tyrrell

Warburton Pike

Purposeful Wanderers: Late Nineteenth Century Travellers to the Barrens

Margaret Hobbs

In 1889 a young Englishman named Warburton Pike set out eagerly from London across the Atlantic Ocean to Canada, to board the Canadian Pacific Railway. He travelled west as far as Calgary, then pushed northward on buckboard to Edmonton, where he found a wagon and Métis driver to take him to Athabasca Landing. York boats ran him down the Athabasca River to Fort McMurray. On Hudson Bay Company steamers he continued his journey on the Athabasca, then down the Slave River. He arrived at Fort Resolution, on the south shore of Great Slave Lake, in mid-August. For the next year, Resolution would be his base for several hunting excursions into the Barren Lands aided by Métis and Indian guides.

Pike would later insist that his journey "was only an ordinary shooting expedition, such as one might make to the Rocky Mountains or the interior of Africa."[1] Pike was well aware of the irony of his description; indeed, there is little that is "ordinary" about any expedition to the Barren Lands. But Pike's journey in the late nineteenth century was notable because it marked the end of a long period of waning European interest in the North and the emergence of a new breed of northern explorers, whose delight in exploring the Barrens for their own sake set them distinctly apart from their earlier counterparts.

Initially, European interest in the Barrens lay in getting beyond them to the Arctic Ocean. Thus to Hearne in 1769, Franklin during his two expeditions between 1819 and 1826 and Back in 1833-34, the region represented an obstacle threatening to undermine the success of their explorations. After Back's trip, only a small number of expeditions entered the region between the later 1830s and the 1850s. These were most often search parties sent out after the legendary lost Franklin party and during these visits the Barrens were still perceived as an obstacle.*

There were no major expeditions through the Barren Lands for the next three decades. And no wonder. Characterized by long cruel winters, raging blizzards and the ever-present threat of starvation, the area to this day does not easily inspire confidence. In summer, for a brief time, the sun shines 24 hours a day, the snow and ice recede, uncovering a myriad of lakes and rivers swarming with marine life. Arctic mammals roam a territory veiled by different types of lichens, mosses and miniature plants. But summer is both short and deceiving in the Barrens. In mid-season the ground remains frozen, winds howl furiously, mosquitoes and blackflies attack in armies and survival is still threatened by famine and exposure.

---

* For an historical survey of travel in the Barrens see George Luste, "History, Travel and Canoeing in the Barrens," elsewhere in this volume.

So by 1889, when Pike wandered north with a "12-bore Paradox and a 50-95 Winchester Express"[2] and very little else, the Barrens lay largely unmarred by humanity. The severity of the environment, together with a long Indian-Inuit tradition of mutual fear and hostility, curtailed Indian efforts to penetrate the region deeply, or cross it altogether. This fear of chance encounters in the Barrens would pose special problems for the white travellers lured to the area in the 1890s, for they were dependent on native assistance to find their way into and out of the Barrens.

The names of Warburton Pike, Frank Russell, J. B. and J. W. Tyrrell, Henry Toke Munn, Caspar Whitney and David Hanbury are unfamiliar to most Canadians today. Yet less than a century ago, popular accounts of their exploits in the Barrens were readily available to a reading audience hungry for northern adventure stories.[3] It appears that these men and their travels once captured the public imagination and have only drifted into anonymity with the passing of time. For them, the Barrens were not an obstacle, nor a land to be feared and avoided. Indeed, this little known wilderness with a formidable history was tantalizing. Still, not many attempted a complete crossing of the heart of the Barrens. Between 1889 and 1902, the time frame for this article, the Tyrrell brothers and Hanbury were the only ones to accomplish this. The others penetrated the territory from the vicinity of Great Slave Lake, thrusting east or northeast and sometimes circling back to their starting point. Whitney, Pike and Munn set out from Fort Resolution, while Russell chose Fort Rae, on the northern arm of the lake, as his point of departure.

As sportsmen, scientists, topographers, ethnologists, or naturalists, these men filtered into the wilderness armed with carefully rationalized intentions. They intended to hunt the elusive musk-ox, collect specimens of northern flora and fauna, map out an unexplored land, or study the habits of the native population. Yet as it has been suggested of those who stampeded to the Klondike in 1898, these individuals "gave all the proper and conventional reasons for going, and set out for quite different ones."[4]

*   *   *

Warburton Pike was definitely the most eccentric if not the most admirable of the new explorers. Born into a moneyed, distinguished family, he was a product of the British public schools and studied for one year at Oxford before he grew restless and quit. After emigrating to Victoria in 1884, he became one of British Columbia's wealthiest entrepreneurs.[5] But as one historian observes, he maintained a life-long "penchant for slumming." "Pikey", as his friends called him "rarely carried any money with him, preferred to go barefoot whenever possible, and because of his ragged clothes and tatty rucksack was often mistaken for a tramp." An embarrassment to many in Victoria's wealthy elite, his friends regarded his unconventional behaviour humorously. Apparently, "only when he received a native Indian woman in the clubhouse," did they consider he had gone too far.[6]

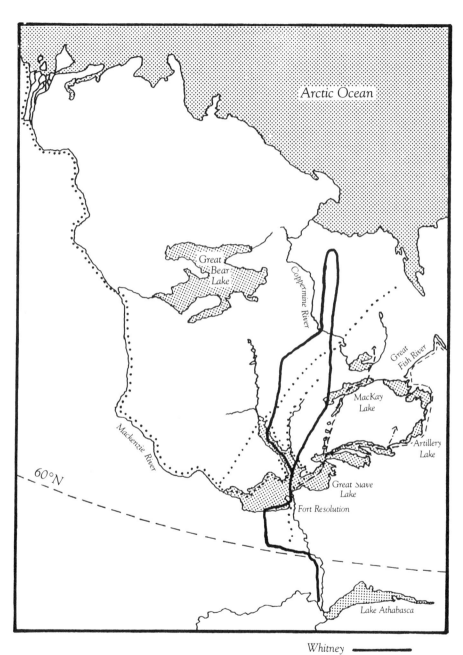

Arctic Ocean

Great
Bear
Lake

Coppermine River

Great
Fish River

MacKay
Lake

Artillery
Lake

Mackenzie River

60°N

Great Slave
Lake

Fort Resolution

Lake Athabasca

Whitney ━━━━━

Russell • • • • • •

Pike – – – – –

Munn –·–·–·–

Pike was a fanatical big game hunter. The profits from his many business ventures, complemented by a private income, afforded him every opportunity to indulge himself in a lifestyle of wandering, hunting and exploring. It was therefore a veteran world traveller and hunter that set out to conquer the Barrens in 1889.[7] Pike was then 28 years old and he fancied himself as an adventuresome gentleman hunter engaged in an epic pursuit of the musk-ox, "a strange animal, a relic of an earlier age." He admitted to a wider interest in simply trying to "penetrate" an "unknown land" and investigate the northern natives, but he insisted that the celebrated published account of his journey was "intended solely for the sportsman."[8] And indeed, the sporting community in Canada seems to have enviously applauded his accomplishments. Following the 1892 publication of his book, the route and highlights of the trip were given lengthy coverage in the popular recreational periodical *Forest and Stream*.[9] Pike's narrative would be an important source of inspiration and information for later Barren Lands travellers, whose trip preparations invariably included the scouring of all available first hand descriptions of the region.

It was getting late in August before Pike's party, led by a Métis guide named King Beaulieu, together with seven of his family and a young Indian boy, left Fort Resolution and canoed across Great Slave Lake to Fond du Lac. By a series of portages, they crossed a chain of lakes which Pike proudly declared "no white man had passed through . . . before."[10] Via these lakes they arrived at Lake Camsell, where they spotted and killed their first band of caribou. A more permanent camp was established at the north end of the lake and on September 17, 1889, six of them began a short journey northward in search of musk-oxen. Very soon, two members of the party turned back to Fond du Lac, while the others pushed onward through Lake Mackay and then portaged to Lac de Gras. After crossing the Coppermine River, they headed north on foot, searching for signs of musk-oxen.

By the end of September winter was rapidly setting in, so the hunters retreated, discouraged that only one musk-ox had been killed. The ice already forming on the lakes forced them to conduct most of their return journey to the Lake Camsell camp on foot. Pike would later acknowledge that he had chosen a bad time to travel, since it was "too late for open water and too early for dogs to be of any service."[11] He would also record his dismay at the outcome of the hunt and his bitterness towards his native guides, whose company he found intolerable. In fact for Pike, this first penetration of the Barrens, so eagerly anticipated, was a considerable let-down.

During a stay of over one month at the Lake Camsell base-camp, Pike marvelled at the sight of the great autumn migration of the caribou, which replenished their dangerously dwindling food supply before they set out again on November 11, 1889. Equipped with dogs and sleds, a small party travelled farther into the Barrens, this time slaughtering several bands of musk-oxen. Pike had intended to winter on the edge of the Barrens upon completion of the hunt. However, his intolerance with his travelling companions, whom Pike insisted were continually trying to cheat him, led him instead to journey back to Fond du Lac on Great Slave Lake, where he arrived in early December of 1889. Shortly thereafter, he very gratefully found himself enjoying the modest comfort of Fort Resolution.

Pike spent the winter involved with leisure activities which included a wood buffalo hunt with James Mackinlay, the Hudson's Bay Company officer in charge of Resolution and in Pike's view, a much more congenial travelling companion than King Beaulieu. Mackinlay, intrigued by the possibility of extending the fur trade to the Inuit, also accompanied Pike on his third Barren Lands trip by way of Back's Great Fish River.[12] On May 7, 1890, their small party led by a Yellow Knife Indian guide, began the crossing of Great Slave Lake by canoe. At Fond du Lac they were joined by several Yellow Knives and their families. Again they travelled by way of Lac de Mort, Wolverine Lake, Lake Camsell, and Lake Mackay. Crossing Lockhart's River to Aylmer Lake, they began their descent of Back's River, making many small excursions "sometimes watching the birds, and sometimes in pursuit of caribou or musk-ox."[13]

By July 23, they had descended the River to Lake Beechey, near which Pike was delighted to discover a recently deserted Inuit camp. After a few days of fruitless searching for further signs of one Inuit, having promised their aides that they would not progress beyond Lake Beechey, they reluctantly began their return voyage, as it was getting late in the season. Upon reaching Aylmer Lake, Pike and Mackinlay chose to follow the course that Back and Anderson had taken to Great Slave Lake, by way of Clinton-Colden Lake and Artillery Lake, across the portage on Lockhart's River (later named Pike's Portage) and on through McLeod's Bay. It was August 24, 1890 when they reached Fort Resolution. Soon after Pike began the long route back to Calgary and then presumably Victoria. He would not remain away from the North for long, though. By the summer of 1892 he was again preparing a journey, this time through the Yukon and Alaska. This trip, considered even more difficult than his Barrens journey, would make him a celebrity among an elite international fraternity of sportsmen.[14]

*   *   *

Just two years after Pike returned from his first northern voyage, an American named Frank Russell canoed and snowshoed the Barrens near Great Slave Lake. Russell represents a complete contrast to the wealthy, eccentric Pike. Born in Iowa in 1868, Russell graduated from the University of Iowa in 1892 and that summer headed north on a scientific expedition. A few years later he received his Ph.D. from Harvard, where he was hired to teach in 1896. A dedicated naturalist, he authored many scientific articles and reviews, a major study of the Pima Indians[15] and a popular account of his Barren Lands visit. In 1901 he began working as an ethnologist for the Bureau of American Ethnology. This budding academic career, however, was clipped short by his early death in 1903 at age 35.

Unlike many of the Barrens travellers of the 1890s, Russell was not at the outset an accomplished sportsman, although he developed an enthusiasm for hunting, and presumably some skill, during his Barrens trip. Travelling under the auspices of the Museum of the University of Iowa, Russell was sent to the vast northern tundra in 1892 to obtain museum "specimens of the larger Arctic mammals, especially musk-ox, and . . . to pick up anything else I could lay my hands on."[16] A year earlier he participated in an ornithological expedition to the Saskatchewan, a journey also funded by the University. During this trip, his association with the ornithologist C.C. Nutting, who had spent nearly fifty years in the "Fur Country" studying its natural history and collecting specimens, aroused Russell's interest in visiting the far North. Ever the sober scientist, this traveller was loathe to admit that his intrigue with the North was more than academic.

Anxious to reach the mythical Barrens, the 24 year old Russell wanted to proceed immediately to Great Slave Lake, but instead, on the advice of his sponsors he spent the first winter near Lake Winnipeg at the Saskatchewan River's Grand Rapids, "in order to become acclimated and to become accustomed to the northern mode of winter travel, before I should attempt to enter the Barren Ground." Arriving at the Hudson's Bay post of Grand Rapids on August 19, 1892, Russell occupied himself throughout the winter. He continued to collect specimens of small mammals and birds, searched old Indian graves for positive identification of Cree Indians of unmixed blood, learned the arts of dog-driving and snowshoeing, and participated in numerous short hunting trips. He demonstrated a particular delight in the latter, setting out on one occasion simply to test his abilities to "kill a moose without the aid of an Indian hunter." January and February of 1893 he devoted primarily to visiting and studying the natives.[17]

Russell left Grand Rapids by sled on February 20 bound for Selkirk. From here he travelled by rail to Winnipeg and proceeded on to Edmonton, Athabasca Landing and Fort Chipewyan. On June 20, 1893, he boarded a steamer for Fort Resolution, then crossed Great Slave Lake. Upon reaching Fort Rae, he decided to take a summer trip to the Barren Ground, listing his objectives as follows:

> to collect ornithological specimens, to secure caribou skins before they had assumed their winter pelage, to search for breeding places or water birds to be visited during the following years, and last, but not least, to get something to eat, as the unvaried diet of tasteless, leathery dried meat was growing intolerable.[18]

Russell, however, seemed to have more trouble than any of the other travellers in obtaining Indian guides to the Barrens—a difficulty he could only explain by their superstitious fear of allowing a white man to penetrate their hunting ground:

> [The Indians thought] that if I sent down the skins of the caribou to be mounted in my country, they would live there forever; which happy fate would induce all the vast herds that roam over the Barren Ground to migrate southward to join them.[19]

As the Indians refused to let him accompany them on their caribou hunt, Russell decided to make his own reconnaissance to the Barrens via the Yellow Knife

River, accompanied only by a young Métis boy, whose services he had secured for "a skin a day" plus board. On July 18, 1893, after receiving directions from four different people, "who all disagreed," they loaded two birch bark canoes and began their journey. Unfortunately, Russell suffered a humiliating start when crowds of laughing natives witnessed his first attempt at solo paddling. "My canoe seemed disposed," he recalled, "to travel in a circle, and as the direction of the revolution could not be foretold, my companion found it safer to give me a wide seaway." In another setting this mishap might merely have been embarrassing; in retrospect, it might even have seemed funny. But Russell was well aware of the practical implications of revealing such signs of incompetence, especially during one's departure and return:

> It was vain to try to reassure myself with the thought that the spectators were half-breeds and Indians whose opinion, however expressed, could not effect my nerves. I did care very much, indeed, for the estimate formed by the forte métis has great weight with the Indians, and my success as a zoological collector depended to a considerable extent on just such trivial considerations. To those people, the appearance presented by a visitor at his arrival and departure is of the utmost importance. Then it is that the smartest colors are worn; the canoeist takes a deliberate stroke, but those beside him can see the bend of the paddle-blade, and the knotting of his muscles, as he grips the handle more tightly.[20]

Russell's luck was not to change. Since the caribou appeared to be well beyond reach, their fishing luck was poor, and their provisions were dwindling, the party was soon compelled to return to Rae, where they arrived on August 5.

At the end of August Russell canoed to Fort Resolution in a largely unsuccessful search for guides for a fall musk-ox hunt and a mid-winter buffalo hunt. As winter approached, however, he was able to make four short trips in search of caribou by dog-sled from Rae. Then on December 7, 1893, Russell set out for Fort Resolution. Accompanied by natives and travelling on snowshoes he battled the snow and wind, reaching Resolution in one week. From here, Russell ventured southward along the Little Buffalo River with a Métis hunter in a fruitless search for buffalo. Returning to Resolution, he then crossed the lake once again to Fort Rae, arriving in early February 1894.

Despite their loud objections, Russell insisted upon accompanying a party of Dog Ribs on their musk-ox hunt early in March. Travelling by snowshoe northeast from Rae they crossed the Coppermine River to the Musk-ox Mountains and beyond. After several unsuccessful attempts, the party finally managed to kill many musk-oxen and returned to Rae by May 4.

Russell decided to chance a meeting with an American whaling ship on Herschel Island, west of the mouth of the Mackenzie, hoping to sail with them back to the United States. With this intention, he set out alone with a dog team from Providence and caught the steamer down the Mckenzie River to old Fort Good Hope. He paddled to Fort McPherson, where he met the French explorer Edouard de Sainville, who travelled with him on the ship to Herschel Island. Before leaving with the whalers, Russell had made extensive ethnological observations, taken notes on the natural history of the North, and collected many specimens, all of which are recorded in detail in his book. But despite Russell's insistence that his motives for travelling to the Barrens were purely academic, his personal fascination with the wilderness environment itself and the challenge and freedom it represented ring through his published account.

*   *   *

In 1893 Joseph Burr Tyrrell, accompanied by his younger brother James William, began the journey that was to make him famous. Of the various white men to visit the Barrens in the late nineteenth century, the Tyrrells represent the only ones born in Canada, amongst few whites since Hearne to completely cross the Barrens. Canadians were spellbound by their epic journey by canoe, snowshoe and dog team. The popular press was quick to record, and no doubt embellish, the events of the expedition and J. W. Tyrrell published a widely read account of the trip. J. B. Tyrrell became a hero overnight. As his biographer observes, "For a time his name was synonymous with the Canadian North."[21]

Having spent their boyhood roaming the territory around the small agricultural community of Weston, J. B. and J. W. acquired an early appreciation of outdoor living. Born into a family of wealth and prominence in 1858 and 1863 respectively, the brothers also grew up in the midst of Canada First nationalism. Confederation had been accomplished by faith in the potential of the Northwest and Canadians proudly declared themselves a race of Northerners. Influenced by this prevailing national sentiment, the North naturally held a special fascination for the Tyrrells.

After graduating from Upper Canada College and the University of Toronto, the brothers each adopted careers which facilitated numerous wilderness excursions. Although James was later to become a civil engineer, he participated in the Barren Lands voyage as topographer and Inuit interpreter. Prior to this journey, J. B. records that James "had spent one winter on the north shore of Hudson Strait, and had served for two seasons as assistant to commander Gordon in the survey of Hudson Bay."[22] In 1900 James Tyrrell returned to the Barrens, engaged in a Dominion Lands Survey expedition.[23] J. B. Tyrrell also varied his professional life. After 1898, he established himself as a successful mining consultant and engineer in the Yukon, where he lived for seven years, and later in Ontario. From 1881 to 1898, however, he was an explorer in the employ of the Geological Survey of Canada.

Since its inception in 1842, the Geological Survey was the primary government agency responsible for the geological and geographical mapping of Canada. Tyrrell was not a typical member of the Survey. Hired one year after receiving his Bachelor of Arts, he was one of the last of the self-trained scientists on the staff, for by the 1880s the Survey as already well on its way to implementing a restrictive hiring policy which demanded that its members be trained specialists and professionals.[24] As the emphasis on professionalism increased, individual responsibilities in the field became more specific. Exploration parties might consist of numerous 'experts' hired either as geologists, naturalists, topographers, or interpreters. In Tyrrell's day, individual explorers were generally expected to develop their competence in all of these fields. In addition, survival in the wilderness often required that they be competent in the handling of a dog team, a canoe, a rifle, and in all facets of wilderness travel. Nonetheless, Tyrrell certainly did not accomplish his explorations without native help. In fact the extent of his expertise in a canoe is uncertain. Several photographs taken on the 1893 journey show him sitting in the centre of the canoe without a paddle, the common style of travel for the earliest European explorers.

J. B. Tyrrell straddled two eras of exploration in other ways as well. He was, for instance, one of the last major reconnaissance explorers, for while his European counterparts of the nineteenth century penetrated and charted unknown territory, twentieth century exploration "for the most part has been a process of providing in ever-increasing detail the data on geological formations, plant growth, soil capabilities and mineral resources of areas where the basic exploration of the terrain has already been done."[25]

Moreover, by the 1890s the Survey was under considerable pressure to strengthen what was becoming its primary commitment to developing the nation's mineral wealth. Reconnaissance expeditions were increasingly criticized by the mining community and the federal government as too costly and too academic. Together they urged the Survey to devote less attention to mapping new water routes, examining geological formations, and recording natural history, and more attention to searching out new sources of readily exploitable resources. In particular, Tyrrell's remote 1893 Barren Lands expedition prompted a loud outcry from the *Canadian Mining Review*, and caused grumbling in the House of Commons, when it was revealed that the expedition had cost about $7,000. Tyrrell recorded in his notebook that "Sir John Thompson [said] that at that we had nearly starved to death and . . . he could not say what it would have cost if we had been well fed."[26] Consequently, the Survey began to buckle under the mounting pressure to conduct its operations closer to settled areas, guided by more pragmatic objectives.[27]

J. B. Tyrrell was 34 years old, his brother was five years younger, when the Geological Survey instructed them to explore the unknown land mass west of Hudson Bay. They travelled to Winnipeg, then to Edmonton by rail and on to Athabasca Landing. On May 31, 1983 they launched the Peterborough canoes that had been shipped from the east and descended the Athabasca River to Lake Athabasca. Their small party included three Indians brought with them from the east and hired because of their expertise in shooting rapids and portaging, and two Métis from the west. From Fond du Lac on Athabasca, they canoed eastward and by a series of portages reached the north end of Black Lake by July 7. They ventured into unknown territory, guided by a crude Indian map. Following a chain of small lakes they ascended Chipman River to Selwyn Lake. On July 17, the party encountered a small band of Indians who refused to guide them northward, and tried to dissuade them from continuing their journey. After some argument the Indians relented, accompanying them across the height of land, where the Tyrrell party continued on past Daly Lake (later named Woholdaia Lake) and descended northward the long Dubawnt River.

By the time they reached Carey Lake on the Dubawnt their food supply was so low that J. B. considered turning back.[28] However, on July 29 they came across massive herds of caribou which temporarily relieved the crisis. As the carcasses were drying, the two brothers were able to spend a few days wandering among the inquisitive animals "armed only with a camera"—an experience James described as "delightful, one never to be forgotten."[29]

By August 7 they had reached Dubawnt Lake, where they remained for eleven days, detained by foul weather and a tiresome search through ice and open water for the outlet of the lake. When they found it, they continued down the Dubawnt River. Before long the party encountered an Inuit family who provided them with directions that they later complained were entirely misleading. Their supply of fresh meat had diminished and they were plagued by uncertainty as to the destination of their course. Their fears were amplified when on August 23 they left Lady Marjorie Lake and the river swung westward, seemingly towards certain death in the Arctic:

> Our hearts sank as the river took us further towards the northwest, for we were making straight for the Great Fish River, which flows into the Arctic Ocean, and while we were only about one hundred miles from that river, we were three hundred and fifty from the nearest point on Hudson Bay.[30]

Fortunately, four days' travel later the river looped eastward, joining what was later known as the Thelon River, which led them past Baker Lake to Chesterfield Inlet by September 7. They were soon travelling down the coast of Hudson Bay past Marble Island. Yet the hardest part of the journey lay just ahead.

By September 15, raging storms, starvation, and exhaustion threatened to end the journey in tragedy. A polar bear kill eventually satisfied their hunger, but James almost died after eating its liver, not realizing it was poisonous to humans. Finally, exhausted and half-starved, they reached Fort Churchill about the 19th of October, only after sending the two fittest native guides on ahead to return with dogs and sleds. From Churchill the Tyrrell brothers set out on snowshoes for the 900 mile overland journey to Winnipeg where they arrived on January 2, 1894. Their extraordinary adventure returned botanical specimens, collections of notes on geology and the Eskimos, and meticulous survey work, all to be examined, recorded, and chartered over the winter in Ottawa.

In spite of the Survey's reluctance to sponsor further reconnaissance surveys, J. B. Tyrrell was sent back to the Keewatin district in July 1894 to continue his explorations on the Kazan River. As he had found a few private sources of funding, Tyrell travelled for seven months into unknown territory on a course parrallel to that taken in 1893. Although the trip was similar in many respects to his previous voyage, it was shorter and more predictable. The journey was also eased considerably by the discovery that the Kazan region was more heavily populated by Inuit than anticipated. The Tyrrells hired several Inuit to take them to Hudson Bay, but upon realizing that the Kazan River flowed into Chesterfield Inlet, and not into the Bay near Marble Island as they had expected, they did not pursue it far beyond Yathkyed Lake. Instead, guided by the Inuit they portaged to Ferguson River, following it downstream into Hudson Bay. Arriving in Churchill on October 1, they headed home at the end of November, stopping briefly in Fort Selkirk on January 5, 1895.[31]

*   *   *

During 1894 the western portion of the Barrens was visited by an Englishman named Henry Toke Munn. Arriving in Canada in 1886 as a young man, Munn settled into an agricultural area north of Brandon, Mantiboa, where he lived with a well-off English family. While Munn demonstrated little of Pike's enthusiasm for "slumming," his social and economic background, which included a public school education, fostered a similar passion for sport, in particular big game hunting. And like Pike, Munn's preferred style of living involved extensive travel and quests for adventure. He moved back and forth between England and Canada, prospected in the Yukon, British Columbia and northern Ontario, served in the Boer War, and constantly sought means of funding new adventures. Although he travelled in various parts of the world, his journeys through northern Canada were the most extensive and memorable. Ten years of travel by inland and sea routes are recalled with nostalgia in two books, *Prairie Trails and Arctic By-Ways* and *Tales of the Eskimo*.

Munn's voyage to the Barren Lands began in May 1894. Successive crop failures had adversely affected his business as a horse trader. So he decided, while awaiting the return of prosperity, to accept an invitation to hunt musk-oxen in the Barrens. His travelling companion was Walter Gordon-Cumming, a well known hunter of big game and "nephew of the famous lion hunter." Departing from Edmonton, they reached Fort Resolution by steamer, scow and canoe via the Athabasca and Slave Rivers. Aided by a Métis guide and a Yellow Knife Indian, they canoed to Fort Reliance, on the eastern shore of Great Slave Lake. Through a series of small lakes and portages, they reached Artillery Lake on July 21. Leaving their canoe and caching some food, they hiked for ten days into the Barrens on an unsuccessful search for musk-oxen. But upon their return to Great Slave Lake they encountered the great caribou migration and were swarmed, for over two weeks, by herds totalling about 2 million caribou. Undoubtedly, Munn reported, this was "the greatest gathering of wild animals of one species in the world. There is nothing left like it to be seen anywhere to-day."[32]

Munn parted with Gordon-Cumming when they arrived back at Fort Resolution. By the end of September, he headed back across Slave Lake for a winter musk-ox hunt, travelling with nine Indians to their camp near Fond du Lac. He spent one miserable month living among them in a teepee. Then in late October 1894 they set off on their hunt with seven dog teams. By November 10 the party was well into the Barrens, where they soon killed a band of musk-oxen.

The meat, however, was devoured by wolves in a blizzard that prevented them from reaching and loading up their kill, so they were forced to wander northeast of Slave Lake in search of food until the end of November.

Munn returned to Resolution for Christmas, but on December 26, 1894 he left for Fort Smith. Here, at the end of January, he met Caspar Whitney, whom he remembered as "a pleasant companion, of a spare, active build, [who] later travelled far and wide, publishing several interesting books."[33] The two maintained their acquaintance until Whitney's death in 1929. Leaving Fort Smith on March 5, 1895, Munn drove his own dog team to Fort Chipewyan and on to Lac la Biche. From there he proceeded to Edmonton and then to Calgary. His Barren Lands voyage was ended, but his association with Canada's North had just begun.

*   *   *

Caspar Whitney was well known to his contemporaries in the United States as an author, editor and sportsman. Born in Boston in 1864, he attended college in California, served as a war correspondent in Cuba and later wrote for the New York *Tribune* in wartime Europe. An avid hunter and lover of outdoor sports, he was editor of *Outing Magazine* from 1900 to 1909, *Collier's Outdoor America* from 1909 to 1913 and *Recreation* during 1913. Whitney spent at least ten years of his life travelling, hunting and exploring in North America, South America, the East and West Indies, Siam, Malay, and India. A prolific author, his adventures in these parts of the world were recorded in many books.

Whitney was thirty years old when he set out north of Great Slave Lake for the Barrens. Like Pike and Munn, he regarded his expedition primarily as a hunting trip to shoot musk-ox, "the most inaccessible game in the world," and wood-bison, "undoubtedly now become the rarest game in the world."[34] As a member of the prestigious Boone and Crockett Club, Whitney was no novice hunter. Founded by Theodore Roosevelt in 1887 "to promote manly sport with the rifle," eligibility for membership was restricted to those who had shot a minimum of three animals of different species of North American large game.[35] But Whitney also wanted to study the habits of the northern Indians and view the habitat of the musk-ox. And after listing the more rational motives for his journey, he pointed to his boredom and restlessness with the urban environment:

> Possibly, too, I went that I might for a time escape the hum and routine sordidness of the city, and breathe air which was not surcharged with convention and civilization.[36]

In the company of Arthur Heming, an artist, Whitney left New York and arrived in Edmonton on the C.P.R. in late December of 1894. The two travelled to Lac la Biche, where they secured a Métis and Cree Indian to guide them by dog sled to Fort McMurray. Within a few days' journey from la Biche, Heming was forced to return home with a back injury. Whitney continued, eventually on snowshoes with another Métis and Indian to Fort Chipewyan, arriving on January 22, 1895. Two days later Whitney was wrapped in blankets on a cariole, nursing an injured ankle and very anxious to reach Fort Smith and James Mackinlay, "the only man who could give me any information" about the Barren Lands.[37]

Upon arrival at Fort Smith he met Munn, headed south from his most recent adventure. During a short wood-bison hunt both were delighted to actually catch sight of these rare animals. Their excitement, however, soon turned to bitterness when the chance for a kill was ruined, in their view, through impatient shooting by the Indians. Whitney claimed that Munn in particular was disappointed, as the Indians had assured him he would return with trophies of bison heads for himself and his friends in the south.

Returning to Fort Smith, Whitney then set out on snowshoes for Resolution, where he planned an early March excursion to the Barrens to hunt musk-oxen. He experienced considerable difficulty in hiring Indians with dogs to accompany him since a winter trip to the Barrens, when food was scarce and travelling hazardous, was considered foolish by Indians and whites of the region. As it was generally impossible to carry in enough provisions to last the whole trip and hunters were dependent on the caribou as their primary food source, the Indians usually timed their musk-ox hunts with the movement of the caribou in the early summer and early autumn. But Whitney was resolved to penetrate the territory in the winter, believing he could travel faster and farther on snowshoes than by canoe when the waters were open.

He finally managed to secure the aid of a Dog Rib Indian, one with a reputation as the best hunter in the country. So despite warnings that he would never return, on March 8, 1895, Whitney set out due north for the Barren Lands. Finding just enough caribou to ward off starvation, they reached Point Lake (on the Coppermine), where Whitney resolved to get as close as possible to the Arctic Ocean. The party therefore pushed on, killing a number of musk-oxen en route. Whitney estimated they travelled within fifty miles on the ocean, but he shared Pike's predicament—the Indians would go no further, despite an offer of a hundred skins to continue to the coastline. Annoyed at their refusal, Whitney travelled west for one day, then began his southward journey. One more herd of musk-oxen was encountered before they returned to Slave Lake. It was the end of April when they arrived back at Fort Resolution. From here Whitney travelled via the Buffalo and Salt Rivers to Forth Smith, where natives and whites were battling a severe famine. By mid-May 1895, he had paddled up the Slave River to Chipewyan, where he took a flatboat up to Fort McMurray. Just one month later Whitney was back in New York, likely cursing the crowded city environment from which he had sought a brief respite.

*   *   *

David Hanbury's travels on the Barrens were unparalleled in the late nineteenth century. Born in 1864 at East Barnet near London, England, Hanbury was educated at Clifton College, later studied surveying and geology and became a committed naturalist. He was about 34 when he came to Canada to conduct two successive journeys totalling twenty months across the Barren Lands and along the Arctic coastline.

Hanbury's activities on his expeditions included note-making on geology, botany, meteorology, enthnology and natural history, and the collection of numerous specimens. Some of the more scientific findings of his expeditions are recorded in an article submitted to the *Geographic Journal*[38] which recounts his second journey, and in the Appendix to his more popularly intended book, *Sport and Travel in the Northland of Canada*.[39] But despite his obvious scientific bias, Hanbury, in contrast to Russell, did not want to be viewed as a scientist in the North. His expeditions were private ones, not sponsored by a scientific or government agency and, like Pike, he claimed his "plain and unvarnished account" dealt only with sport and travel, "no attempt having been made to accomplish elaborate geographical or other scientific work." In his book, Hanbury preferred to identify himself as a sportsman and a "wanderer."[40]

Hanbury made an unsuccessful attempt to begin his westerly crossing of the northern plains in the summer of 1898, but having arrived too late in the season to head northward from Fort Churchill, he was forced to postpone his trip until the next year. On May 12, 1899 he was guided by an Eskimo to Marble Island, where he had cached a canoe the preceding summer. Arriving at Chesterfield Inlet by canoe on June 8, he proceeded inland to Baker Lake, reaching the Kazan River on July 12. After a five day delay to await the partial melting of the ice ahead, the party followed the shore of Baker Lake to begin the ascent of the Thelon River by July 19. Following the "Ark-i-linik" or Thelon River they passed Schultz Lake and then Aberdeen Lake, where they intercepted the annual migration of large herds of caribou. Continuing on past the mouth of the Dubawnt River they entered unexplored territory "without guides and without supplies of any kind." Depending entirely on their rifles and nets for foods, they reached the forks of the Thelon, followed its western branch (which became the Hanbury River) and crossed over the divide to Clinton-Colden Lake, where the previously unexplored portion of the trip ended. They then travelled on to Fort Resolution by way of Artillery Lake, losing one canoe in the rapids on Lockhart River below Artillery Lake. Arriving at Resolution by September 25, Hanbury paddled on to Fort McMurray by the Slave and Athabasca River. He arrived in Edmonton by dog sled at the end of October 1899.

Hanbury's next voyage through the Barren Lands was truly an astounding accomplishment. On July 13, 1901, he set out by canoe from Fort Resolution to retrace his route of 1899 back to Chesterfield Inlet. His Indian guides were moving slowly, wanting to return home. Hanbury saw this as a threat, the ultimate aim being to extort from him "more pay and presents." He was therefore consoled when, upon arriving on Abbott Lake, the Indians "were in strange country and I was the sole guide of the party."[41] But at the west end of Schultz Lake he again was compelled to hire guides, this time Inuit, to take him to Marble Island, where he had arranged to have a whaler supply him with provisions for the northward journey. To his disappointment, when he reached the Island, there was no sign of the whaler. Winter was dangerously close, so he searched around for news of the whaler's whereabouts, backtracking to Baker Lake where he cached the canoes. Early in October of 1901 Hanbury finally met the whaler, planning to winter on Hudson Bay at Depot Island. After obtaining provisions he returned to Baker Lake, preferring to spend the winter with the Inuit at their camp. During that winter he took part in numerous hunting expeditions for musk-oxen, sometimes entering territory where he boasted, "no white man had ever been."[42]

In late December Hanbury began his return trip by dog sled to the whaler in order to prepare for a journey to the Arctic coast. It was therefore March 9 before he set out from the Baker Lake camp with a party of Inuit and twenty dogs. They passed Schultz and Aberdeen Lakes and reached Ti-bi-elik Lake on April 3, 1902. Two days later they turned northward and treked deeper into the Barrens on snowshoes, reaching Pelly Lake by April 14, 1902. Soon they were off again on a journey marked by amazing luck in hunting. Remarkably, in just over two weeks, they arrived at the Arctic coast to the west of McTavish Point. From there Hanbury followed the coastline to the west beyond Coronation Gulf to the mouth of the Coppermine, went up the Coppermine to the Kendall River and over to Great Bear Lake. Hanbury completed his journey by travelling up the Mackenzie to Resolution, arriving September 28. It was the middle of December 1902, when he arrived in Edmonton.

*   *   *

The late nineteenth century Barren Lands travellers constituted an elite group of male professionals and recreationalists with similar social and economic backgrounds. Drawn from the middle and upper middle classes of Britain, the U.S. or Canada, all but Munn were university educated and most could boast of successful and respectable careers. Some were wealthy enough to fund independent expeditions and travel extensively for months at a time and others were sent north as salaried explorers or scientists. Most were products of affluence and privilege and were surely in a position to reap the full benefits of 'civilization.' Why then, did they choose to flee this world that offered them its choice rewards? What forces drew them to such an inhospitable environment as that which had mythologized the Barrens?

Certainly they were not motivated by hopes of financial gain. J. B. Tyrrell, for example, was much wealthier in his later career as a mining consultant than as an explorer. The Geological Survey was not noted for its high salaries and during Tyrrell's 1894 explorations he was actually compelled to draw his summer's salary to cover the extended costs of completing the expedition. In a letter to his wife Edith he commented uncertainly, "Probably I shall get it back, after a while."[43] As Tyrrell was accustomed to and expected an opulent lifestyle, a career in wilderness exploration required considerable sacrifice. And in fact he would eventually leave the Survey partly because of a longstanding salary dispute.

Many of these men arranged their lives around a compulsion to travel and explore, often by demanding modes to difficult regions. Sometimes, the act of travelling itself seemed more important than the actual destination. Munn, for instance, recalling his initial decision to come to Canada, wrote:

Obeying the call of some atavism in my blood, I found that I had to travel, but the toss of a coin decided whether I should go to the Argentine or to Canada, the two countries I selected almost haphazard from the map.[44]

Munn followed his instinct, journeying to many parts of the world, but like most of the others, he paid particular attention to the Canadian North. Whitney, however, did not focus his travels primarily on the North. Rather, his travelling history suggests a preference for warmer climates and it is uncertain whether he ever returned to the North after his Barrens expedition. Nevertheless, it was invariably little known wilderness areas far removed from civilization that were eagerly sought by the travellers.

The motives underlying their wilderness journeys in general and northern trips in particular were complex and varied. But they generally were intertwined with the travellers' ambivalence about civilization and assumptions about wilderness.

Invariably the travellers asserted that their particular journey, or certain stretches of it, had never before been traversed by white men. Sometimes the thrill was increased by the realization that northern natives had not even crossed the territory. It was clearly important that they be the first in some respect. But behind their boastful claims there often lay more than ego. Some reacted wih a respectful feeling of privilege that nature had permitted them to be the first to view its special beauties. This sentiment is apparent in James Tyrrell's description of their discovery of Lake Aberdeen:

It was a lovely calm evening when the track of our canoe first rippled the waters of this lake, and as we landed at a bluff point on the north shore and from it gazed to the eastward over the solitary but beautiful scene, a feeling of awe crept over us. We were undoubtedly the first white men who had ever viewed it, and in the knowledge of that fact there was inspiration.[45]

Lakes and rivers never before seen by whites were regarded by the travellers as true discoveries. Such discoveries enhanced their sense of self-importance, strengthening their psychological ties with the first European explorers who roamed the North. Not surprisingly then, the names of Franklin, Hearne and Back recur persistently. When they crossed the former paths of these early explorers, they were elated. Such men were their heroes. Most notably, J. B. Tyrrell would sustain his idealization of Hearne, Turner and Thompson throughout his life, devoting considerable time and energy to recreating their lives by editing and publishing their journals.

Undoubtedly, these men valued the comforts of southern urban life. As Munn wrote in a teasing letter to Whitney before the latter emerged from the wilderness:

Ye gods! think of the luxury of a big hot bath, a good cigar and—but why should I fill your mind with envy and all uncharitableness? Truly, when I think of all you have left behind for the barrenness of the Barren Grounds, I agree with Puck: "What fools these mortals be."[46]

Imagining the luxuries awaiting their return was, for many of the travellers, a common pastime that seemed to ease the pain of cold and hunger.

But the explorers could also feel trapped by civilization. Indeed, their writings reflect an anti-urban bias which coloured their perceptions of the North, enhancing its appeal on the one hand and yet disappointing them on the other. Cities were often portrayed in their journals as artificial, confining, dirty, petty, destructive, and ultimately dull. Conversely, the wilderness represented escape, freedom, challenge, adventure and beauty. The travellers frequently perceived themselves as superior to the average urban dweller by their ability to reject the ideals of civilization and survive the hazards of nature. Whitney best expressed these attitudes and rhetorically captured the spirit of the wilderness explorer in the following passage.

> To him who has scented the trackless wilds, and whose blood has gone the pace of its perils and freedom, there comes, every now and again, an irresistable impulse to fly from electric lights, railroads, and directories; to travel on his feet instead of being jerked along in a cable-car; to find his way with the aid of a compass and the North Star, instead of by belettered lamp-posts. At such a time and in such a mood the untamed spirit chafes under the pettiness of worldly strife, and turns to the home of the redman.
>
> 'Tis a strange fascination, but strong as strange, this playing at monarch of all you survey; this demand upon your skill and endurance and perseverance in a continuous game of hazard with life as the stake; this calling home where you throw down your blankets. The mind reaches out to the freedom and the openness of a life that rises superior to the great machine called civilization, which moulds us all into one proper and narrow and colourless whole.[47]

Travelling in an untouched wilderness was believed to be an elevating, transforming exierince. Mere survival demanded a re-ordering of priorities and an endless ability to adapt. Life in the North was harsh, yet simple, and infinitely more 'pure' than the urban ideal. Upon completing a northern journey, one re-entered civilization feeling alien and detached, but ultimately superior:

> How little the fenced divisions of ordinary every-day life seem when you have returned! How petty one feels on rejoining the hysterical mob which hurries forth each morning from dwelling to office, and gathers again each night from office to dwelling.[48]

Among its many other faults, civilization was sometimes seen to enforce a false separation between man and nature. In the North these distinctions were severed. Immersion in the wilderness offered the chance to rediscover one's 'natural' self in relation to a natural environment. Pike almost pitied those who had not the opportunity to develop this sensibility:

> Surely we carry this civilization too far, and are in danger of warping our natural instincts by too close observance of the rules that some mysterious force obliges us to follow when we herd together in big cities . . . a dweller in cities is too wrapped up in the works of man to have much respect left for the works of God, and to him the loneliness of forest and mountain, lake and river, must ever appear but a weary desolation.[49]

But despite such passionate oubursts, the adventurers were unable to maintain a view of humanity and nature which was non-anthropocentric. Perhaps, in part, their quest to harmonize their inner selves with nature was defeated by a quest of a different sort—one which was rooted in their ultimate acceptance of southern values. As young men bred on Victorian ideals of manliness, their voyages were clearly associated with an assertion of their masculinity. Behind their more objective interests in the North lay a hankering to pit the strength of their bodies and their wits against the hostile environment of the Barrens. A Barren Ground trip was, in the words of Whitney, "the hardest a man could make";[50] in an age which placed a premium on the masculine ideal, it promised to test the limits of their potential. The land itself became the medium through which they could prove themselves, for survival in the northern wilderness drew upon all one's inner reserves of strength, endurance, self-reliance, patience and skill. It was thus with a sense of great pride and accomplishment that J. B. Tyrrell looked back on his first field trip with the Survey in 1883 to the foothills of the Rockies and summarized, "I went out a boy and came back a man."[51]

Hardships and close confrontation with death were an important component of this masculine quest. It is therefore not surprising that the perils encountered were so often recounted with enthusiasm and pride. Even Russell—ever the detached academic observer—admitted feeling thrilled when his canoe was drawn into the Boiler rapids, tossed among the rocks and threatened with destruction. And Hanbury was disappointed to find his paddle along the unexplored stretch of the Thelon River calm and uneventful:

> The journey turned out to be so absurdly easy, that I more than once regretted that I was deprived of the pleasure of meeting and surmounting difficulties.[52]

J. B. Tyrrell was unique in his tendency to downplay adversity. Well trained in genteel modesty, Tyrrell rarely indulged in obvious self-flattery by trumpeting his heroics. His letter to Edith following the 1893 expedition, during which Tyrrell's entire party almost died of starvation and exposure, typically reflected his mastery of understatement: "The summer and autumn brought us much hardship and starvation but I am now in better health than ever."[53] Clearly, however, Tyrrell enjoyed meeting and overcoming difficulties. Neither his nor the other travellers' preference for charting a new course, for example, stemmed simply from their eagerness to find where it led, as Tyrrell's biographer contends.[54] It was also linked to the process of the quest and the anticipation of unknown challenges and dangers ahead.*

Related to the desire to be first, the quest for a wilderness retreat, and the search for masculine identity, is another prominent motive—the hunt for big game. While the Tyrrell brothers were primarily hunters of meat, not trophies, Pike, Munn and Whitney were sport hunters, enamoured by contemporary ideals of sportsmanship. What exactly constituted good sportsmanship was a topic of

---

* For an analysis of the traditionally masculine quest patern see William James, "The Canoe Trip and the Quest Pattern", elsewhere in this volume.

considerable debate in southern recreational circles,[55] yet underlying the concept were certain tacitly understood rules of conduct considered crucial to the development of both manly vigour and honourable character.[56] Much to the travellers' chagrin their native aides continually violated this code of proper conduct. Pike eventually gave up trying to force the Indians to conform to white hunting ethics and simply warned prospective hunters to "leave at home all the old-fashioned notions of shooting etiquette" when visiting the North:

> If you see a man in a good position for a shot, run up, jostle his elbow, and let your gun off; if an animal falls, swear you killed it, and claim the back-fat and tongue no matter whether you fired or not; never admit that you are not quite sure which animal you shot at. It is only by strict attention to these rules that a white man can get a fair division of plunder when shooting with half-breeds and Indians.[57]

The rules of sportsmanship governed more than one's relationship with fellow hunters. The notion of fair play also applied to the process of the hunt itself. Indeed, it was considered crucial that a hunt for sport be distinguishable from mere slaughter. According to one writer in *Forest and Stream*, the way to maintain this distinction was to give "every reasonable chance" to the game, while keeping a few for oneself.[58] While the Barrens travellers could be thrilled by the chase and kill of the buffalo and caribou, many expressed disgust with their hunts for musk-oxen. For Pike, the hunt of his fantasies turned out to be "a sickening slaughter, without the least pretense of sport to recommend it."[59] Similarly, Russell told sportsmen to stay away from musk-ox country unless they enjoyed "cruel butchery":

> You do not feel the triumphant exhilaration which results from successfully pursuing the noble moose or elk; in fact you can duplicate the sensation felt on such an occasion at far less expense and less hardship, by hiring a pack of hungry curs for an afternoon, and turning them loose into your neighbor's sheep pasture. When they have rounded up the flock, you can take your stand at a safe distance and shoot down the sheep! The musk-ox is not a sporty animal.[60]

Although Munn was despondent with the failure of his musk-ox hunt in the Barrens, he would much later confess that he never felt completely comfortable about killing game. Even in his keenest hunting days, he reflected, "I always hated to see the reproach in their eyes—even when it was a shot purely necessary for food to justify it." Eventually, he renounced his love of hunting, trading in his gun for a camera:

> The noblest head of wapiti or moose, the biggest black or grizzly bear, a fine mountain sheep or a goat would be safe from me to-day at ten paces, provided he, in turn, let me observe him in peace. The camera is the weapon I would shoot him with.[61]

Throughout their journals the travellers complained of what they saw as the Indians' indiscriminate love of slaughter and corresponding tendency to over-kill. As usual, Pike was the harshest in judgement, declaring the Indians, and to a lesser extent the Inuit, the "enemies" of "persecuted animals like the caribou and musk-ox."[62] In contrast, the travellers insisted that they had "no wish to shoot for the mere killing."[63] They prided themselves on their restraint in shooting only as many animals as they required for food or a 'reasonable' number for sport. Sharing many of the concerns of late nineteenth century conservationists, these hunters sometimes advocated increased and extended legal protection for northern wild-life—if only to ensure an adequate supply of game for future hunting excursions. In fact, somewhat ironically, recreational hunters were often in the vanguard of the early North American conservation movements. Indeed, Theodore Roosevelt and his fellow Boone and Crocket Club members were arguing the need for conservation well before the term was coined in 1902. Both Caspar Whitney and later Warburton Pike had ties to this exclusive organization, the former as a member and the latter as an associate member.

*   *   *

The various hopes and dreams that launched the travellers on their northern journeys so often clashed with their actual experiences in the North. Tensions between expectations and reality were especially evident in the white explorers' relationship with the Indians. The scorn with which the travellers regarded Indian hunting practices was typically extended to many other facets of their life and character.

While the young adventurers needed the natives as guides and teachers in the North, they bitterly resented their dependence in a foreign land and felt humiliated to be so helplessly reliant on a group of people who, they complained, "only wait to rebel and desert till a time when they think you can least do without them."[64] Russell, especially, was painfully conscious of his own alienation and dependence, finding himself an unwitting victim of persistent abuse. The Indians' lack of respect for him damaged his self-esteem and had adverse practical implications as well. Recalling, for example, his unpleasant experiences with a party of Dog Rib Indians and Métis, Russell commented querulously:

> I was simply a passenger, with no authority whatever over my companions' movements; I furnished tea for the party and wielded a paddle. Aside from the discomfort and hardship of such an arrangement, it gave the Indians the idea that I was a servant and not a 'master', as they term the officers of the Company and explorers travelling through the country. As a result, it was hard to convince them that I really could pay when their assistance was required.[65]

Although Russell was not as guilty as some of the others, the explorers generally sanctioned the stratified division between natives and whites, reacting with indignation when the Indians stepped beyond their 'servant' role. The travellers arrived in the North fully expecting the northern Indians to hire themselves out as guides and travelling companions for months at a time, at a moment's notice. When the Indians refused, or were unco-operative and insubordinate, they were regarded as "lazy" and "deceitful."

J. B. Tyrrell on the whole possessed a more charitable view of the Indians than did the other travellers; but then the Tyrrells were also the least dependent on the services of local Indians, having brought guides with them to the North.

Of course, J. B.'s outlook was hardly egalitarian. He merely assumed the superiority of whites and found little need to articulate it. This attitude is best reflected in the Tyrrell's appalling treatment of their native aides upon their return voyage in 1893. On the last stretch of their journey from Churchill, when dogs and sleds were available, the Tyrrell brothers lay wrapped comfortably in blankets on the carioles while their two Indians companions were expected to walk, or rather run, to keep up with them. Not surprisingly, they were unable to maintain the pace set by the dogs. After travelling 40 to 47 miles a day on snowshoes, J. W. said the Indians soon "became crippled" and could go no farther. The Tyrrell's solution was simply to leave their loyal aides behind and make alternate arrangements for their return voyage.[66]

In contrast to the Indians, the Inuit rarely elicited anything but praise from the travellers. Unlike the "sullen," "slovenly" Indians, the Inuit were seen as the personsification of the 'noble savage' ideal. Commonly described in patronizing terms as "happy and contented children, always laughing, and merry, good-natured and hospitable,"[67] the explorers were delighted when they discovered traces of the Inuit in the Barrens. If they stumbled upon a deserted campsite and could not find its inhabitants, they were always careful to leave behind presents, such as a plug of tobacco or a tin plate, to demonstrate their friendliness.

If the late nineteenth century explorers had perhaps hoped to briefly recapture their non-industrial roots through their travels in the northern wilderness, ironically, they were themselves harbingers of civilization. Despite their awareness of its flaws, they believed not only in the inevitability of the advance of civilization, but also in its ultimate desirability. Frequently they viewed the northern wilderness in imperialistic terms. Whitney, for example, waxed eloquent in wilderness romanticism, yet dispassionately asserted that "everyone knows that the savage must disappear before the civilized man." In the final analysis, he only wished authorities would be more rational in their approach:

> At present [the Indian] distrusts and sees only that he is being 'civilized' off the face of the earth, and remembers the white man in his successive roles of welcomed guest, greedy hunter, settler, and exterminator. I am not dealing in heroics . . . but if we are to attempt the civilization of those that remain let us first endeavour to gain their confidence, and then follow it up by methods which they can grasp.[68]

Hanbury, on the other hand, could not understand why the federal authorities ever bothered with the treaty arrangements of 1899 and 1900, complaining that "they are Indians still, and the return for the time, trouble, and money expended on them seemed to me very inadequate."[69] The Tyrrells built a faith in the future potential of Canada which rested largely on assumptions of large-scale development. Considering the occupational pursuits of both brothers it is not surprising that neither was disturbed to ponder the day when the unknown territory they once traversed would be occupied by prospectors and miners. But the most imperialistic vision of the North was held by Munn. Looking back in the early 1930s he was bursting with pride to have witnessed the expansion and development of Canada. Recalling once having viewed hundreds of antelope in a location near

Medicine Hat, he described in idyllic terms the scene which emerged to take its place:

> Today, with prosperous farms on either side, we see an Indian driving his Ford along the fine highway at the same place, or the tourist in his luxurious limousine, on his way to Banff and the marvellous highways through the Rockey Mountains.[70]

Frank Russell shared many of the attitudes and assumptions of the other travellers, however he demonstrated the most interesting insight into the process of development and questioned his own responses to the North. At the outset of his voyage, Russell was somewhat naive in his rigid adherence to the academic code of objectivity and rationality. He appeared almost prepared to greet the natives as friendly laboratory specimens. Nevertheless, his early association with the Athabascan Indians prompted him to sympathize with the plight of the northern natives and to note the disruptive effects of 'civilization' on their lives. He noted the squalor and starvation, the decline of the buffalo and caribou and he listened to the natives' grievances regarding the treaty arrangements with the Indians further south. Russell was moved beyond his objectivity upon hearing of the government's broken treaty promises and manipulative tactics. Yet as his contact with the natives intensified on his Barren Lands expedition, his impressions became much less than favourable. Resentful and disillusioned, Russell told of setting out on one hunting trip, with "little hopes of killing any musk-ox, but in excellent humour for slaughtering a few Dog Ribs."[71]

Three years later, when Russell recorded his impressions on the Indians in retrospect, his views were considerably modified. He was the only traveller to admit his tendency to impose the norms and standards of white society upon the Indians. His recognition of that fact led him to re-interpret his association with them:

> During the three years which have passed since my residence among the Dog Ribs, I have come to have a better understanding of the 'Indian mind'. They were more intelligent than I supposed, but I made the mistake of judging them by our standards, and my first impression was followed by disappointment. . . . They were never stupid, but always lighthearted, even in the most depressing circumstances.[72]

But in the end, Russell concluded that white contact had modified the Indians' lifestyle very little, pointing out numerous examples, such as the education of native children in schools, where civilization was improving the Indians' quality of life. He never fully returned to his earlier critical assessment of the effect of civilization on the Indian population.

*   *   *

These purposeful wanderers of the late nineteenth century represented a new breed of northern explorers. Unlike their earlier counterparts, they were generally more interested in experiencing the mythical tundra than in getting beyond it to something else. They were youthful, middle or upper- middle-class men, often in the process of carving out a respectable profession. Most were very absorbed with urban affairs. Yet all of them felt a compulsion to temporarily escape civilization.

Conscious of the transience of wilderness in an urban industrial age, the Barrens held a special appeal to these travellers. Tantalized by images of vast stretches of unexplored territory and of a terrifying beauty unmarred by civilization, they rushed northward to taste a completely natural environment before it was too late. Inspired by the memory of the first explorers to penetrate the Barrens, they hoped to revitalize their links with heroic figures of the past. Some hoped also to track rare game or collect scientific specimens of plant and animal life. And the travellers also anticipated a unique opportunity to test the limits of their masculine potential and demonstrate their manhood. Although determined to escape civilization, these wilderness-seekers unavoidably carried their class baggage with them. Ultimately, they represented the forerunners of modernity, and remained imprisoned within an inherited cultural value system which was predominantly white, genteel, and urban.

The travellers were clearly a restless lot; change, diversity, and challenge distinguished their preferred lifestyles. Once they succumbed to the exploring instinct, they could not easily be satisfied with a life of security and convention. By nature they were adventurers and wanderers. Somewhat anxious, however, to preserve a respectable image, they offered various rationales for their travels. As scientists, sportsmen, topographers, or translators, they were each armed with a legitimate excuse for a northern adventure. They became purposeful wanderers— a flattering self image that balanced romance and respectability.

ENDNOTES

1. Warburton Pike, *The Barren Ground of Northern Canada* (London and New York 1892), p. v.

2. Pike, *The Barren Ground*, p. 2.

3. Nineteenth and early twentieth century Canadian fiction was heavily dominated by stories of romance and adventure which by the 1890s were increasingly focused on the north. See G. Roper, R. Schieder and S. R. Beharriell, "The Kinds of Fiction, 1880–1920", in C. Klinck, ed. *Literary History of Canada* (Toronto 1965), p. 296.

4. Pierre Burton, *Klondike* (Toronto 1972), p. 408.

5. Pike and his business partner (and fellow hunter) Clive Phillipps-Wolley launched many business ventures which included "mining copper in the Cassiar Mountains," and running "a steam paddle-wheeler and pack trains into the Klondike gold field." Patrick Dunae, *Gentlemen Immigrants: From the British Public Schools to the Canadian Frontier* (Vancouver and Toronto 1981), p. 117.

6. Ibid., p. 118.

7. Ibid.

8. Pike, *The Barren Ground*, pp. v, 274, vi.

9. See H. G. DuLog "Barren Grounds of Canada", *Forest and Stream*, Jan. 26, 1893, pp. 70–71.

10. Pike, *The Barren Ground*, p. 34.

11. Ibid., p. 65.

12. For Mackinlay's account see James Mackinlay, "A Manuscript Written on Mr. Warburton Pike's visit to Back River in 1890", *Arctic Circular*, vol. 10, no. 3, 1957, pp. 32-50 and no. 4, 1957, pp. 51-69.

13. Pike, *The Barren Ground*, p. 173.

14. Dunae, p. 119. Pike published a popular account of his 1892 trip in *Through the Sub-Arctic Forest* (London and New York 1896).

15. This study, originally part of the Twenty-Sixth Annual *Report of the Bureau of American Ethnology, 1904-1905* was recently re-published as a book. See Frank Russell, *The Pima Indians* (Tucson, Arizona 1975).

16. Frank Russell, *Explorations in the Far North* (Iowa 1898), p. ii.

17. Ibid., pp. 44, 7.

18. Ibid., p. 70.

19. Ibid., p. 71.

20. Ibid., pp. 72, 73.

21. Alex Inglis, *Northern Vagabond: The Life and Career of J. B. Tyrrell* (Toronto 1978), p. 51.

22. J. B. Tyrrell, "Report on the Doobawnt, Kazan and Ferguson Rivers and the North-West Coast of Hudson Bay," *Annual Report*, Geological Survey of Canada, vol. 9, 1986, p. 6f.

23. For the report of this exploration, not included in this study, see "Report of J. W. Tyrrell, D. L. S., Exploratory Survey Between Great Slave Lake and Hudson Bay, Districts of Mackenzie and Keewatin." Sessional Paper #25, Department of the Interior, *Annual Report*, 1900-1901, pp. 98-131.

24. Morris Zaslow, *Reading the Rocks* (Ottawa 1975), p. 131.

25. Alex Inglis, *Northern Vagabond* (Toronto 1978), p. 56.

26. J. B. Tyrrell, "Notebooks recalling the years 1889-1897," M.S. 26 Box 134, Rare Books Department, Fisher Library, Toronto.

27. M. Zaslow, *Reading the Rocks*, p. 203. This trend eventually culminated in the Survey's temporary takeover by the Federal Department of Mines.

28. Inglis, *Northern Vagabond*, p. 25.

29. J. W. Tyrrell, *Across the Sub-Arctics of Canada*, (Toronto 1897), pp. 78-79.

30. J. B. Tyrrell, "An Expedition through the Barren Lands of Northern Canada," *Geographical Journal*, vol. 4, 1894, p. 445.

31. The full details of this journey are recorded in Tyrrell's report for the Geological Survey. See J. B. Tyrrell, "Report on the Doobawnt, Kazan and Ferguson Rivers and the North-West Coast of Hudson Bay," pp. 16f-26f.

32. Henry Toke Munn, *Prairie Trails and Arctic By-Ways* (London 1932), p. 58.

33. Ibid., p. 78.

34. Caspar Whitney, *On Snow-Shoes to the Barren Grounds* (New York 1896), pp. 2, 39.

35. For the history of this club see James Trefethen, *Crusade for Wildlife: Highlights in Conservation Progress* (New York 1961).

36. Whitney, *On Snowshoes*, p. 39.

37. Ibid., p. 112.

38. See David T. Hanbury, "Through the Barren Ground of North-Eastern Canada to the Arctic Coast," *Geographical Journal*, vol. 22, August 1903, pp. 78-91.

39. D. Hanbury, *Sport and Travel in the Northland of Canada* (London 1904).

40. Ibid., p. v.

41. Ibid., pp. 32, 33.

42. Ibid., p. 83.

43. "Personal correspondence of J. B. Tyrrell to M. E. Tyrrell," January 9, 1895, M.S. 2, Box 9, 1892-96, Rare Books, Fisher Library, Toronto.

44. Munn, *On Snowshoes*, p. 7.

45. J. W. Tyrrell, *Across the Sub-Arctic of Canada*, pp. 112-113.

46. Whitney, *On Snowshoes*, p. 135.

47. Whitney, *On Snowshoes*, pp. 2-3.

48. Ibid., p. 3.

49. Pike, *The Barren Ground of Northern Canada*, p. 274.

50. Whitney, *On Snowshoes*, p. 292.

51. Quoted in Inglis, *Northern Vagabond*, p. 78.

52. Hanbury, *Sport and Travel in the Northland of Canada*, p. 11.

53. J. B. Tyrrell to M. E. Tyrrell, Jan. 7, 1894, M.S. 26, Box 134, Rare Books Room, Fisher Library, Toronto. Oddly enough, Tyrrell is said to have been somewhat of a hypochondriac while in an urban environment.

54. Inglis, p. 52. Note however that Tyrrell's love of adventure in remote regions waned as jealousies and conflict mounted in the Survey. With his eye on a teaching position at the University of Toronto, his impatience with the Survey led him on numerous occasions to yearn for a more ordinary existence. In 1896, during the peak of this disillusionment, he wrote to Edith: "how lovely it would be to have a quiet house in the country, within easy reach of the city, from which one would not be obliged to wander off into the wilderness every year." J. B. Tyrrell to M. E. Tyrrell, June 30, 1896, M.S. 26, Box 134. Rare Book Room, Fisher Library, Toronto. As Tyrrell later in life became more involved with the pragmatic activities of a prosperous mining career, his instinct to explore for the sake of exploration was possibly undermined again. In fact, one hardly recognizes the eager adventurer of 1893 in his reponse years later to a friend who expressed interest in retracing his Dubawnt route to Hudson Bay: "Why on earth would you want to do that? You can go there by plane you know." Quoted in Inglis, p. 52.

55. See for example the following commentaries in *Forest and Stream*: Aug. 17, 1895, p. 133; Nov. 2, 1895, p. 325; "True Sportsmanship," Nov. 2, 1895, p. 377; "Sportsmanship Again," Nov. 28, 1895, p. 444; "The Right and the Wrong of Hunting," April 7, 1900, p. 267.

56. On the relationship between sport and the "masculine mystique" involving both a physical and moral ideal see Joe Dubbert, "From Battlefield to Ballfield: The Rise of Sport, 1880-1920" in his book *A Man's Place: Masculinity in Transition* (New Jersey 1979).

57. Pike, *The Barren Ground*, p. 108.

58. "True Sportsmanship," by Kelpie, *Forest and Stream*, Nov. 2, 1895.

59. Pike, *The Barren Ground*, p. 145.

60. Russell, *Explorations*, p. 124.

61. Munn, *Prairie Trails*, p. 24.

62. Ibid., p. 52.

63. Whitney, *On Snowshoes*, p. 269.

64. Ibid., p. 106.

65. Russell, *Explorations*, p. 80-81.

66. Inglis, p.

67. Hanbury, *Sport and Travel in the Northland of Canada*, p. 42.

68. See Whitney, *On Snowshoes*, pp. 22-23.

69. Hanbury, *Sport and Travel*, p. 26.

70. Munn, *Prairie Trails*, p. 8.

71. Russell, *Hunting Musk-Ox With the Dog Ribs* (Toronto 1970), p. 26.

72. Russell, *Journey to the Far North*, pp. 158-159.

The Mounted Police in the Barren Lands: The Pelletier Expedition of 1908

John Jennings

It was observed by Apsley Cherry Garrard, one of the survivors of Captain Scott's ill-fated Antarctic expedition, that "polar exploration is at once the cleanest and most isolated way of having a bad time that has yet been devised."[1] Much the same could be said for the exploration of sub-Arctic Canada, with the difference that this region was slightly less clean when the mosquito and black fly were in season, and even more isolated. The astonishing fact is that a vast area of the Barren Lands of Canada was one of the last places on earth to be explored, long after scores of Europeans had meandered for several centuries through polar regions, searching for the elusive Northwest Passage. Even "Darkest Africa" was rather well known by the end of the nineteenth century, at a time when the knowledge of a huge area between Great Slave Lake and Hudson Bay continued to rest largely on a few vague Indian descriptions.

Perhaps this territory remained unexplored because it did not catch the popular imagination. It had already been determined as early as the 1740s by those searching for the Northwest Passage that Chesterfield Inlet did not lead to China, so after the expeditions of Samuel Hearne and George Back, interest in the area lapsed until the end of the nineteenth century. Then, as so often happens, there occurred a sudden surge of interest and in less than a decade several hundred thousand square miles of territory were explored by canoe and snowshoe.

Suddenly, in the 1890s, the area was properly discovered by several eccentric, mostly British, sportsmen and by the Geological Survey of Canada in the form of the two Tyrrell brothers. All of these men, most notably Warburton Pike, David Hanbury, and the Tyrrells, were there partly for the purpose of gathering scientific information, but they shared another sort of motivation as well. They all had a deep scientific curiosity; yet more important, perhaps, they were all besotted with the North and were part of a small fraternity that found a deep spiritual satisfaction in isolation, hardship and endurance. Their purpose was to explore, but they likely would have found little happiness in doing so by snowmobile or airplane.* Their activity, as well as their approach and method, reflect the changing national perspective of the North.

The next traveller in this region, and one who would have been quickly embraced by this select fraternity, was the first Mounted Policeman in the area,

---

* See Margaret Hobbs, "Purposeful Wanderers: Late Nineteenth Century Travellers to the Barrens" elsewhere in this volume.

Inspector Ephrem Albert Pelletier. It was Pelletier's job in 1908, in effect, to join the western and the eastern Arctic by canoe, using the newly discovered Hanbury-Thelon route between Great Slave Lake and Chesterfield Inlet. Though important in Mounted Police history, it is a trip which has not been properly recognized. For instance, Farley Mowat in *Tundra* has informed us that "in 1908 Inspector Pelletier patrolled some distance up the Thelon; but since there were no people in the inland plains except the Eskimos, and therefore no crime, the police saw little need for further patrols."[2] Mowat's misleading description, obviously based on a meagre knowledge of the subject, hardly prepared the reader for one of the major trips in Barren Land history. By the end of their journey, Inspector Pelletier and his party had travelled 2,575 miles by canoe and snowshoe from Fort Smith, on the Slave River, to Norway House. It is perhaps unfair, however, to single out Mowat's ignorance concerning this trip, for it is one that is familiar only to northern experts.

Inspector Pelletier's patrol is absent from the popular literature of the North for two reasons. First, he was not exploring virgin country, and had the advantage of travelling with J. W. Tyrrell's extremely detailed maps of the route. Second, his trip would not appeal to those who deal in sensational writing since his unassuming competence ensured a somewhat uneventful journey.

The sad truth is that people like Scott of the Antarctic and Sir John Franklin have become famous less for their courage and daring, which were considerable, than as a result of their incompetence. They would be less well known if they had not needlessly led so many people to their death. Pelletier, unlike Scott and Franklin, put less faith in the invincibility of the British Empire than in careful planning and sound judgement.

Pelletier's expedition across the Barrens could be considered an aberration if not seen in context for, as Mowat has pointed out, Pelletier stated at the end of his report that there was no need to make other such patrols and the Police did not retrace his route for some time. But his patrol was part of a logical and consistent plan on the part of the Mounted Police to assert a presence in the North ahead of other whites. This is the same philosophy which had been so effective in western Canada when a fledgling nation had created the North West Mounted Police in 1873 to stake its claim to the West, to ensure peace and fair dealings toward the Native population, and of course, to help in the process of shunting these people to one side so European settlement could proceed.

Following its precedent in the West, the Federal Government in the last decade of the nineteenth century initiated a policy in the North of low-budget sovereignty through the agencies of the Geological Survey and the North West Mounted Police. Until this time the government had almost completely ignored the North, largely due to its preoccupation with western settlement. But as whites began to drift to the North, the government now considered it necessary to assert a presence. Just as the original Mounties had been sent west to deal with the whisky traders of Whoop-up Country, in the 1890s the Police were sent north to monitor the pursuit of happiness by the prospectors and whalers, mostly

Americans, who were beginning to invade the country and undermine Native society.

Well before the Klondike gold rush, a Police contingent had been sent to the Yukon to investigate the area. When news of gold ignited a stampede to the Yukon, the Police were in position at the top of Chilcoot Pass to welcome some of the most hard-bitten characters in the western world to Canadian territory and advise them on the finer points of Canadian law. By 1898, when the full force of the gold rush hit the Yukon, the Police were well entrenched and through their tight control and policy of wide-ranging patrols, were able to dictate a remarkably peaceful atmosphere.

Although their main northern preoccupation for the next several decades continued to be the Klondike, the Police were also establishing themselves in the more remote parts of the western and eastern Arctic. In 1903 two posts were established; one at Herschel Island under Sergeant F.J. Fitzgerald (who later led the famous lost patrol of 1910- 11), and one under Superintendent Moodie at Fullerton, situated just north of Chesterfield Inlet in Hudson Bay. The purpose of both posts was to establish a Canadian presence in areas that were becoming inundated with foreign whalers, who often showed few scruples in their relationships with the Inuit.

Inspector Pelletier was a member of this first post in the eastern Arctic. In his report for 1904-5, Superintendent Moodie included a description of the life of this first 11-man contingent at Fullerton.

> The winter passed quickly and pleasantly. The weather was not exceptionally cold, the lowest temperature being 52 below zero. Football and baseball daily, weather permitting, races and other sports, a number of concerts and a weekly dance.[3]

By the time of Pelletier's journey in 1908, the Police had established a definite presence in all parts of the North where Europeans were beginning to penetrate.

It was decided by the Commissioner that the time had come to establish jurisdiction over the inland section of the eastern Arctic, and create a patrol route between the western and eastern Arctic. Certainly this policy must have been prompted by the expectation that the travels of Pike, Hanbury and the Tyrrells in this area would encourage others to follow suit. Therefore, it was decided to send a party to evaluate the feasibility of a permanent route from the Mackenzie River to Hudson Bay, to report on the location and condition of Indian and Eskimo bands, and to appraise the need to establish permanent posts along the route. So Inspector Pelletier and three other Policemen set out on the longest and most difficult Police patrol to that time, a patrol that was to last nine and a half months and to eventually cover 1325 miles by canoe plus 1250 miles by dog sled.

*   *   *

Pelletier was a good choice to lead such a patrol. He had been stationed at Fullerton in 1904 and before that in the Yukon for two years, where he travelled extensively by canoe and dog team.[4] In 1906 and 1907 he had led two pioneering patrols from Norway House, at the north end of Lake Winnipeg to Fort Churchill on Hudson Bay, with the purpose of opening a mail route between Regina and the new Police post at Churchill. Pelletier began his first patrol on Boxing Day, 1906, with three dog teams and Indian guides at a dollar a day. He commented in his report that few white men, not even Hudson's Bay Company agents, would hazard a trip into this country without Indian guides. The generosity of Pelletier's remarks concerning his Indian guides is worth noting, because it contrasts sharply with many of the remarks made about Indians by a number of other explorers. A majority of northern explorers, from Franklin to Hanbury and the Tyrrells, left the impression that their Indian guides and helpers were often lazy, demanding, unfriendly and even unreliable. Explorers such as Samuel Hearne and George Back seem to be the exceptions to this observation. Most often, European explorers were rather overbearing toward their Indian guides and hunters and lacked a proper respect for their abilities.

Certainly Pelletier did not share these attitudes. He quickly acknowledged their superiority on their home ground and obviously established a rapport with them based on this respect.

> In general they are good sturdy men, good runners and dog drivers. They are very faithful and patient, look to your comfort generally and are quick to pick up your ways and habits. The more you allow them to do for your comfort the more pleased they seem to be . . . the less you do of manual work the more they think of you. By driving my own dog team I lost prestige with them . . .[5]

Pelletier made good time to Churchill and back, averaging over 28 miles a day and in one stretch averaging more than 43 miles a day on this round trip of more than 1,000 miles.

A few months later, Pelletier repeated the journey during the summer of 1907, this time by canoe. As with his previous trip, he had extensive Indian help. They took three canoes, one 19 footer and two 18 footers. Most of the equipment was carried in one canoe because the other two each carried five huskies, who were being taken to Churchill. Pelletier's description of this canoe route does not sound the slightest bit attractive. Much of the country was flat and soggy. Many of the portages were torture; they often sunk past their knees in mud. The black flies, mosquitoes, midges and bulldogs were "ubiquitous." One night, after spending the day portaging through mud and fallen timber, they camped on a beaver house! Again Pelletier had great praise for his Indian companions who had taken the Police over this awful route without complaint. He concluded in his report that it was not a route to be recommended for summer travel, partly as no one in his right mind would stay in the country during the summer. He also commented that he had found oars fitted to the canoes most valuable and lanteen sails had proved efficient and easily handled. The ideal canoe for this country, in Pelletier's opinion, was 19 feet with good depth and a 44 inch beam. There should be no keel and it should be constructed of either basswood or cedar. The party used white lead and copper tacks for repair and tin cans, flattened with an axe, were found satisfactory where material was necessary for punctures.[6]

In all likelihood, Pelletier was using Peterborough canoes.* Certainly Hanbury and the Tyrrells did, as did the Mounted Police in the Yukon. It is probably also safe to assume that, while in the Yukon, Pelletier would have patrolled quite extensively by canoe. The police had not used canoes to any great extent until they came to the Klondike, but certainly by 1905 they were patrolling, in the Dawson area alone, more than 3000 miles a year by canoe.** So by 1908, when Pelletier set off on his Barren Land trip, he was a seasoned traveller in every sense.

*   *   *

Pelletier left Fort Resolution on Great Slave Lake on July 1, 1908,*** accompanied by three other Mounties, Corporal M. A. Joyce, Constable R. H. Walker, and Constable P. R. Conway. They had departed from Edmonton at the beginning of June, proceeding by horse, scow, steamer and canoe to Fort Resolution.

The party travelled in two canoes, each carrying about a thousand pounds (three months' supply). One canoe was 18 feet with a 42 inch beam, and the other was 18½ feet with a 43 inch beam. Both were 18 inches deep, weighed 120 pounds, and were constructed of longitudinal varnished cedar. They were fitted with oars for pulling against strong winds on lakes and had 55 foot lanteen sails.

The four Mounties, though certainly not the first to travel the route, were probably the first whites to travel in this area without Indian or Métis guides or canoemen. Pike had lived with an entire band. Hanbury hired two Red River Métis to take him across the Barrens in 1899, when he became the first European to explore the Hanbury-Thelon route. The Tyrrell brothers on their epic trip of 1893 sat in the middle of their respective canoes, while their 6 hired Indian and Métis canoemen did the difficult paddling and all the portaging[7]. It is not the intention here to demean these early explorers. Their accomplishments were considerable indeed, but could they have done the same without the assistance of the native experts in the field?

From Resolution, Pelletier's party paddled and sailed 240 miles to the

---

* See John Marsh's article "The Heritage of Peterborough Canoes" elsewhere in this volume.

** C.S.P., Mounted Police Report, 1905, Dawson City Report. The annual patrol mileage for Dawson for that year was over 200,000 miles, the vast majority of it being by horse (150,000 miles) or by dog team (18,000 miles).

*** C.S.P., Mounted Police Report, 1909, pp. 141-168. Unless otherwise indicated, all subsequent quotations detailing this expedition have been drawn from this source.

east end of Great Slave Lake without incident except that one morning at about 6 a.m. they ran into such huge waves that they had to put to shore. As there was no wind, this situation was somewhat puzzling until Pelletier discovered that a large cliff had given way in their vicinity. They arrived at Charlton harbour, the eastern extremity of the lake, two weeks after leaving Resolution, having been retarded by very strong head winds.

After passing a stone chimney, the only remains of George Back's winter camp at Fort Reliance, they began the long portage route to Artillery Lake, catching lake trout weighing up to 25 pounds as they went. They avoided the Lockhart River, the obvious route to Artillery Lake, because it was too dangerous. Hanbury had lost his canoe and all his equipment here while trying to line down a very energetic set of rapids and might have died had he not been found by Indians. Instead, Pelletier followed the traditional Indian portage route that was now named after Warburton Pike, the first European explorer to follow it. This route led through a series of small lakes that J. W. Tyrrell named for the Indian and Métis canoemen of his 1900 survey; Harry, French, Acres, Kipling, Burr and Toura. Pelletier acknowledged the great assistance which Tyrrell's very detailed maps of one inch to a mile provided him over this section.

On this portage, which marked the beginning of the Barren Lands, the Police spotted their first caribou. On the night of July 15 at Toura Lake, deer kept passing to and fro close to our tents in large numbers. On the 22nd near the foot of Artillery Lake we saw thousands and thousands of deer [caribou] mostly bulls. . . . Gradually the ridges on each shore and the traverse itself were alive with them. It was a wonderful sight seen late at night.

Again, eight days later, at the far end of Artillery Lake, Pelletier wrote that, while making good time with the sails, they were held up by caribou crossing their route.

The hills on both shores were covered with them and at a dozen or more places where the lake was from half to one mile wide, solid columns of deer, four or five abreast, were swimming across and so closely that we did not like to venture through them for fear of getting into some mix up.

Unfortunately, they did not see the Artillery Lake Monster, described by Indians as 20 or 30 feet long, with slender horns or feelers.

A short time later they met a band of Dog Rib Indians, who were drying caribou meat and tanning the skins. These were the last people the Police saw until they began to encounter Eskimos at Beverly Lake. The Indians appeared prosperous and gave the Pelletier party an enthusiastic welcome by firing their guns in quick succession.

Pelletier remarked in his report that these Indians had no permanent camps in this area, but followed the caribou.

They have very little to do with white men except at Fort Resolution during treaty time. All their year's supply of fur is traded for the coming year's supply of clothing, food, ammunition, etc.. They do not appear to be of a slaughtering disposition, ie., do not seem to kill more game than they need—nothing goes to waste. . . . The greatest objection or complaint I was given in regard to them is that when trading they are slow at making up their mind as to what they want, also wishing for more than the trader is willing to give, which I consider a very slight offence.

When Pelletier remarked on the vast sea of caribou he had just witnessed, hardly believing that so many could exist in the North, the Indians informed him that the main herd was a few miles up the Lake.

After leaving the Indians, the Police ascended the Casba River into Casba Lake (now named Lockhart River and Ptarmigan Lake) and then across a very short portage into Clinton-Colden Lake. Here they were caught by such a gale that their tents would not stay up and they slept under the canoes. They remained windbound for several days, huddled under the canoes, drinking tea heated on their spirit stove.

By the end of July the Police had crossed the height of land between Clinton-Colden Lake and Lake Deville and were now in the Hudson Bay drainage. Good weather allowed them to sail through lakes Deville, Smart and Sifton. But this same weather brought out the blackflies in their billions so the travellers were now to share with the caribou the torture of those tiny beasts.

Even with Tyrrell's maps it was not easy to find the route out of Lake Sifton, so Pelletier climbed the only hill in sight to get a view of what he described as an immense lake dotted with islands and long points of land. He was able to identify the exit from the lake by looking for sea gulls, which prefer shallow running water. The next day, July 31st, the Police arrived at Timber rapid which separates Lake Sifton and Lake DuBois. Part of this they portaged and then, in shooting the rest, they had the slight mishap of grazing a rock while they avoided bumping into caribou. They were so thick that the Police had to stop and watch them cross within a paddle length.

By August 2nd the party had reached the head of the Hanbury where they stopped just long enough to load up with trout and grayling in the rapids. Pelletier described this country as low and arid with very little wood. They were now in fast water. "There are many sharp bends and very short stretches are seen at a time, thereby adding zest to the adventure." The Hanbury section of their route seemed to be their favourite part of the trip, especially Dickson canyon which J. W. Tyrrell had described as the "wildest and grandest" section of the entire route.[8]

The junction of the Hanbury and Thelon was reached on August 7th, ending the most difficult and exciting part of the trip. Now, on the wider and slower water of the Thelon they began to run into real timber again. They were leaving the country which the Indians labelled "no-stick" on their maps and entering that of "plenty-stick." The Thelon River was known by the Indians as the Thelewdezzeth, meaning fish river, and by the Eskimos as the Arkilinik, meaning wooded river.

Pelletier described an impressive stand of timber near the junction of the two rivers which might possibly have been the place where John Hornby and his two companions built their cabin in the winter of 1926-27 and proceeded to starve to death. In the light of their tragedy, it is interesting to note that Pelletier reported that there was virtually no game in this area and said that it appeared to be an area into which neither Indians nor Eskimos travelled. David Hanbury had concluded much the same.

Here the Police also spotted their first musk-ox. "He was on a small island lying down asleep, and looked very much like a large overturned sod." His appearance quickly changed to that of a "bird in flight", his fur waving up and down as he lumbered off. Although they saw innumerable musk-ox tracks, they were only lucky enough to see two more, both of whom stood gazing "stupidly" at them before running off.

These descriptions of musk-ox by Pelletier, and indeed by most Barren Land travellers, are in marked variance with those of J. W. Tyrrell who claimed that his party was charged on three different occasions by musk-ox bulls[9]. Perhaps this story should be regarded with the same credulity as one contained in his account of the exploration of the Dubawnt River.

> At nightfall, after a long day's struggle with the opposing elements, as we were hauling the canoes ashore towards the shelter of some rocky cliffs, we were suddenly set upon by a pack of huge grey wolves. A great gaunt, hungry-looking brute with dilated eyeballs led the attack . . . he was promptly bored from end to end with a slug from my brother's rifle.[10]

Wolves simply do not attack humans. Indeed, there has not been an authenticated wolf attack on humans in Canada (by a healthy unprovoked wolf). This is the same J. W. Tyrrell who shot at loons after dark to stop their "diabolical screams" and had the appallingly bad judgement to shoot a large black bear in the head after dusk[11]. No experienced hunter, who cherishes life, would shoot a large bear in the head under conditions of poor visibility. Needless to say, Tyrrell left a wounded bear thrashing about in the bush after dark. One's respect for the brothers Tyrrell is sorely tested.

But Tyrrell does redeem himself. At the end of his 1901 report, he stated:

> For the preservation of the musk oxen—which may be so easily slaughtered—and are rapidly diminishing in numbers, I would suggest that the territory between the Thelon and Back rivers be set apart by the government as a game preserve.

Three years later, in his first report from the new Mounted Police post of Fullerton (Just north of Chesterfield Inlet), Superintendent Moodie reported that he had taken it upon himself to prohibit the export of musk-ox hides from Hudson Bay because he feared there was a danger of their extinction. Today there is a vast Thelon Game Sancturary precisely where J. W. Tyrrell recommended. Someone in Ottawa clearly did read the reports.

Pelletier had an uneventful trip down the Thelon, past huge tracts of prairie country which he thought would make the very best ranching country. On

August 12th he met his first group of Eskimos at the western end of Beverly Lake, apparently as far inland as the Eskimos ever came. They preferred the open country which had fewer flies in summer and harder snow in winter, and only came up the Thelon to procure wood for their sleds, kayaks and tents.

Again, on Beverly Lake, a second party of Eskimos were seen.

> On approaching the shore I called out 'Chimo! Chimo!' which is the usual form of greeting when meeting Eskimos in these lands. We were much surprised to hear a 'Good Morning' in answer. Walker expressed his astonishment by saying 'Holy smoke!' to which the native, misconstruing his meaning, replied very fervently: 'Me no smoke; me no tobacco!' We made a landing, and I discovered that the Chief of the camp was Ameryah, commonly known as Lucky Moore. He speaks good English; he is one of the natives who accompanied Hanbury on his long voyage to the Arctic coast and up the Coppermine River in 1901-2. The canoe Hanbury gave him he still had, very carefully hauled on the beach. He was well dressed with white men's clothes, and had very little the appearance of a native. . . . He was much interested in the maps I had, and recognized with great glee and gusto every prominent point on the tracing, which speaks highly for the maps made by J. W. Tyrrell. We gave them a few presents of tobacco, matches, needles, hooks, knives, etc. in return for which they gave us a few deerskin coats and boots. . . They all expressed wonder at seeing no Indians or natives accompanying us.

The Police were now entering more exposed country. On several occasions they were windbound, forced to sleep under their canoes since their tents would not stay up. They lost much time in this stretch because of wind, not reaching the lower Thelon River east of Schultz Lake until August 25. Here they had the only mishap of the entire trip. One canoe stuck on a submerged rock in slack water, which had not been seen because the sun was in their eyes.

The next day, with sails hoisted in favourable winds, Baker Lake's 60 mile length was crossed in a day and a half. At one point the waves were so high that the second canoe completely lost sight of the first. At the bottom end of Baker Lake another group of Eskimos was encountered. They greeted the travellers with great enthusiasm and invited them to a feast of caribou meat and tongues. These Eskimos obviously made a most favourable impression on Pelletier for he reported that they were all perfectly self-sufficient, had all the necessities of life, and had laid in a good stock of meat and deerskin for the winter. Caribou were very plentiful in this area; Pelletier reported seeing caribou every day from Beverly Lake to Hudson Bay.

On August 31 the party reached Ellis Island, at the mouth of Chesterfield Inlet, the supposed end of their expedition. They were met by the ship *McTavish*, arranged by Superintendent Moodie at Churchill. Here Pelletier said goodbye to his three companions who were to remain at Fullerton for the winter. They boarded an Eskimo whale boat and Pelletier began the trip to Churchill on September 2nd. But the weather, which had thus far been relatively benign, struck with a vengeance. Rain, fog, and strong winds caught the *McTavish* as they started.

At midnight (September 4th) we were suddenly awakened by heavy pitching and noise of wind through the rigging. Constable McMillan . . . reported the anchors dragging . . . It was pitch dark, a northwest gale blowing, and in a very short time we were surrounded by white foam, waves breaking over the reefs. We were slowly drifting to shore . . . Every wave brought us nearer to the shore. We were lifted again, and struck broadside on a bare reef which at high water is covered with a foot or so of water.

The Police were forced to salvage what they could from the *McTavish* and abandon her. Fortunately, they were within sight of an Eskimo camp and when the weather slackend the Eskimos came to their rescue, providing them with a whale boat to take them to Fullerton. Pelletier decided that it was too late in the season to attempt the journey to Churchill by canoe, risking the inevitable autumn gales. He planned instead to wait at Fullerton until the weather was suitable for travel by dog team. So on September 10th, exactly the same day that the Tyrrell brothers reached this same point in 1893 and started their canoe trip down the coast to Churchill, Pelletier headed for Fullerton.

The Tyrrells were overtaken by winter and came very close to killing themselves by continuing the trip by canoe. The ice was rapidly forming and they were forced to go out of sight of shore to find open water. It was then found almost impossible to get back to shore and they spent one harrowing night, frozen, soaked by the spray, almost starving to death, and literally bailing for their lives, trying to regain shore. They were very lucky to do so, but they were so spent after thirty hours on the open sea that several members of the party could no longer walk. Fortunately, the western Métis in the party were still strong enough to go ahead to Churchill on foot and bring back help[12]. The Tyrrells were in such bad shape that they had to be taken out of the country on dog sleds, driven by Indians and Métis they hired at Churchill.

The sort of difficulties which the Tyrrells encountered in Hudson Bay were obviously to be expected, so Pelletier after "close investigations about game to be found along the way", departed from Fullerton on November 30th with three Police, Sergeant McArthur, Corporal Reeves and Special Constable Ford, and two Eskimos, Pook and Tupearlock. Their equipment consisted of two 18 foot sleighs, pulled by nine dogs each, with 800 pounds of food and gear on each sled. Pelletier calculated on 10 days' food for the dogs and 15 for the men, plus sea biscuit for 40 days. They also counted on shooting caribou along the way.

They reached Churchill on January 11th, having been stormbound for 12 of the 43 days it took to travel the 450 miles. Fortunately, there was plenty of game in the country and the Eskimos shot 28 caribou between Fullerton and Churchill. The party was never in danger of privation, but it was a tough trip. Christmas day was spent stormbound, the primus stove had just broken, the dogs had broken into the sea biscuits and eaten a good part of them, so Christmas dinner consisted of tea and frozen raw caribou. Although Pelletier stressed in his report that at no time during the trip from Fullerton to Churchill did they suffer privations or find themselves in a precarious position, he did admit to some mild discomforts.

The worst feature of a long journey like this . . . in a country where no fuel is to be procured, is the absolute impossibility of drying clothing, bedding, etc. The moisture from the body accumulates, and there is no means to dry clothing . . . and every day sees it harder to put clothing on in the morning, and the bed harder to get into at night, until both clothing and bedding become as stiff as a board from the ice. . . .Sleeping with one's clothes on only makes matters worse.

It was almost a month before Pelletier left Churchill on the last leg of his trip to Norway House and Gimli. His report states rather cryptically that he was delayed because of difficulties in procuring an outfit and then was improperly provided with dogs and sleds. No guides could be procured. Correspondence contained in Pelletier's Mounted Police personnel file is rather more explicit. While waiting at Churchill, as he assembled his outfit, he wrote a formal letter of complaint to the commanding officer at Churchill, Superintendent Moodie, accusing him of obstructing his patrol and taking his best dogs. He threatened to report him to the Commissioner.

> I want to have nothing to do with your Churchill dogs. I have succeeded in bringing those Fullerton dogs here in good condition. These Fullerton dogs are part of my present travelling outfit and I do most seriously object to having them taken away from me to be replaced by your inferior dogs, 'your culls'[13].

Clearly there was animosity between the two men, for Moodie also wrote to the Commissioner, complaining of Pelletier's arrogance and constant demands while at Churchill, adding that when Pelletier had served under him at Fullerton in 1904-5 he had been extremely insolent. "I trust that I may not again come in contact with Insp. Pelletier either on duty or otherwise."

Pelletier had also complained bitterly about the sleds that Moodie provided him with, but both dogs and sleds must have served their purpose since the rest of the trip to the end of the railway at Gimli, a distance of 800 miles, is described in half a page. He set off from Churchill with three Mounted Policemen and no guides. Sergeant McArthur and Corporal Reeves had come with him from Fullerton and Constable Travers joined the party at Churchill. They travelled with two sleds and twelve dogs, averaging about 43 miles a day over country with which Pelletier was familiar from his patrols of 1906-7. Pelletier arrived at Gimli on March 18th, 1909, having covered 3,347 miles from the starting point of Edmonton in 9½ months.

Even if Superintendent Moodie was right about Pelletier's arrogance and insolence, it is certainly to the latter's credit that he made no inflated claims about the difficulty of his trip or its significance.

> The route between Great Slave Lake and the Hudson's Bay, although not presenting any serious difficulties is by no means an easy one. The Hanbury River is the most dangerous stretch.
>
> As to using this route as a permanent yearly patrol, the time is not yet ripe for it. There is no one living on the longer part of this stretch . . .
>
> The natives themselves, first, the Yellow Knives and Dog Rib Indians, yearly come to Fort Resolution . . . They seem to be well off and hold a fairly good reputation. They have no permanent camp, and a police detachment would do them no good.
>
> Secondly, the Eskimos at the Hudson's Bay end of the route are very few and far between. They are well provided with arms, ammunition and trading goods, which they procure either from the Hudson's Bay Company or the whalers in the Hudson's Bay. There is no crime committed by these people, although totally ignorant of the law and Christianity, they have old customs and laws of their own which are very fair and Christianlike in every respect . . .
>
> In my opinion there is no need for a police post north of Churchill at the present. The work of collecting customs from the whalers could be done from Churchill . . . There is no need to enforce game laws in that country. The natives do not kill more than they actually need. Game is plentiful and there is no fear to be entertained as to its becoming scarce or extinct. The country is too vast and the natives too few.

So ended the longest and most difficult patrol thus far in Mounted Police history. It was soon eclipsed by the spectacular patrol of Inspector F. H. French in 1917-18 which covered over 5,000 miles of the Barren Lands in its search for the Eskimo killers of H. V. Radford and T. G. Street. One might suggest that if Pelletier's patrol had been hunting for murderers or had perished from starvation as did Fitzgerald's on the 1911 McPherson to Dawson patrol, it would be better remembered. Instead the competence of this patrol has relegated it to obscurity.

After the Tyrrell brothers, Pelletier and his party were the first Canadians to conduct a major expedition through the Barren Lands. Both of these groups were among the very first to use the modern cedar strip canoe in Barren Land travel. They shared with David Hanbury a great admiration for their Peterborough canoes, finding them ideally suited for rugged travel.

Pelletier's years in the North spoiled him for normal Police duty; he was thoroughly bitten by its lure. After his patrol of 1908, he threatened four times to resign unless posted to Norway House. His mother, an old friend of both Fred White, the Comptroller of the Mounted Police, and Sir Wilfrid Laurier, pleaded with both men to let her son continue to serve in the North because he hated civilization and the routine of Police duty in the South. But Fred White and A. B. Perry, Commissioner of the Mounted Police, finally became thoroughly irked by Pelletier's demands and accepted his resignation from the Police in 1910.

Certainly Pelletier had developed a burning love for the North, but there was another reason for his incessant demands for a posting at Norway House. On his patrol of 1907 from Norway House to Churchill he had discovered gold. As soon as he left the Police he formed a mining company, The Ojibway Mining Syndicate, to develop his find on the east shore of Lake Winnipeg, about 75 miles north of West Selkirk.

Perhaps Pelletier struck it rich, but if he did so, it was at the expense of a very promising career with the Police. If he had been able to better direct his impetous energy, he might have become an important name in the history of the North.*

Though his patrol did not achieve the notoriety of the famous Police patrols of the period, he deserves a place in the pantheon of northern explorers, for he shared with them that combination of rare qualities which set them apart from ordinary mortals. Pelletier and his companions combined those qualities of extreme toughness and determination, both mental and physical, without which the North could not have been opened to southerners. These were the qualities fundamental to Canada's assertion of sovereignty and authority over the North.

---

* Pelletier's personnel file includes the information that he was a major in the First War (he had been a lieutenant in the Boer War), that the Dominion Parks Branch asked for his advice for it's Reindeer-Musk Ox Commission, and that he offered his services again to the Police when the Second War began. He died in relative relative obscurity in 1951 at St. Ferdinand d'Halifax, the town where he was born and grew up.

ENDNOTES

1. Quoted in Nancy Mitford, *The Water Beetle* (London, 1962) p. 16.

2. Farley Mowat, *Tundra* (McClelland and Stewart, 1973) p. 275. It is more surprising to find that Morris Zaslow, certainly one of Canada's most eminent northern historians, in *The Opening of the Canadian North* (Toronto, 1979), has Pelletier patrolling the Barrens in the wrong year, with the wrong number of companions, and he has him ascending the Lockhart River, which Pelletier studiously avoided.

3. Canadian Sessional Papers, Mounted Police Report, 1905, Part IV, p. 3.

4. Public Archives of Canada, Record Group 18 (Mounted Police), Vol. 3444, Pelletier Personnel File (Officier #122). Pelletier had joined the Police in 1901 as an inspector, after serving in the Boer War as a lieutenant in the Second (Special Service) Battalion of the R.C.R. of Infantry. He was born in 1880 at St. Ferdinand d'Halifax, Co., Megantic, P.Q.

5. Canada, Sessional Papers, Mounted Police Report, 1907, pp. 130139.

6. Ibid., pp. 140-153.

7. See Warburton Pike, *The Barren Ground of Northern Canada*, (N.Y. 1967); David Hanbury, *Sport and Travel in the North of Canada*, (N.Y. 1904); J. W. Tyrrell, *Across the Sub-Arctic of Canada*, (London 1898).

8. Canada, Sessional Papers, 1901, Department of the Interior, Report of J. W. Tyrrell (appendix #26 to the report of the Surveyor General) p. 119.

9. C.S.P., Dep't of the Interior, 1901, Tyrrell Report, pp. 118, 121.

10. J. W. Tyrrell, *Across the Sub-Arctic*, p. 98.

11. Ibid., p. 73.

12. Ibid., Chapter XV.

13. P.A.C., R. G. 18, vol. 3444, January 21, 1893.

George M. Douglas at Hodgson's Point.

George M. Douglas
and the Lure of the Coppermine

Shelagh D. Grant

The object of the present unostentatious expedition was to make a preliminary investigation of the Coppermine mountains, to determine whether there was any analogy between these deposits and those of the Lake Superior district, and to decide whether the prospect was sufficiently promising to warrant investigation on a further more comprehensive scale.

George M. Douglas, 1914.

The wilderness regions north of frontier settlement have long held a special fascination for Canadians. At the time of Confederation, the image of a land beyond was given further definition by the vague notion that a great destiny lay in future development of this vast inhospitable land. In 1898, the Klondike gold rush added a new dimension to the mystique of the North—the promise of unexploited mineral wealth. Coinciding with a period of growing nationalist sentiment, countless books and articles on the Yukon stirred the imagination of southerners, creating new heroes and great expectations while at the same time reinforcing a romantic vision of the country's northern heritage. Lands formerly traversed only by explorers, fur traders, missionaries and Mounted Police were eyed with increasing interest by prospectors and developers. One such individual was George Mellis Douglas who in 1911 led a small party to the Coppermine mountains to investigate the nature and extent of reported ore deposits. The Douglas story is of particular interest in that it marks a transitional phase between the "purposeful wanderers" of the late nineteenth century and the mid-twentieth century scientists, prospectors and surveyors whose countless forays into the North were conducted primarily in the interest of their profession. The age of discovery gave way to an age of development. George Douglas represented both.

*   *   *

The expedition led by Douglas was very much a family affair funded by an elderly cousin who had amassed a considerable fortune in the mining industry.[1] Accompanying George were his younger brother Lionel, an officer on leave from Canadian Pacific Steamships and Dr. August Sandberg, a metallurgist and geologist. The plan was to establish a base camp on Great Bear Lake and from there to conduct two field trips to the Coppermine area: a preliminary survey in late summer by way of canoe and a more extensive investigation early the following spring travelling overland by dogsled. Although the purpose was defined in strictly scientific terms, the expedition was ultimately shaped by the character and interests of its leader. As a consequence, the schedule of activities was directed by professional objectives, whereas rewards were measured in terms of spiritual experience rather than material gain. In the opinion of George Whalley, who first met Douglas while researching the biography of John Hornby, the adventurous mining engineer was "more interested in getting to the Arctic Ocean and seeing it, than in hope of gaining wealth from the results of prospecting."[2] In this regard, Douglas's journey might be described as a pilgrimage to the seas once plied by his maternal ancestor, Sir Edward Belcher, in his search for the lost Franklin expedition. In other respects, the trip took on characteristics of some present day travellers as Douglas attempted to follow in part the routes previously traversed by Samuel Hearne in 1771, Captain John Franklin in 1822, Dr. John Rae in 1851 and David Hanbury in 1902. Conscious of re-living history, he purposely sought out old campsites and landmarks recorded in earlier reports and on several occasions would compare his own impressions of landscape or river travel to those described by the explorers. Yet regardless of personal interests and ambitions, the official purpose for which the expedition received its funding was completed to the satisfaction of both the party and its benefactors.

The detailed narrative published two years after his return, *Lands Forlorn: A Story of an Expedition to Hearne's Coppermine River*, provides an exceptional insight into a very uncommon man.[3] Reflecting unusual literary skills and historical knowledge, the account also points to an inner tension in the author's character: an efficiency and self-discipline expected of a mining engineer in combination with a genuine empathy for the northern wilds. George Douglas was at home in the natural world, but his inspiration was philosophical rather than scientific. Whalley, who came to know him well in later years, described some of the inherent inconsistencies.

> . . . his romanticism was of the purest, most innocent sort, lacking self-consciousness, with no trace of morbidity. His incorrigible generosity, his strong will, his infectious enjoyment of other people's idiosyncracies, his inflexible because incorruptible personal integrity — all these things made him a strange if always admirable figure in a corrupt and positivist world.[4]

The apparent paradox in the objectives demanded by his profession and his love of the wilderness were easily compromised in the 1911 expedition. Later, the conflict would haunt the thoughtful mining engineer whose favourite book was Thoreau's *On Walden Pond*. By nature Douglas was energetic and conscientious with a calm manner that tended to inspire confidence. Humble as well, he described himself as leader of the expedition "by chance more than by any other qualification."[5] Although sometimes impatient and critical of ineptitude, he nevertheless displayed an unusual sensitivity and understanding of man and nature.

Douglas was atypical of most Canadians at the turn of the century. Much of this individuality can be traced to family background and boyhood experiences. He was a third generation Canadian, born at Halifax in 1875. His father, a retired Army surgeon, was an avid canoeist and member of both the Toronto Canoe Club and the American Canoe Association. Dr. Douglas was also a restless man, moving his family from Nova Scotia to Quebec, then Montreal and eventually to Toronto. Enroute to the 1883 ACA regatta in the Kawarthas, he noticed the "for sale" sign on a farm located just north of Lakefield.[6] On impulse he purchased the Northcote estate on the shores of Lake Katchewanooka, where George and his younger brother spent many happy hours exploring the lake country. They were not "taught" or "taken" canoeing; it was simply a way of life. Added to the usual youth adventure stories were the tales their mother told, of Sir Edward Belcher, of Arctic exploration, of the dangers and exploits in a strange and alien land. Quite understandably, the sons equated romantic adventure with the Canadian Arctic. A further and by no means minor influence was his father's colourful personality and penchant for challenge and excitement. When the Northwest Rebellion broke out in 1885, Dr. Douglas volunteered his services and travelled west with Maj-Gen. Middleton. After a number of delays on the Saskatchewan River, the enterprising surgeon set off alone in a small folding canvas canoe. His account of this journey appeared in both *Field and Stream* and *Badminton Magazine*. A decade later, the same canoe would carry him across the English Channel from Dover to Calais.[7] Unquestionably, the spirit of adventure was passed on from father to son. When his wife died in 1894, Dr. Douglas applied for a new commission in the British army to pay for his sons' education. The two boys accompanied their father to England and much to their distress the farm was sold. In Britain, George Douglas entered into an apprenticeship which included three years at sea. After receiving his engineer's papers, he was offered employment in North America by an older cousin, the Canadian born Dr. James Douglas who had risen through the ranks of the Phelps-Dodge Company to become a successful mining promoter and financier.[8] Following assignments in Mexico and the United States, George Douglas returned to Lakefield for a visit in 1906 and was successful in buying back the family homestead. The summer of 1908 was the first of many spent at Northcote until his retirement there in the 1930s.[9]

*   *   *

His first trip to the Barrens evolved from a discussion with his cousin concerning investigation of potential mineral development in northern Ontario. As an alternative, James offered to grubstake an exploratory study in the Coppermine region.[10] Without hesitation, Douglas accepted and began to collect books and documents dealing with Arctic exploration. Included were reports by Samuel Hearne, Franklin, Richardson, and John Rae. Of particular interest was David Hanbury's *Sport and Travel in the Northland of Canada* which provided a detailed account of a 1902 canoe trip up the Coppermine and Kendall Rivers, overland and down to the mouth of the Dease River on Great Bear Lake. Using this trip report as his guide, Douglas planned the reverse route. He also obtained a sketch map from the Geological Survey, ostensibly the work of J.M. Bell and Charles Camsell in 1900. In the fall of 1910, Douglas sat down to work out a detailed plan.

Meticulous care was taken in provisioning the expedition. Most equipment and two canoes were purchased in the East, one larger canoe and food in Edmonton, and a York boat at Fort Simpson. On the advice of "seasoned travellers," he waited to buy toboggans, snowshoes and fur clothing at the northern trading posts, a move he regretted after discovering that superior quality and selection had been available in the South. Commiserating over the time wasted in acquiring these items, Douglas claimed "it was one of the many instances to show how unreliable the advice may be of men who have been a long time in that country, and their commonly curious failure to appreciate the importance of time." He took great pride in his selection of boats — here the more romantic side of the competent organizer emerges. The two 18-foot canoes were handbuilt in Lakefield from specially selected wood "by men who took a keen personal interest in their work." One was christened *Polaris* after the North Star, the other *Procyon* a star of the first magnitude in the constellation Canis Minor. The freight canoe purchased in Edmonton was built by the Peterborough Canoe Company of longitudinal basswood strips with close ribs and rigged with a lug sail. This craft was named the *Aldebaran*, also a star of the first magnitude, the eye of Taurus. The York boat acquired to transport the heavy load of supplies up the Great Bear River was called the *Jupiter* after the largest planet in the solar system.*

*   *   *

On 11 May 1911, the Douglas party departed from Edmonton on the long journey down the Athabasca-Mackenzie waterway to Fort Norman. Travelling by canoe, river scow and Hudson's Bay Company steamer, they arrived at the northern trading post in early July. Enroute down the Mackenzie, Douglas met Robert Service who was headed for the Yukon, and the American scientists Radford and Street—who were brutally murdered that same summer by a group of Eskimos.[11] Although few crossed paths in the interior, there were a surprising number of travellers in the Canadian Northwest and chance acquaintances were commonplace. At Fort Norman, Douglas met Cosmo Melvill and John Hornby, two Englishmen who had travelled for two years in the Barrens from a base camp on Great Bear Lake. Melvill continued southward but Hornby on hearing the party's plans decided impulsively to return to the old winter camp, purportedly to aid a young Oblate priest in establishing a mission among the Coppermine Eskimos.

This accidental meeting between Hornby and Douglas set the wheels of fate in motion; intermittent contact over the next year led to a continuing association through correspondence and occasional visits. It was a curious relationship for two men so diametrically different. In contrast to Douglas' meticulous organization and calm, self-assured manner, Hornby might be described as erratic, careless, ill-prepared and prone to faulty judgement which frequently led to near disasters. His fascination for the Barrens drew him back time and again until a legend grew around the exploits of the quixotic Englishman. Edmonton was mecca for the departing and returning adventurers of the Northwest, and the local newspaper kept its readers informed of the latest escapades of the

---

* According to Mrs. Douglas, his interest in astronomy was a consequence of his three years spent at sea.

"Northmen."[12] Not surprisingly, Hornby became a virtual hero because of his tales of close encounters with death, and it was not until his tragic demise with two companions in 1927, that his associates dared put forward any public criticism. Years later, George Whalley would approach Douglas as Hornby's closest "friend" in an effort to solve the mystery of this curious individual. Ironically the publication of *The Legend of John Hornby* in 1962 brought the story of George Douglas to the attention of a new generation, but this time more as "Hornby's friend" than in recognition of his own achievements. In 1911, however, it was the lure of the Coppermine which forged a common bond between these two men of such diverse character.

After experiencing some difficulty in hiring natives to assist in tracking operations up the Great Bear River, the Douglas party eventually set out on July 8th, leaving behind the *Procyon* to be used if return via the Porcupine and Yukon Rivers became necessary. Ice on the river banks slowed their progress, but they managed to reach the ruins of Fort Franklin in six days. After a brief word with Hornby and Father Rouvière, who arrived the next morning, the two brothers and Sandburg continued on across the wide expanse of Great Bear Lake. Plagued by rain and fog, they finally reached the site of old Fort Confidence on Dease Bay and proceeded up the river by the same name until halted by rapids. They arrived at the proposed location of their base camp on July 24th, 44 days after leaving Edmonton.

Although offered the use of lodgings built by Joe Hodgson, a former Hudson's Bay Company factor, Douglas quickly rejected the idea, describing the structure as "a rude, poorly built log shack." An adjacent site was chosen for their cabin, tents erected, the *Jupiter* unloaded and everything stowed before nightfall. According to plan, Lionel would remain behind to build their winter quarters while George Douglas and "the Doctor" made a preliminary journey to the Coppermine. With provisions to last fifty days, the two departed in the *Polaris* on July 28th only four days after their arrival at Hodgson's Point.

Progress up the Dease River was slow and tedious as low water necessitated wading the canoe through seemingly endless stretches of shallow rapids. Even more time was wasted in an attempt to identify Hanbury's "Sandy Creek," a tributary of the Dease. After two days of frustrating search, they proceeded up the shallow stream, wading and portaging until reaching the divide. The overland trek to the Dismal Lakes was 6½ miles long and took over two days as they covered the ground seven times, taking three loads each and both carrying the canoe. Here they met their first Eskimo who fled in apparent fright after a short meeting. Arrival at Teshierpi Lake was celebrated by "an extra good feed" supplemented by "desiccated raspberries as a special treat." The raspberries were an unexpected disappointment, but the juice was mixed with a little brandy brought along "for emergencies" and the concoction light-heartedly christened "Teshierpi Toddy."

After crossing the Dismal Lakes and heading down the Kendall River, the two men began to tire under "the constant strain of steering down the boulder-strewn rapids." In the last set before reaching the Coppermine, they struck a large

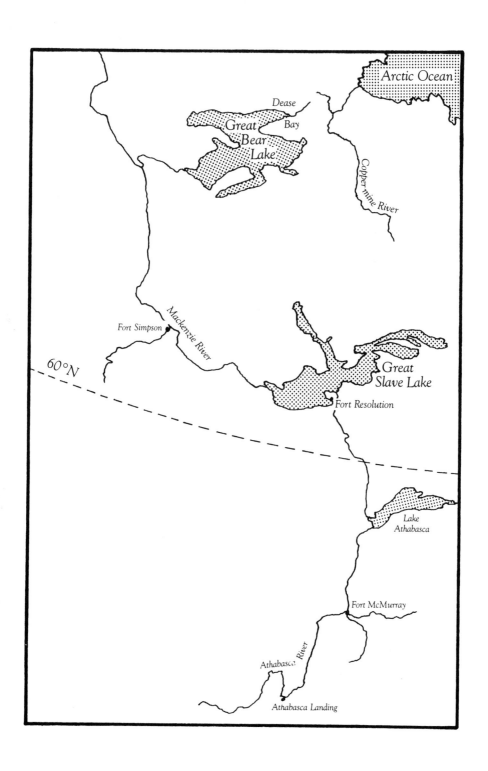

Arctic Ocean

Dease
Bay

Great
Bear
Lake

Copper mine River

Fort Simpson

Mackenzie River

Great
Slave Lake

60°N

Fort Resolution

Lake
Athabasca

Fort McMurray

Athabasca River

Athabasca Landing

rock which holed the canoe and were able to reach the shore only minutes before it sank. A day was spent resting, hunting, prospecting and repairing the *Polaris* before resuming their journey downriver. Camping at a point where the river cut through the mountains, Sandburg began his geological reconnaissance while Douglas set off in search of caribou. Over a week was spent in the general area and although Douglas would have liked to have continued to the ocean, "the return would have taken more time than we could afford." The ascent back up the Kendall was nerve-wracking. Douglas compared his state of mind to similar feelings expressed by Hanbury when he had passed that way nine years earlier:

> . . . ascent of a dangerous river, or rather I should say a river where continued caution is absolutely necessary to prevent an accident, is apt to get on the nerves. Every day the attention is strained and every night you are obliged to camp close to the thunder and swish of the rough, heavy, and rapid water which you know you will have to tackle the following morning.[13]

When Douglas and Sandburg reached the lake plateau, their mood changed abruptly. They believed their worst trials were over; it was now downhill. The surroundings also had undergone a dramatic transformation. Ten days ago it had been summer; now the hills bore their attire of yellow willows and birches, accented by brilliant red mosses. Mauve and cerise sedges lined the water's edge. The weather, previously sunny, soon turned "thick and stormy" with some frost and snow encountered on the divide. The first portion of the descent was tedious, the cold adding greatly to the discomfort of wet clothing as they waded the canoe down the shallows of Sandy Creek. By the time they reached the Dease River, autumn had disappeared. The trees were leafless and the sedges "withered to a dark yellow;" nights grew darker and the aurora borealis was sighted for the first time. At the last lunch stop before reaching the base camp, they tidied up the *Polaris* and gave their utensils an extra scouring "following the time-honoured fashion of the sea to make port with everything ship shape." On September 11 the two reached Hodgson's Point, 45 days after their departure and 5 days earlier than estimated.

A welcome surprise greeted them. In a month and a half, Lionel had created a masterpiece out of scrub spruce. The 14' by 16' log cabin, with corners neatly squared, was chinked with moss and caribou hair, mudded inside and out, and roofed with small spruce poles, more caribou hair, dry sand and a top covering of waterproof canvas. In keeping with northern tradition, a pair of antlers adorned the peak. A large fireplace with a quartzite mantle stood in one corner. Two windows brought from Fort Simpson brightened the interior. The sand floor was covered with wooden blocks and the walls were papered with pages from old magazines. Food and utensils were neatly stowed on open shelves and the four folding chairs obtained from the Hudson's Bay Company steamer added a touch of modernity to the otherwise rustic hand-built furniture. With only minor assistance from a local native, Lionel had erected a structure aesthetically perfect by northern standards, and designed for optimum comfort and utility. In contrast, the cabin built by Hornby for Father Rouvière was described by Douglas as simply "a shack."

For the next six months the expedition was on hold. The Bear Lake Indians visited frequently but were not encouraged to linger. According to Douglas, when they "found we didn't want anything and that there was very little to be got out of us, they soon went their own ways." Unlike earlier travellers, Douglas preferred to rely on his own initiative and firmly rejected the use of Indian guides. This decision was likely influenced by problems incurred by Hanbury and Hearne, and by awareness of the long standing friction between Indian and Eskimo. His initial prejudice against the Natives was unquestionably adopted from his readings, as stated in the first pages of *Lands Forlorn*:

> The Indians of the Mackenzie Valley have earned a most unenviable character, for thorough unreliability and inefficiency. All travellers who have accomplished anything agree in describing them as worthless, shiftless, careless, unreliable, and generally contemptible.[14]

Experience softened his attitude somewhat. After initial contact with the Fort Norman Indians, he admitted that "the opinion we had formed of the Northern Indians generally, was certainly improved by our small experience with these men." Yet, apart from assistance needed in tracking the York boat up the Great Bear River, Douglas stubbornly refused native help and discouraged close relations. During later trips north, according to his widow, he came to know and appreciate Indian philosophy through closer contact with individuals.

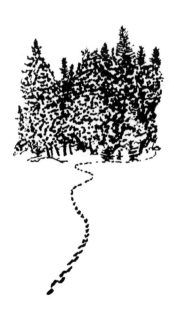

During the winter months, there was sporadic interaction with Hornby and Father Rouvière although the two parties remained quite independent of each other. They did join forces for a short excursion in October, but apart from one brief trip to Hornby's cabin located about six miles away, the visiting was very one-sided with the Englishman and the priest travelling to Hodgson's Point. Douglas was noticeably non-commital in his opinion of Hornby, whereas he described Rouvière as having "added greatly to the pleasure of our life in winter quarters."

Unlike Hornby, the Douglas party came prepared for all events and took extra pains to ensure mental and physical well-being.

> We had good grub and good equipment, our camps were always comfortable, and we took trouble preparing our meals. We had learned the necessity of taking good care of our bodies; they were mere machines for the conversion of heat into energy and required the careful attention necessary for every high class machine.[15]

Although well supplied with adequate food to sustain them over the winter, they were successful in hunting both ptarmigan and caribou to provide fresh meat throughout the winter months. By contrast, Hornby and Rouvière were forced to rely on dried meat obtained from the Indians. In addition to concern for their physical health, special efforts were made to ensure optimum emotional stability. Douglas believed that wintering-over in the Barrens should not be treated as a casual experience, that "protracted residence in that country lowers standards of reliability and efficiency, and warps accuracy of judgement." Elaborate plans were set out to provide a rigid routine that incorporated change to avoid monotony, equal sharing to defer personal conflicts, periods of rest to balance work sessions and reading times interspersed with cards and chess. Throughout the winter, intellectual stimulus was furnished by reading "good novels" and Michelet's *History of France* borrowed from the Hudson's Bay Company factor at Fort Simpson.

A degree of privacy was provided by strict division of labour rotated on a weekly basis. During the day, household chores, hunting and collection of firewood were carried out on individual assignment, thereby limiting group gatherings to the early morning and evening. Pride in personal achievement was derived from preparation of an exceptional meal, a well-stacked wood pile or a successful hunt, and collective satisfaction grew from awareness that the winter plan was succeeding. There were no apparent personality conflicts and no unforeseen circumstances to threaten their physical well-being. Anticipation of change was the key weapon against boredom. Even the menu reflected this strategy. Aside from variation dependent on availability of game, Sundays offered breakfast coffee instead of tea, hominy instead of oatmeal. For supper, maple syrup was added to the usual bannock. Yet just as change was instituted to relieve tedium, there was also an attempt to duplicate the comforts of home: a table made from old flooring obtained in Fort Simpson was painted yellow and adorned with a table cloth of blue serge.

Preparedness also played a major part in the strategy. Undoubtedly influenced by accounts of near starvation due to the absence of fish or game, Douglas had ensured that food supplies were adequate for the total time of the expedition. He also adhered to this principle on his two trips to the Coppermine for he believed hunting would unnecessarily take time away from geological explorations. Similarly, their equipment was of the highest quality and included many items designed to counter the detrimental effects of harsh climate and isolation. For example, the photographic supplies included premium cameras, ample film and developing materials lest delay and adverse weather conditions deteriorate the exposed film. This meticulous attention to detail and organization was quite alien to free-spirited adventurers like John Hornby, but for the Douglas party it assured a productive and enjoyable experience, free from undue discomfort or mishap. Critics might argue that George Douglas had merely transplanted southern insitutions into the North and in doing so, destroyed the challenge; admirers would simply point to Hornby who boasted of living "with the savages, leading a wild and natural life"[16]—and smile. Although seemingly over-prepared and over-organized, the results were an unqualified success as the long winter months passed quickly with no hint of tension or hardship.

For the spring journey to the Coppermine, Douglas originally hoped to manhaul the toboggans, a plan which was quickly abandoned after a few short trials. Since Hornby was familiar with the use of dogs and particularly "anxious to make the trip to the coast," it was agreed he should join them—with a rather curious provision. Despite Douglas' resolve to travel without native assistance, Hornby was allowed to take along a young Indian boy as a "travelling companion," thus enabling the Englishman to "follow his own devices" once they reached the Coppermine. If it had not been for Hornby's expertise in dog-handling, it appears doubtful he would have been invited. On April 30 the party set out with two toboggans each drawn by three dogs. The overland trek followed a more direct route to the Coppermine but was undertaken in relays in order to transport the copious supply of food and equipment to the base camp. In mid-May, the snow disappeared just as the last toboggan load arrived at the camp. From then on the dogs and the men carried the packs.

At Bloody Falls, the party encountered the first sizable group of Eskimos, a friendly lot who created a very favourable impression. Douglas wrote with apparent surprise that "it was a delight to meet these vivacious, well-bred people after the sulky Indians; their manners indeed were just as good and similar to our own." In a later encounter, he again remarked on their "well-bred ways usual with people of culture." This firsthand experience with the Coppermine natives caused him to question the advisability of white contact and attempts to convert them.

> Perhaps it may be a pity that the latter (the Eskimo) cannot be left strictly alone; competent observers declare civilization means nothing but inevitable ruin and misery for them.[17]

In view of his expressed admiration for Father Rouvière and the work of the Oblates in general, this suggestion may appear somewhat contradictory. Yet Douglas' criticism of native behaviour, unacceptable by his standards, was not derived from a general racial bias. He believed that the unpleasant aspects of their conduct were directly attributable to contact with white man's civilization.

More from anticipation than actual accomplishment, the climax of the expedition was their arrival on the Arctic coast. Only the Douglas brothers hiked the nine miles from Bloody Falls. The others remained behind: the geologist to take notes and Hornby in hopes of further encounters with the Eskimos. But to the Douglas brothers, it was an occasion to be celebrated as they unfurled their flags and "took pictures of each other proudly standing on the ice of the Arctic Ocean." Aside from achieving the northern limit of their travels, there must have been a deep personal satisfaction to have reached the Arctic waters once sailed by their great-grandfather Admiral Belcher. The rest of the trip would be "a retreat ever southward."

The party journeyed back quite leisurely to allow for more geological note-taking. By June 18 they finally reached Lake Rouvière where the Oblate priest was attempting to establish an Eskimo mission. Here the Douglas brothers separated from the rest, preferring to travel by Hornby's leaky canoe which had been stored there the previous winter. In their estimation, paddling was "a perfect joy" compared to hauling toboggans or packing dogs. This last segment of the voyage was described in nostalgic terms as they passed familiar landmarks and old campsites for the last time. The log cabin which they had left in a field of snow now appeared strange and unfamiliar surrounded by greenery and wild flowers. But there was little time for relaxation if they were to make contact with the southbound steamer. Immediately they began preparing for their departure on June 26, less than a week after returning from the Coppermine.

Significantly, relatively few pages are devoted to the homeward trek. The excitement was over and return to civilization held no great attraction. There is a certain flatness in the balance of the narrative. Ice jams, swarms of mosquitoes and grey skies did not enhance the long journey around Great Bear Lake. Words such as "disagreeable," "bleak," "desolate" and "dismal" were used with unusual frequency and the lack of an expected welcome at Fort Norman did little to improve the men's spirits. Reflecting a note of cynicism, this disappointing event was attributed to the fact they had "failed to conform to the convention requiring that the explorer should come to the first post ragged and half-starved, eating his moccasins and mits ." Douglas became increasingly critical and impatient of delays as they travelled south. Understandably, the record of the last day on the Athabasca River focused more on recollections than on current happenings.

> My last memories are pleasant ones only: of quiet waters and comfortable camps, of fine nights and fine days, of short spells of work, of long spells of rest; sitting at ease in the scow, lazily watching, through an atmosphere of uncomparable purity and ineffable calm, the naked trees reflected in the tranquil stream in all their beauty of line, and the faint silver threads of gossamer floating in the still air. Time itself had come to a standstill; such afternoons seemed as though they might last forever.[18]

His writing style which had begun in a methodical and abrupt manner underwent a gradual transformation, with the final chapters reflecting a somewhat idyllic romanticism derived from a profound personal experience.

Somewhat uncharacteristic for a man returning south after a year in the wilderness, Douglas initially claimed to have no great difficulty in adjusting to civilization. He simply took up life where he had left off. This reaction was no doubt facilitated by the fact that he was returning to Northcote rather than to an urban environment. But no such experience leaves one completely unaffected.

> Some time passed before we began to feel in many subtle ways the results of a long absence. In regard to the great world, we were the same people who had left eighteen months before, but while we were relatively unaltered, our world had gone its appointed course, and unhastening, unceasing the appointed changes had been wrought. It was ground irrevocably lost; no skill, nor energy, nor address could recover it. The times had changed, the change in ourselves had no reference to them but made conformity to established usages more difficult.[19]

The world had not waited for their return, a fact accepted with some regret. Douglas was also aware that his reluctance to conform to conventional practices had increased with the Coppermine experience. Non-conformity may be defined as eccentricity, a characteristic often ascribed to individualists and certainly a common trait among northern travellers of the period.

In the tradition of previous explorers and adventurers, Douglas sat down on his return with pen in hand to narrate the details of the expedition. Aside from bringing the far North closer to the armchair adventurers in the South, *Lands Forlorn* remains an invaluable source of knowledge and inspiration for those who follow his path. And like other northern travellers, Douglas could find no words of his own to conclude the book. Instead, he quoted a poem to explain how the three men had departed, leaving behind "as hostage of each heart all that was most our own." George Douglas left part of himself in the Coppermine, and took back in return only memories.

*   *   *

When Douglas left Great Bear Lake in 1912 he fully intended to return the next summer. His cousin, though pleased with results of the investigation, had serious reservations. Predicting that "the region may become one of the great copper producers of the world," and that commercial production was now more feasible due to the party's discovery of lignite deposits on Great Bear Lake, the mining promoter and financier warned that accessibilty was a major problem which could only be resolved by building a railroad either from the south or easterly to Hudson Bay.[20] Whether or not James Douglas would have agreed to further study became irrelevant; by the summer of 1914 war intervened. To his great disappointment George Douglas was rejected by both the Royal Flying Corps and Navy because of deafness, an affliction since childbirth. In 1916 he was back working in Mexico and a year later married. By the end of the war, a change in circumstances prevented any immediate return to the Coppermine. Apart from the sudden death of his cousin, who had taken such an interest in his aspirations, there was considerable confusion arising from attempts by the Canadian government to restrict foreign oil and mineral exploration in the Northwest Territories.[21] Douglas continued working on various assignments primarily in Mexico and Arizona, but now spending more and more time at Northcote.

In the summer of 1928, he returned once again to the Northwest Territories, this time to the southeastern shores of Great Slave Lake. The official purpose was to verify a government surveyor's report of possible copper deposits in the area. By now, other companies had joined in the search and one Toronto-based company was now trenching* in the Coppermine Mountains.[22] On this occasion, Douglas was sponsored by the United Verde Copper Company of Arizona.[23] While not explicitly stated, there also appeared to be a personal motive in the second trip. Not only did it coincide with John Hornby's disappearance, it was conducted in an area which the unpredictable Englishman had cited in his last letter as an alternate destination.[24] Moreover, Douglas admitted to taking along extra food and equipment "in case we came across Hornby."[25] Not until his return did he hear of Hornby's death by starvation on the banks of the Thelon River.

Although the use of bush planes had ended the need for long arduous trips by canoe and dog sled, Douglas and his companion set out as before with two canoes and full rations to cover the entire journey. The larger freighter was not only equipped with a lug sail, but now sported a blunt end to carry a small outboard motor. The smaller butternut strip canoe with elm ribs was to be used over portages. In the tradition of the earlier expedition both craft were named for stars: the *Mizar* and *Alcor* respectively. The 850 mile journey along the southeastern shores and up the rivers into the interior represented the first serious geological study of the area, but similarity to the first journey ended here. No copper of significance was found and there was little evidence of the excitement he had experienced on the Coppermine expedition.

---

* "Trenching" involves excavation to determine the extent of mineral deposits.

In a speech delivered on his return to the Canadian Mining and Metallurgical Association, Douglas was unusually cautious over the future of mining in
the Great Slave Lake basin and warned that any notable growth in development
would have to be preceded by construction of a railway from the Peace River
Country to Hay River. Equally notable was his pessimistic concern for the
natives. He repeated an earlier observation that northern natives having the least
contact with white civilization were the happiest, best mannered and least offensive. Once more he suggested that the best recourse might be to exclude all white
trappers and small traders from the area in order to save "the fur and the Indians it
supports." But he now rejected the idea as impractical and concluded with the
pessimistic prediction that "the fur trade is doomed, and most of the Indians with
it." He saw no benefit for the Indians in developing water power, lumber, fishing
or mineral resources and claimed that a great increase of government support for
the northern natives was inevitable.[26]

His reaction to the second trip was also quite different from 16 years
earlier. With the exception of a few paragraphs on the history, topography and
potential development of the area, the article entitled "A Summer Journey Along
the Southeast Shores of Great Slave Lake" was little more than a detailed description of the trip preparation and equipment. There was no daily log or mention of
the route followed. In fact the format was virtually identical to the tripping
manuals of the period.* Concern was for safety and optimum efficiency as
opposed to the previous focus on travel and adventure. In addition to advancing
age, Hornby's death may have been a contributing factor to an apparent change
in attitude. Douglas spoke of "personnel" being of "prime importance in an
expedition planned to explore a little-known country." Although his reference
was directed toward geologists, the wider implications of his philosophical theo-
rizing were unmistakable:

> Knowledge, the mere acquisition of basic facts or accepted hypotheses, may be acquired
> in comparatively few years; but wisdom, as one of the great Victorians said, comes slowly
> .... So by the time a geologist has acquired maturity of judgment he may be incapable of
> meeting the physical stress imposed on the members of a small expedition to a rough and
> remote country .... The powers of youth and the wisdom of age are rarely combined in
> an individual.[27]

If *Lands Forlorn* was written for the purpose of sharing a memorable experience,
"A Summer Journey" was designed more as a lesson.

Douglas returned to the Northwest Territories on four more occasions
and each time became more disconcerted. Now semi-retired, he went to Great
Bear Lake as a consultant in the winter of 1932, and again the following spring
when he witnessed the frantic activity involved in the start-up of the Eldorado
Mine. In 1935 and 1938, he returned to Great Slave Lake on further prospecting

* See B.W. Hodgins, "The Written Word on Canoeing and Canoe Tripping Before
1960," elsewhere in this volume. The nature of Douglas' article was similar in both
style and content to the tripping manuals of this period.

assignments. His last trip coincided with the opening of the Consolidated Mining and Smelting operation at Yellowknife and according to an acquaintance, he was deeply affected by "the high pressure development he at last saw, the feverish and disorderly scramble for mineral wealth, the untidy spawning of the town of Yellowknife." As for the new northerners, "Why" he exclaimed, "these men aren't even polite to the Indians!"[28] Depressed over the damage wrought by his own profession, George Douglas no longer had any desire to return. The romantic vision of his northern wilderness was now tarnished by the realities of southern progress and development.

By the time World War II broke out, Douglas had permanently retired to Northcote where he led a relatively quiet life away from the frantic pace and modern conveniences of urban society. To many he appeared somewhat eccentric as he paddled the nearby lakes and rivers alone or in the company of his wife, retracing the favourite haunts of his childhood. An interest in history continued to occupy much of his thought as evidenced in a rather prolific daily correspondence. Although lengthy conversation had become tedious due to increasing deafness, he spent many hours with George Whalley in an attempt to untangle the mysteries of the errant John Hornby. Even after 50 years, Douglas' feelings for the Englishman reflected a curious mixture of amusement, impatience, affection and scorn.[29] Whether by fate or good fortune, *The Legend of John Hornby* appeared in print barely a year before Douglas passed away at the age of 88. He was content in the knowledge that the true story of Hornby's irresponsibility had been told, alerting the public to the fact that wilderness travel required caution, preparedness and expertise.

*   *   *

The broad spectrum of northern adventurers in the early twentieth century suggests a generation seeking both material and spiritual answers. For the Canadian born, wilderness travel was often a search for national identity, an attempt to relate to earlier explorations and to the northern frontier psychology inherent in the growth of the new Dominion. For the American, it was more a personal challenge, a test of character and physical endurance conducted in the name of science or sport. To the Englishman, adventure in far off lands was a tradition. Apart from intense pride in the British heritage of exploration, vestiges of the imperial vision continued to lure sons of the upper class to former colonies throughout the Empire, to India, Africa, Southeast Asia and Canada. The challenge was frequently inspired by the bedtime stories of their youth, or in some cases simply as a means of escape from an increasingly urbanized society. By contrast, most Canadians were in the North by reason of their occupation: missionaries, fur traders, Mounted Police and members of the Geological Survey. With the arrival of bush planes in the North, a new breed was added: the geologists hired by private exploration companies. Much later northern travellers of a different sort appeared: the short term vistors who chose to follow the paths of earlier explorers and wanderers. As a mining engineer inspired by his northern heritage, George Douglas was a native Canadian with a foot in both past and future worlds.

For early twentieth century adventurers, a journey into the Barren Lands demanded both physical strength and a special wisdom. Some succeeded where others failed, and even failures gained recognition for their heroic attempts. Yet only a very few of those "Northmen" are widely remembered today. Their goals and achievements had more of a personal nature compared to the great explorers of the past who sought the Northwest Passage to Cathay or the overland route to the Pacific. The new travellers ventured into unknown territory for individual satisfaction rather than for national purpose. Their major public contribution was in the form of books and articles which reinforced the mystical lure of the far North, a lure which remains today drawing canoeists and back-packers into remote regions. But times have changed. Over the years, travels which once seemed nearly impossible to readers of their chronicles have been re-enacted by countless Canadians motivated by both professional and personal interests.* Moreover, the North has moved closer to the South with the aid of modern transportation and communications, and the art of canoe- tripping has undergone change with the introduction of new equipment and food processing. The Northmen now belong to history and as a consequence their writings have become an invaluable resource, providing insight into the changing character of northern adventures as an integral part of our Canadian heritage.

If Warburton Pike was the first of a new breed of travellers in the Barrens,** then Douglas represents a further transitional phase linking the seekers of challenge and excitement to the twentieth century professionals. In contrast to the somewhat egocentric adventurers of the late 1800s, Douglas was a selfless man who sought neither fame nor fortune. He did not revel in overcoming hardship as much as he sought to prevent it. His desire for independence, as reflected in his refusal to rely on natives for food or guiding, also set him apart from his contemporaries and predecessors. In the tradition of the Tyrrell brothers and other Canadians, Douglas was able to satisfy his longing for wilderness travel through his vocation. Yet even here there is a subtle difference: financial support came not from government or institutions, but from private industry and perhaps more significantly, from American capital.

George Douglas achieved more than a personal ambition in his journey

---

* The dichotomy between personal and professional objectives is still prevalent today as many young people join scientific field parties more as a means of working in the wilderness than as agents of its destruction. As long as resource exploitation and northern development offer employment in remote regions of the Canadian North, there will be men and women who will try to satisfy personal objectives through occupational opportunities.

** See Margaret Hobbs, "Purposeful Wanderers: Late Nineteenth Century Travellers to the Barren Lands," elsewhere in this volume.

to the mouth of the Coppermine. His geological studies of the ore bearing mountains promised new areas of opportunity to the geologists and mining promoters. In a sense, he was the forerunner of the modern prospector. Building upon the century old reports of Samuel Hearne, he extended the limits of serious mineral exploration to the shores of the Arctic Ocean, to the mysterious land beyond, known formerly only to explorers, police, traders and natives. Yet despite the esteem earned in professional circles, his greatest satisfaction was derived from the personal experience of northern adventure. In some respects, Douglas was a contradiction, a paradox. Whereas success in his occupation was measured most often in material wealth, for this mining engineer it held little allure. He was described as a man who was at one with nature, at ease in the wilderness, yet his exploration achievements would speed the advancement of civilization even deeper into the far North.

Douglas left another legacy to northern travellers of future generations. His labour of love, *Lands Forlorn*, is now a collector's item sought by those with a special interest in turn of the century canoe tripping or exploration of the Coppermine region. In the Canadian tradition, there will always be those who travel northward with canoes and packs to follow the paths of their forefathers. As so aptly described by Canadian historian A. R. M. Lower,

> . . . only those who have had the experience can know what a sense of physical and spiritual excitement comes to one who turns his face away from men towards the unknown. In his small way he is doing what the great explorers have done before him, and his elation recaptures theirs.[30]

Relatively few of us have had the opportunity to experience the exhilaration of reliving our history. George Douglas was one Canadian who truly loved and lived his northern heritage, at a time of marked transition for the nation's perception of the North.

ENDNOTES

1. Unless otherwise noted, biographical details were obtained from Mrs. Kay Douglas, widow of George and still residing in Lakefield, Ontario.

2. George Whalley, *The Legend of John Hornby* (Toronto: Macmillan, 1962) p. 76.

3. Unless otherwise noted, short quotes, details of preparation and description of the trip itself were taken from George M. Douglas, *Lands Forlorn: The Story of an Expedition to Hearne's Coppermine River* (New York 1914).

4. Whalley, p. 76.

5. Douglas, *Lands Forlorn*, p. 7.

6. Trent University Archives, Edward Guillet Papers, B-74-003/1 File 1, "Memories of George Douglas," 17 August 1959. Also see correspondence from Douglas to Edward Guillet, 19 April 1953.

7. Ibid., letter from Douglas to Guillet, 9 May 1944.

8. Wesley Stout, "Want to Buy a Ghost Town," *The Saturday Evening Post*, 26 May 1951, pp. 147-148.

9. Guillet Papers, "Memories of George Douglas."

10. Whalley, p. 52.

11. Ibid., p. 50.

12. Frederick B. Watt, *Great Bear, A Journey Remembered* (Yellowknife 1980), p. 3.

13. Douglas, *Lands Forlorn*, p. 126.

14. Ibid., p. 8.

15. Ibid., p. 93.

16. Whalley, p. 173.

17. Douglas, *Lands Forlorn*, p. 231.

18. Ibid., p. 269.

19. Ibid., p. 270.

20. Douglas, *Lands Forlorn*, p. iv.

21. D. H. Breen. "Anglo-American Rivalry and the Evolution of Canadian Petroleum Policy to 1930," *Canadian Historical Review*, LXII:3 (September 1981), pp. 290-301.

22. Richard Finnie, *Canada Moves North* (Toronto 1948), p. 116.

23. George Douglas, "A Summer Journey Along the Southeast Shores of Great Slave Lake," *Canadian Mining and Metallurgical Bulletin* (February 1929), p. 347.

24. As quoted in Whalley, pp. 259 and 263.

25. Douglas, "A Summer Journey," p. 349.

26. Ibid., pp. 349-360.

27. Ibid., p. 347.

28. Finnie, p. 117.

29. Whalley, p. 3.

30. A.R.M. Lower, *Unconventional Voyages* (Toronto 1953) p. 24.

Women of Determination: Northern Journeys by Women Before 1940

Gwyneth Hoyle

The North—magnificent, magnetic, mysterious—was and remains for wilderness travellers the ultimate challenge. The North is more than the geographic North. It is also the mythical North, the wilderness frontier beyond the limits of civilization. In the early part of the nineteenth century the Canadian wilderness was close at hand. Scattered communities had carved a tenuous civilization out of the enveloping forest. Those wishing to experience the primordial did not have to travel far from the centres of population. As the century advanced, as railways crossed the continent, and settlers cleared and planted the land, the frontier was pushed ever northward. Wilderness could still be experienced within a day's travel of most cities, but the truly unspoiled wilderness was receding into the North.

The mass of writing on the subject might suggest that northern travel of a recreational and exploratory nature was a male preserve, ignoring the small but significant proportion of northern travellers who were women. Women, too, have spirits which crave the adventure of the unknown and the silence of the northern wilderness.

The wives and families of Hudson's Bay Company officers had crossed the country, seated in the centre of the great *canots du maître*.[1] Governor Simpson's wife travelled hundreds of miles by canoe, and the wife of the Governor's secretary, Frances Hopkins, captured the excitement of running rapids with the voyageurs in her paintings. These women had not necessarily chosen to make such trips; their travels were really imposed on them by duty and necessity. But there is a small, elite group of women who ventured North by their own choice. These women had the original germ of the idea, they initiated the plans and they took the responsibility for carrying them out.

Before these women could set out on their travels they had first to overcome the objections and arguments of well-meaning friends and relatives. To begin with, it was unthinkable for a woman to travel alone, or in the company only of men or native guides, without the protection of a husband or a suitable female companion. To do so was to endanger her person or risk her reputation. Women were not encouraged to think of themselves as physically strong, but rather as gentle creatures who needed the stalwart male to support them. Even their long-skirted fashions fostered this notion. A further restraint was the economic factor. Mounting an expedition can be expensive, and few women had the independent means to tackle it.

In spite of these roadblocks, a few determined women made extensive and remarkable northern journeys before 1940. They did this for their own reasons, out of interest, for pleasure, or to fulfill a personal mission. During World War II, the great influx of women into the work force challenged many of the traditional assumptions about women's "proper" role. But with some important exceptions, it was not until the 1960s that the number of women scientists and recreationalists to travel North really burgeoned.[2]

The first women who blazed trails in the northern wilderness had character and determination. Their writings chronicle the struggle against the forces of nature to reach their destinations, and the impact of living in close contact with a vast unspoiled nature. They are worthy pioneers of the Canadian heritage of wilderness travel.

Anna Murphy Jameson (1794-1860)

She was born Anna Murphy, the daughter of an immigrant Irish artist. The family was clever and artistic, but poor. By the age of 16 Anna found employment as a governess and was helping to support her parents and younger sisters. Travel to the continent was the norm for wealthy English families so, as a governess, Anna was taken along. She quickly found her way into the art galleries and churches, indeed with more freedom to do this on her own than her employer's wife had. A naturally observant and articulate person, her impressions filled the pages of her diary and letters to her family, and eventually were published as a fictional account of a young woman's travels.[3]

In her late twenties, after five years of hesitation, Anna Murphy was married to Robert Jameson, a struggling lawyer four years her junior. Anna's first book was published with the help of her husband's literary circle of friends which included Charles Lamb and the Coleridge family. Both Anna and Robert were strong-willed and determined; the marriage was doomed to failure from the start.

Mrs. Jameson's first literary success made her a minor celebrity, leading to further publications in the new periodicals, as well as to a social circle which included writers, artists and prominent members of the upper classes.

Robert Jameson was appointed as a judge in Dominica, one of the string of tiny islands that make up the Lesser Antilles in the Caribbean. The appointment lasted four years, for Jameson an exile in a colonial backwater. After a brief return to England he was appointed Attorney General of Upper Canada, a position of considerable importance in more congenial and progressive surroundings. There had been no thought of Anna joining him in Dominica, but in Toronto he felt that his wife's presence would be an advantage to his position, and after a year of negotiations the arrangements were completed.

Mrs. Jameson arrived in Toronto in December of 1836. She came by way of New York where she spent a month visiting publishers and arranging for an American edition of some of her work. With her flair for society she made the acquaintance of Washington Irving, America's internationally known author, and John Jacob Astor, one of New York's wealthiest merchants.

By contrast, Upper Canada in the depths of winter was dreary, and Toronto society insufferably dull. Mrs. Jameson had achieved some degree of celebrity as an author in England and Germany, and was used to moving independently in the sparkling society of literary and social circles. In Toronto, she was faced not only with bitter cold, but also with a narrow, provincial society which recognized her only as the wife of the Attorney General and knew nothing of her accomplishments. To add to her despondency, her relationship with Jameson, always problematic, was not enhanced by years of separation.

The first glimmer of pleasure in her surroundings came with a winter visit to Niagara by horse and sleigh. "Let but the spring come again and I will take to myself wings and fly off to the west".[4] For a writer of travel books living with an uncongenial husband, travel was the obvious solution.

To these ends, Mrs. Jameson set off in the middle of June 1837 on a tour through southwestern Ontario. Two months later she had completed a circuit right around Lake Huron. Apart from some letters of introduction and a few names of potential contacts, she was unhampered by schedules or deadlines, free to adapt her travels to each opportunity that presented itself.

The journey began with a steam-boat crossing to Niagara, then by road to Hamilton, Brantford, Woodstock, London, Chatham, and across to Detroit. That may sound like a day's drive until one remembers that the roads were frequently corduroy or worse. Only rarely was there a stage coach between towns, in the absence of which the traveller hired a farm wagon with a boy to drive it. Accommodation varied from clean and attractive to mean and miserable. All was noted and commented on in Mrs. Jameson's book *Winter Studies and Summer Rambles in Canada.*[5]

From Detroit there was regular service along the American shore of Lake Huron by steamboat. A 24-hour journey brought her to the Island of Mackinaw, where Mrs. Jameson was introduced to the Indian agent and ethnologist, Henry

Schoolcraft, and to his wife, who was half Chippewa, half Scottish. The island was populated almost exclusively by Indians of the Ottawa and Pottawattomie tribes, whose customs Mrs. Jameson observed enthusiastically.

After 10 days on the small island Mrs. Jameson, accompanied by Mrs. Schoolcraft and her children set off with an hour's notice for Sault Ste. Marie by bateau—a clumsy, flat bottomed boat with a fixed sail in the middle, rowed by five French-Canadian voyageurs. The journey of about 200 miles took two days and nights, the travellers sleeping uneasily in the boat on a board and blanket.

At Sault Ste. Marie, Mrs. Jameson attained the distinction of being the first European woman to shoot the ³/₄ of a mile of rapids in a 10-foot canoe propelled by an Indian. Her reaction was ecstatic: "I recommend it as an exercise before breakfast. Two glasses of champagne could not have made me more tipsy and more self-complacent."[6] Mrs. Johnston, Mrs. Schoolcraft's mother and a full blooded Chippewa, adopted the traveller as a daughter, giving her the Chippewa name, Wahsahgewahnoqua, meaning "the woman of the bright foam."

From Sault Ste. Marie, Mrs. Jameson travelled again by bateau, rowed by four voyageurs, in the company of the Johnston family along the north shore of Lake Huron to Manitoulin Island. This journey of 170 miles took 3½ days. They pitched a tent on shore at nights and cooked their meals by campfire. The myriad of mosquitoes, the fear of rattlesnakes, even a thunderstorm with drenching rain did not discourage the eager traveller.

Their arrival at Manitoulin Island coincided with the payment of treaty money to the Indians of the district by the Chief Superintendent of Indian Affairs representing the Governor of Upper Canada. The Indians, numbering about 3700, arrived in parties of canoes from as far away as 500 miles, some of them wearing scalps to decorate their clothing. The ceremonies on this occasion were made-to-order for the observant writer.

The final leg of the journey was accomplished in style, in the canoes of the Indian Department superintendent, paddled by expert voyageurs. The party consisted of two 25-foot birchbark canoes, one paddled by seven and the other, carrying mainly baggage, paddled by eight. The whole party consisted of 21 men and Mrs. Jameson, who described her experiences.

> My blankets and night-gear being rolled up in a bundle served for a seat, and I had a pillow at my back; and thus I reclined in the bottom of the canoe, as in a litter, very much at my ease; my companions were almost equally comfortable. I had near me my cloak, umbrella, and parasol, my notebooks and sketchbooks, and a little compact basket always by my side containing eau de cologne and all those necessary luxuries which might be wanted in a moment, for I was well resolved that I would occasion no trouble but what was inevitable.[7]

Jameson's single tent was erected a little distance from the others. Her bed was made of fresh boughs covered with a bear skin and then blankets, and after a day of rain, hot madiera was served in the tent at bedtime!

The journey to Penetanguishene took four days, during which time Mrs. Jameson anticipated the pleasure of sleeping once more in a bed. But she found that nine nights in the open air, on rocks and boards, had spoiled her for the comforts of civilization; she felt suffocated by the small room and curtained bed.

The remainder of the journey included a 16-mile portage in a little wagon and a steamer across Lake Simcoe to Holland Landing. From there the road was excellent, passing by prosperous and well cultivated estates. At 3 a.m., as the moon was setting, Mrs. Jameson arrived on her doorstep, having been two months absent on what she called her "wild expedition."

Mrs. Jameson's contacts with the native people interested and delighted her. Any hardships of travel were far outweighed by the pleasures of living in the natural world, under mainly ideal conditions. Her book contrasting the monotonous, torpid life of Toronto's winter, with her summer's ramble around Lake Huron found a receptive public in England, but not in Upper Canada.

Mrs. Jameson's actual destination had been west—the most accessible wilderness; had she travelled fifty years later it is almost certain her direction would have been north. While the area she visited would not qualify as North today, in 1837 it lay beyond the outer edges of civilization. And for a woman travelling alone, without the benefit of scheduled transportation, it was high adventure in a quest for the wilderness experience.

*   *   *

Elizabeth Taylor (1856-1912)

Scheduled transportation made possible the first recorded pleasure trip to the North undertaken by a woman. Elizabeth Taylor was the daughter of James Wickes Taylor, popular American consul in Winnipeg for 23 years. James Taylor had a love of Canada and of wilderness, clearly communicated to his daughter.

Elizabeth Taylor, who had travelled widely with her father in childhood, later went by herself to Norway, France and England. She was something of an artist, botanist, ornithologist and general scientist. She is described as tiny in stature and rather frail and anaemic, but her spirit and enthusiasm more than compensated for her physical deficiencies.

In 1888 her first venture into the wilderness was an experiment to test herself under difficult conditions away from the comforts of civilization—a 13-day canoe trip from the village of Red Rock in Northern Ontario, 60 miles north to a mission station on Lake Nipigon and back. The trip was made in a large canoe, with two Indian guides. A missionary's wife acted as chaperone, accompanied by her young son and her Indian woman servant. Elizabeth Taylor was 32, on her first real camping trip. It involved early starts and late stops, 18 portages, the first of them 2½ miles in heat, fog and drizzle, black flies, mosquitoes and punkies ('no-see-ums') by the thousands, everything wet and disagreeable, the terrain rough and rocky. Balancing the hardships were 38 different birds seen and heard, 45 varieties of flowers collected, her first trout caught with a flyrod, and the excitement of running spectacular rapids. A sudden cold rainstorm gave her a congestive chill, and she fainted at the end of a long portage, but doses of whiskey and the excitement of shooting more rapids while lying in the bottom of the canoe seemed to cure her. When they arrived back at Red Rock, Joseph Esquimaux, the guide, had been so impressed with her pluckiness that he tried to persuade her to go on an additional trip, offering to take her without payment. Unfortunately, as there was no suitable female companion prepared to go along, Elizabeth had to forego the pleasure.

In 1892 the question of a chaperone did not arise. It was in this year that Elizabeth Taylor achieved her ambition to travel to the delta of the Mackenzie River. The extension of a branch line to Edmonton by the Canadian Pacific Railway in 1891 made it possible to travel to Peel's River and back in one summer—it was certainly not considered acceptable for a woman to winter in the Arctic. Her father's friendly contacts with Hudson's Bay Company officials were invaluable in arranging her transportation to the North.

At the time planning of the trip began, Elizabeth was living in a small apartment in Paris, studying art. She wrote to a friend, "I have begun my independent career by ignoring all conventionalities and having a young man call here."[8] The young man was Ernest Thompson Seton, also in Paris to study art, and the subjects discussed were the merits of Jaeger flannels, air mattresses, binoculars, how to skin birds, and what to take along for the preservation of wildlife specimens.

There were also visits to her Paris couturière. "I have a lively recollection now of a struggle I had with a dressmaker in Paris—her impassioned appeals for a *little* train, her dismay at the full skirt when only 'bell skirts' were being worn."[9] The well-dressed northern traveller wore a long skirt, a cape with detachable hood, gaiters, and cuffs—all of waterproofed wool—with a blouse, knickerbockers, a felt hat and horse-hide boots.

The journey northward, begun in Edmonton, was accomplished in a variety of conveyances, beginning with a team of horses to Athabasca Landing, then a steamboat to Grand Rapids. Her stateroom on that boat, furnished with only a hay tick, was leaky. Later, in the absence of grass for the oxen, used to take the cargo over one of the portages, Elizabeth's hay tick was donated as fodder. At some rapids the cargo was transferred to York boats and the rapids were shot with the passengers in other York boats. Then they transferred to another wood-burning steamer down river, well past the danger. Where the river had risen dangerously with the spring run-off, they had to camp several days until the water dropped.

After six weeks they arrived at Fort Smith at 1:30 a.m.:

> We put up our tents on the edge of the hill and we went to bed in broad daylight at 2:30. We were quite tired out. I put in a very uncomfortable night: had caught cold on the boat, couldn't breathe, the light hurt my eyes and the mosquitos found their way under the bar. Then my tent collapsed. I spent the rest of the night lying among the ruins. Emerging from the tent I heard a low, discontented rumble and grumble all about, but as I crept out it changed to a shriek of joy and they all cried 'Hurrah! Here she is! Come on! Come on! and they all made for me. I am not exaggerating when I say that at least 4000 mosquitoes were swarming about me in a moment. [10]

After Fort Smith they were clear of the rapids. The difficult part of the trip was behind them—until the return journey. On the steamer "Wrigley," the Mackenzie Delta was reached in six days.

Her first meeting with Eskimos surpassed expectation:

> As a fat old woman toddled down to meet me, her broad face shining with whale oil, her dress inside out to keep it clean, her husband's hair in a bunch on top of her head, her toes turned in and her elbows turned out — I felt that I had fully realized my ideal. With convulsive giggles she grasped my hand firmly with one of hers, while with the other she patted me affectionately on the shoulder. Evidently I impressed her as presenting an utterly absurd appearance, for after looking me all over, she would shut her eyes, shake her head from side to side and go off into a fit of laughter.[11]

Altogether the trip took three months. Elizabeth made extensive collections of flowers, birds, and butterflies, all of which were sent to Washington. Her work was mentioned in Edward Preble's "A biological investigation of the Athabasca Mackenzie Region" published by the U.S. Department of Agriculture, Department of Biological Survey.

While this journey to the North may seem tame in comparison to the canoe trips undertaken by men at the time and women soon after, it was significant enough to warrant including Elizabeth Taylor in the United States government's 1908 list of great explorers in the North American regions—the only woman to achieve this distinction. Though the transportation was scheduled, the journey was arduous (especially the stretch between Edmonton and Fort Smith), and was perceived as quite remarkable for a woman travelling alone — a measure of the public's perception of both womanhood and the North at the time.[12]

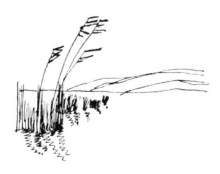

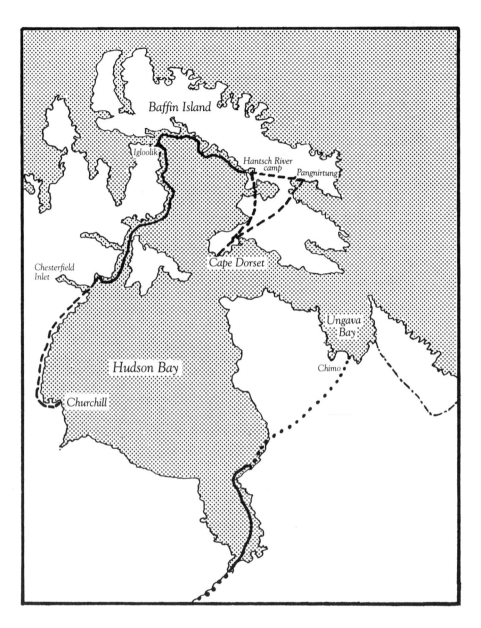

Baffin Island

Igloolik

Hantsch River
camp

Pangnirtung

Cape Dorset

Chesterfield
Inlet

Ungava
Bay

Chimo

Hudson Bay

Churchill

Manning – boat
        – snowshoe & dog team
Tasker – ship
        – canoe
Hubbard – canoe

Mina Benson Hubbard (approx. 1870–1950)

On the other side of the continent, in 1905, Mina Benson Hubbard was engaged in an entirely different sort of northern adventure. Her story had its real beginning in 1903, when Leonidas Hubbard Jr., journalist and assistant editor of the magazine *Outing*, travelled from his home in Congers, New York, to Labrador, on an expedition of exploration sponsored by his magazine. The object was to explore and map the Nascaupee and George River systems, entering at Hamilton Inlet, and coming out at Ungava Bay. For this ambitious undertaking he had two companions: Dillon Wallace, a New York lawyer, and George Elson, part-Cree Indian from the James Bay region acting as guide and woodsman, although the terrain to be travelled was actually unknown to him. They had one canoe, and one very sketchy map drawn at the end of the previous century by A. P. Low of the Geological Survey of Canada. The interior of Labrador was virtually unexplored at the time.

Many events conspired against the success of this venture: a late start in mid-July, a summer of unusually bad weather, the lack of a guide who knew the territory, and the absence of an accurate map. By mid-September they had failed to reach the big lake, Michikimau, which would lead them to the headwaters of the George River. Their supplies were dwindling and winter weather was closing in. In mid-October Hubbard died of exhaustion and starvation. The other two men succeeded in reaching the food cache and eventually civilization.

Two years later the writer's widow, Mina Hubbard, prepared for a similar journey to complete her husband's work. Born Mina Benson, in Bewdley, near Peterborough, Ontario, she graduated from the Brooklyn Training School for Nurses in New York. She married Leonidas Hubbard on January 1, 1901. Now with the advantage of the information and experience obtained from the first expedition, with a larger crew, and with a start three weeks earlier, the work begun two years before was successfully completed.

The crew consisted of the same George Elson who had accompanied Leonidas Hubbard and had recovered his body and photographic material from the interior of Labrador in the winter following his death. Elson brought with him two Cree Indians from Missanabie, and also a "part-Eskimo"* who had taken part in the unsuccessful rescue attempt in 1903.

In two canvas-covered canoes they carried about 1000 pounds of supplies and ammunition. In addition, Mrs. Hubbard carried a revolver, a hunting knife, fishing tackle, two cameras, a sextant with an artificial horizon, a barometer, and a thermometer. Beside her regular camping clothes and supplies, she carried a blouse for Sundays, an air mattress, a small feather pillow, and a hot water bottle.

As they left Northwest River on June 27th, ahead of them lay a journey of 550 unmapped miles to Ungava Bay and a deadline of the last week of August,

---

* "Part-Eskimo" was an error on the part of Mrs. Hubbard. The man was actually Montagnais Indian. Cooke, Allen, "A Woman's Way", *The Beaver*, Summer, 1960.

when the only ship of the year would be calling at the Hudson's Bay post.

The journey up the Nascaupee was very slow, poling up the rapids, tracking the canoe, and carrying over many long and heavy portages. Progress on the worst days was as little as 1½ miles. Mrs. Hubbard was head of the expedition—she had initiated it, her money was paying for it, and she would have to make any vital decisions in the course of the expedition. Yet in the tradition of the time she travelled as a passenger in George Elson's canoe. Her tent was erected for her and her meals were cooked and served in her tent if the flies were bad, as they usually were through July. When it was discovered that the air mattress pump was missing, she thought to send someone back over a day of portages and rapids to find it, knowing that she could not sleep without her mattress. Fortunately this was unnecessary, as one of the men merely blew it up by mouth.

George Elson, having been with her husband, felt doubly charged to conduct Mrs. Hubbard safely to her destination in order to safeguard his own reputation as a guide. Never before having travelled in the wilderness with a woman, he was anxious that she should not stand too close to the edge of the rapids in case she lost her footing, and concerned that she should not get lost on portages or climb hills by herself to search out the way ahead. At first Mrs. Hubbard found the protectiveness irksome. On one occasion while the men were completing a long portage, she went off rebelliously to explore on her own. Firing her revolver to let them know where she was, she apparently disappeared around another hill, appearing and disappearing quickly. The men were nearly frantic with worry and, when they caught up, were quite exhausted from the exertions of the chase combined with the portaging. Significantly, Mrs. Hubbard later perceived her rebellion as unfair, became reconciled to the protectiveness, and no longer chafed against it.

Apart from the physical difficulties of ascending a wild river, there was the concern to find the route, always remembering that it was the failure to do this that had led to such tragic results for the first Hubbard expedition. Mrs. Hubbard, particularly in the early stage of the journey, experienced very strong emotions knowing she was travelling over the route her husband had travelled, having read his descriptive journal.

When at last they reached Lake Michikimau, the watershed to the George River and the lake for which her husband had searched in vain, it was already August 8th. The exceptionally fine weather of July was past and they were held up for several days at a time by storms. But when they could travel they made very good time on the downstream journey.

After a week on the George River, they met their first natives, an encampment of Montagnais women and children, the men having gone across country to the trading post. The Indians thought the journey to Ungava Bay would take two months, a severe blow. Here one realizes Mrs. Hubbard's extraordinary courage as the leader of the expedition. It was her decision to push forward, knowing that she would be responsible for the welfare of four men, possibly during the whole of the winter if they should miss the ship.

Three days later, on August 20th, they came to an encampment of Nascaupee Indians, who declared that they were within five sleeps of Ungava Bay. The final section of the George River was completed without incident. They reached Ungava Bay on August 27, in plenty of time for the ship which had been severely delayed and arrived on October 22.

They had covered 576 miles between June 27th and August 27th, 43 days of travelling, 18 days in camp. The mapping which was done showed the Nascaupee, Seal Lake, and Lake Michikimau to be in the same drainage basin and, contrary to A.P. Low's earlier conclusion, the Northwest Arm and the Nascaupee were one and the same river. In addition, Mrs. Hubbard had made extensive notes on the topography, geology, flora and fauna of the country.

What could have persuaded this young woman to leave her comfortable home outside New York City to travel in the uncharted wilds of Labrador? The obvious and stated reason was to complete the work started by her husband. The unstated and possibly more compelling reason was the desire to vindicate Hubbard's reputation and spite his travelling companion, Dillion Wallace, whose book, *The Lure of Labrador*[13] described Leonidas Hubbard affectionately, but pointed out some errors in judgement and planning. Wallace believed these errors had cost them dearly, almost resulting in his own death as well as Hubbard's. Mrs. Hubbard was deeply offended by this criticism of her dead husband. Moreover, she was angered by Wallace's refusal to give her Hubbard's topographical notes and photographs of the expedition.

When it became known that Wallace was planning a return to Labrador to try again to find the George River, George Elson went to New York and persuaded Mrs. Hubbard that if she would lead an expedition, he now knew the correct route and was sure that they would be successful. And so it happened that both the Hubbard and the Wallace expeditions left the Northwest River Post in Labrador on June 27, 1905. The excitement in the tiny settlement was intense.

Mrs. Hubbard makes no mention in her book *A Woman's Way Through Labrador*, of Wallace's second journey. Wallace, in the preface to a sixth edition of *The Lure of Labrador*, recounts his successful second attempt but ignores Mrs. Hubbard's accomplishment. The animosity between them shows itself in this charged silence and in a careful reading between the lines. It was a powerful factor in sending Mrs. Hubbard on a mission which few women, before or since, would have dared to attempt.[14]

Mrs. Hubbard's book gives a flavour of the wilderness journey, with a feeling for the remarkable person making this pilgrimage. Camped at the height of land, about to begin the downstream section, she wrote:

> Here at its beginning on the boggy margin of the stream, we went into camp. Here I saw the sun set and rise again, and as I lay in my tent at dawn, with its wall lifted so I could look out into the changing red and gold of the eastern sky, I heard splashing of water near, and looking up saw a little company of caribou cross to the head of the stream and disappear toward the sunrise.

How little I had dreamed when setting out on my journey that it would prove beautiful and of such compelling interest as I had found it. I had not thought of interest—except that of getting the work done—not of beauty. How could Labrador be beautiful? Weariness and hardship I had looked for, and weariness I had found often, and anxiety, but of hardship there had been none. Flies and mosquitos made it uncomfortable sometimes but not to the extent of hardship. And how beautiful it had been, with a strange wild beauty, the remembrance of which buries itself silently in the deep parts of one's being.[15]

In those words Mrs. Hubbard speaks for all who are touched by the wilderness of the North.

*   *   *

Florence Tasker (approx. 1880-1950)

The reputation gained by George Elson as outstanding guide and companion resulted in another expedition by a woman—Florence Tasker. In 1908 article written after the successful adventure, Mrs. Tasker devotes a paragraph to George Elson and his connection with both Hubbards. Indeed even the title, *A Woman Through Husky-Land*[16] resembles Mrs. Hubbard's title, *A Woman's Way Through Unknown Labrador*.

Mrs. Tasker, travelling with her husband, Stephen, a 32 year old marine engineer from Philadelphia,[17] explored an unmapped corner of northeastern Canada. Of Mrs. Tasker no details are known. It can be presumed that the Taskers were well-to-do and educated since they had the leisure and money to mount a 5-month journey purely for sport and adventure. It is also probable that Florence Tasker was a little younger than her husband.

Their expedition began at the town of Missanabie on the Canadian Pacific Railway northwest of Sudbury, and took them by 18-foot Peterborough canoe down the Missanabie and Moose Rivers to Moose Factory. From there the whole outfit was carried reluctantly by the 75 ton supply steamer, *Inenew*, up the east coast of Hudson Bay only as far as Great Whale River—reluctantly because the captain of the *Inenew* considered their undertaking dangerous and foolhardy. Because their canoe was too heavily loaded for safe travel along the remaining 100 mile stretch of Hudson Bay coast, natives with a canoe were hired to carry the extra load. The natives would go only as far north as Richmond Gulf, so the Taskers' plan was revised to fit this circumstance.

The two heavily laden canoes worked their way north along the barren, inhospitable coast of Hudson Bay. For the first two days their passage was sheltered by large rocky islands a mile or two from land. Here the shore of Hudson Bay is solid rock, smooth and sloping up gradually for a mile toward great perpendicular walls. It was always possible to land the canoes, and to camp by streams of fresh water trickling down the rock wall. After five days on the great open bay a swift current swept them through the narrow channel into granite-walled Richmond Gulf. The hired canoe left them there, and the original party found its way to the Larch River which empties into Ungava Bay at Fort Chimo.

The successful completion of such a journey was an enormous achievement, testimony to Mrs. Tasker's strength of character. Careful reading of her account suggests that she was an active participant rather than a passenger. "All hands were busy with the paddles," she writes, and "The portages . . . the alders, willows wrapped their outstretched arms so clingingly to my portions of the outfit," Such statements imply that she both paddled and carried her share on the portages.

Mrs. Tasker recorded the journey with candour, leaving no doubt that it was difficult and dangerous. Mid-August was late in the season and the weather was uniformly bad—wet, cold, and either still and humid, or accompanied by stinging winds. Altogether they saw very little sunshine. The mosquitoes were omnipresent and voracious. The portages were rough and difficult.

Shocked by the pervasive poverty and starvation among the native people, the Taskers were generous with their food supplies in encounters with destitute natives. After all, they fully expected to meet up with caribou herds later. But the caribou did not materialize and by the end of the trip their own rations were reduced to tea, biscuits and a few beans.

Mrs. Tasker describes the journey with sardonic humour, but with a strong sense of compassion for the people of the North. She has nothing but praise for the two native guides, George Elson and Job Chappies, who were unfailingly cheerful, good natured and skillful. She would long remember the magnificent rapids and the grandeur of the Hudson Bay coast where they passed herds of seal and a school of white whales. But clearly, she was not eager to repeat the experience:

> As we crossed the suspension bridge at Niagara Falls, and I felt that I was again on my native soil, I swore a mighty oath to never cross those boundaries again. But will some one kindly tell me what I am to do with a husband who, before a year has passed, comes to me with newly laid plans for another journey into unknown regions? Oh, for the strength and wisdom to keep on saying, 'No!'[18]

The whole venture was completed without mishap, lasting from June 20th leaving Missanabie, to arrival at Fort Chimo on September 3rd. In total the journey was over 4000 miles, 1500 of those by canoe. The extreme portion of the trip was across 500 miles of unmapped wilderness—travelled twenty years previously by the government surveyor A. P. Low. For this exploration, Stephen Tasker was made a fellow of Royal Geographical Society of London. While Florence Tasker may not have initiated this adventure, she shared in its planning and she participated as an equal, paddling, portaging and making camp—a woman well ahead of her time.

Lady Clara Vyvyan (1885-1976)

By 1926 women had ceased wearing long skirts, and were thus able to travel more comfortably than they had in pre-World War I society. In that year, two English women from Cornwall conceived the idea of a trip across Canada and back, making the outward journey by way of the North, crossing the great divide into Alaska, and completing it by coastal steamer to Vancouver Island.

Lady Clara Vyvyan and her friend, Gwen Dorrien Smith, had previously completed a successful walking tour in the Balkans and felt they were ready for further challenges. At the time of their northern trip, Lady Vyvyan was Clara Coltman Rogers, born in 1885 on a Queensland, Australia, cattle station, into a family which is recorded in *Burke's Landed Gentry*. She was educated at the London School of Economics and was a professional writer specializing in books on Cornwall, her ancestral home, on gardens and on travel.

Most of this tour involved conventional transportation on ships and trains. In planning the journey north from Edmonton, they were fortunate to have as their neighbour in Cornwall a director of the Hudson's Bay Company who put them in touch with useful contacts in Canada. The plan that evolved was for them to travel to Edmonton by train. From Edmonton to Aklavik, the Hudson's Bay Company supplied the transportation, very similar to the experiences of Elizabeth Taylor at the beginning of the century. From Aklavik they would go by canoe with two Indian guides over the Continental divide into Alaska by way of the Rat and Porcupine Rivers to Fort Yukon. After that their travel would be by scheduled steamers, and transcontinental train.

The cost estimated by the Hudson's Bay Company was a staggering sum of $1350. To minimize costs they booked steerage class passage across the Atlantic, and tourist accommodation on the railway west. By contrast, in Winnipeg they were able to live in style with a cousin who was part owner of a hotel, and there they were entertained by Lady Tupper, daughter-in-law of Sir Charles Tupper, and others who were interested in their adventure.

The real preparation for the adventure began at Edmonton, where they had 4 days to procure steamer tickets and their complete outfits. A Hudson's Bay Company officer who knew their proposed route was able to advise them. He informed them that it would take 10 days to track up the Rat River to LaPierre House, where they would obtain guides to take them downstream to Fort Yukon. They should provide 3 pounds of food per person per day, but could reprovision at LaPierre House, so 12 days food would give them a safe margin. He emphasized the difficulties of travelling up the Rat River, and warned that the Indian guides would not take orders but must be treated on a friendly and equal footing.

In addition to buying their outfits in Edmonton, they had to provide themselves with large amounts of cash, so that each woman carried $500 in a bag around her neck. When their shopping was completed, their outfit consisted of six canvas bundles, a rifle, a despatch case, one suitcase and a rucksack, weighing a total of 175 pounds, plus 250 pounds of food, reckoning 3 pounds for 4 persons for 21 days. Fortunately, they had ignored the advice that they could reprovision at LaPierre House.

The steamboat to Aklavik was a carefree and beautiful introduction to the North. The scenery and the people, both on the boat and on shore, are described with pleasure.[19] A fortuitous accident delayed them for two weeks in Aklavik. A strained tendon in Gwen Smith's foot made two weeks of complete rest imperative if she was to undertake the trek up the Rat River.

At Aklavik they learned from the Hudson's Bay post manager that there was nothing but an empty cabin at LaPierre House. This site had been marked on the atlas they had used in England, and was a pivotal point in all their plans. At LaPierre House they were to obtain guides for the downriver part of their canoe journey. Their Rat River guides could not possibly take them on to Old Crow, the first point where guides would be available. The distance for the upriver guides to walk back to Aklavik carrying their provisions was too great. The only solution was for the two women to canoe 115 miles from LaPierre House to Old Crow on their own. No dangerous rapids were reported in that stretch of the Porcupine River, but the women had never expected to handle paddles at all. In fact, while Gwen Smith was at home in rowboats and sailboats, and had once paddled a small canoe, Clara Rogers had never been in a canoe in her life. Fortunately, she had time on her hands, and found an expert to teach her.

The two guides chosen for them by the Hudson's Bay post manager were Louchoux Indians. Lazarus Sittichili was everything they could have hoped for in a guide: extremely strong, very skilled, thoughtful, and totally reliable. Jimmy Koe, his helper, was a boy trained in the mission school, who chose to make the trip in order to learn from Lazarus.

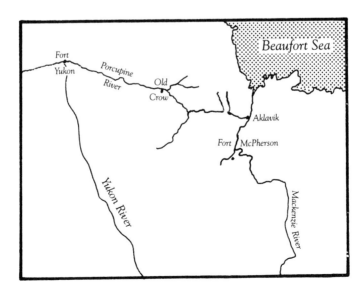

By July 7th, they were ready to leave Aklavik, and for the next nine days they ascended the Rat River. Ascend is too easy a word—in fact they struggled most of the way. The two women, much of the time on foot, clambered over deadfalls, searched for dry footing on muskeg, and picked their way through rough rocky terrain, always in clouds of mosquitoes. Meanwhile, the two guides paddled against the current, lined the canoe up through rapids, waded, pushed, pulled and struggled in the icy water. Melting ice was still falling into the river in chunks. The river was in flood. Heavy, showery, weather added to their miseries, raising the water level and threatening their campsites. But ascending is exactly what they were doing, and when they could raise their eyes from their footsteps, the women could see the Richardson mountains coming ever closer. There was a whole day when they were stopped by the rising river, and they wondered whether the guides would refuse to go on. Lazarus was not fluent in English and communication between them came slowly, but gradually their respect for him increased and their trust became unshakable. The guides took them an extra day's journey beyond LaPierre House, and there they parted, each guide being paid $210, at the rate of $14 a day, established by Stefansson, for 10 days upstream and 5 days of walking back.

The women parted from the guides with regret. At first, a feeling of awe, of total aloneness, and a depth of solitude enveloped them in a vast empty world. But the mosquitoes had disappeared as they reached the height of land, and after a while a new feeling of freedom gradually dawned on them. They took time to have a bath and wash the clothes which had not been removed, even for sleeping, in the last ten days. And then they pushed onward.

The 4½ day journey down the Porcupine River was pure enchantment, peaceful, golden, restful, and without incident. Moving along with the current, and without the constraint of guides, they enjoyed the freedom of sleeping late, and even without a tent, waking one morning to see a caribou watching them. Swift water, swirling currents, and snags from fallen trees were their chief concerns, but their greatest anxiety was the lack of an adequate map of the area and the fear that they would pass Old Crow without noticing, and be swept into the dangerous rapids. But Old Crow appeared on schedule. The local trader gave them hospitality and helped them to hire a guide to take them on to Fort Yukon. The remaining five days flowed on like the river, the current helping them to make sixty or seventy miles a day. Suddenly, they were in Fort Yukon, having travelled nearly 600 miles by canoe.

This was an epic journey for two women, then in their forties, to undertake and complete. Clara Rogers published two brief articles on the adventure.[20] Soon after this she married Sir Courtney Vyvyan, a widower much older than herself. Following his death and after the war, she returned to writing travel books, among them an account of a walking tour of the Rhone River from its source high in the Swiss mountains to the estuary on the Mediterranean. She was 67 when she set off with rucksack and billy-can to walk the 500 miles, some of it alone and some of it with friends. Finally, in 1961, with only her personal diaries and the two published articles to refresh her memory, she wrote *Arctic Adventure*[21] recalling the northern trip made 35 years before.

Travel to remote places and writing about it were Clara Vyvyan's life. Her choice of routes emphasized a geographic totality, whether it was following a river from source to mouth, or completely exploring a region. Her northern trip, encompassing half a continent and crossing the continental divide by canoe, was typical of this large vision. The compelling aspect was the remoteness and the challenge for these two strong-willed, adventurous, British upper-class women.

*   *   *

Lillian Alling

Most of the women travellers gave full accounts of their adventures in books or magazine articles. The exception was Lillian Alling, who crossed the continent— mainly on foot—from east to west, between the years 1927 and 1929. She remains shrouded in mystery.[22] Lillian Alling was a young Russian immigrant, homesick and lonely in New York City. Working as a house maid, she could not possibly save enough money to buy a steamer ticket back to Europe. Instead, she studied maps, chose her route, and set off on foot, with her carefully hoarded savings and a stout iron bar for protection, with the Bering Straits as her destination. She headed west to Chicago, then north to Minneapolis and Winnipeg, refusing all offers of lifts.

In late September, 1927, she appeared on the Yukon telegraph trail, in northern British Columbia. The snow was already covering the tops of the moun- tains, and she was lightly dressed, wearing only ordinary running shoes on her feet. The provincial Police from Hazelton, B.C., intercepted her. She had only $10, a small knapsack and her iron bar, and by her own account she was heading for Siberia.

For her own protection, the police charged her with vagrancy and, because she could not pay the fine, she was put into Oakalla Prison, near New Westminster. There she had shelter and good food for two months. On her release, work was found for her so that she could accumulate some savings.

Near the end of June, 1928, Lillian Alling was off again on her pilgrim- age. By July 19th, she had arrived at Smithers, over half the length of the province away, having walked at least 30 miles a day. The police gave her permission to continue, provided she check in with each of the cabins along the telegraph trail through the mountains into the Yukon. The linesmen who staff these lonely maintenance cabins took a great interest in her journey and her welfare. They provided her with hot meals, remodelled their shirts and trousers to replace her worn outfit, and one man presented her with a mongrel, outfitted with pannier bags, to keep her company.

After the mountainous stretch, Lillian Alling appeared only briefly at isolated farms, maintaining tight-lipped silence about herself and her destina- tion. Her long-expected arrival at Dawson in a small boat was reported enthusias- tically in the local press,[23] and she was regarded as a heroine and a "mystery woman." She worked as a cook in one of the camps for the winter, living as a recluse. In the spring she launched her boat on the broad expanse of the Yukon River. Her four-legged companion had met with an accident, so she had skinned it, stuffed the hide, and carried it along with her. She reached Nome, Alaska, and there she left the boat and was seen with a little cart which carried her few possessions and the body of her dog.

The trail ends on the bleak shores of the Bering Strait—it is not known whether she succeeded in persuading Eskimos to take her across to Siberia. Lillian Alling had already accomplished alone a 6000 mile journey across the continent, driven by one overwhelming desire—to return to her beloved homeland, the Steppes of Russia.

Lillian Alling

Ella Wallace Manning (1910-   )

Since the mid-nineteenth century, women have lived and travelled in northern Canada because they were married to Hudson's Bay Company traders, or to missionaries, and more recently to government employees. A few married knowing they would be going directly to a northern post; for example, Letitia Hargrave, whose husband was already an officer at York Factory on Hudson Bay when he returned to Scotland in search of a bride. Others found themselves married to men who then chose, or were sent, to northern outposts.

Marriage has been called a voyage of discovery. Marriage to a man one has not seen for several years and with whom communication has been limited by his remote location is a major exploration. Add the condition that the marriage is to take place in the Arctic, where the couple is to live under the primitive conditions of the native population, and it is easy to understand why all of Ella Wallace's friends tried to persuade her not to accept the cryptic telegraphed proposal received one spring day in Montreal in 1938.

Tom Manning had been in the north since 1936 as a member of the British-Canadian Arctic Scientific Expedition. He had a reputation for being one of the "hardest travellers" alive, considered by the Eskimos as equal to the best of them—a rare compliment.[24]

All efforts to dissuade Ella Wallace from embarking on this seemingly foolhardy adventure failed, and she sailed on July 8th on the *Nascopie* for Cape Dorset, taking an old Harris tweed suit, a large stock of toothbrushes, and very little else.

They were married very soon after her arrival by the Bishop of the Arctic, using for a wedding ring a brass ring made by the *Nascopie* chief engineer. Their first home was aboard the *Polecat*, Thomas Manning's two-ton boat, the length of a freight canoe, which was fitted with a primitive inboard engine and sails. On land home was an umbrella-shaped tent which they shared with an Eskimo couple, who would travel and live with them to help with the mechanics of daily life on Baffin Island. Mrs. Manning was soon fitted out with sealskin boots, shirt, breeches, and eventually with caribou-skin garments.

Once they had their supplies organized, they set off up the west coast of Baffin Island in the *Polecat*, towing two freight canoes full of supplies, with the Eskimo couple and a child named Lizzie who had been brought along as company for the Eskimo woman. The area where they would live was unexplored and unknown even to the Eskimos living with them. They expected to be about 300 miles from the nearest Hudson's Bay post, so their supplies would have to last for over a year. In addition to the five people there were seven dogs and four pups. They had no wireless transmitter and there were no natives within 250 miles. All this Mrs. Manning accepted without a qualm, not realizing how much better equipped were other expeditions at the time.

The scientific mission studied all kinds of things—from the ruins of stone houses of an ancient culture, to ornithology and mammology. They made flower collections and did geographical surveys, mapping unknown areas, taking star fixes for latitude and longitude.

Late in August, they reached the Hantsch River and chose a spot for the winter camp. The tent was set up and arranged like a native house. The bed was raised for warmth; it would be the sitting place, as well as the sleeping place, the sewing room, and the nursery. A row of boxes was placed so as to suggest that the Eskimo family and Mannings each had their own space, and each had their own cooking kits, quite usual even if two Eskimo families were sharing a tent.

The Eskimo woman was very lazy, which turned out to be in the Manning's favour. Mrs. Manning soon learned to do everything for herself, including making caribou clothing, and cooking with the seal oil lamp. In October a baby was born to the woman, who had made no preparations for it. The baby was a wonderful plaything for the mother who was constantly waking it up, bouncing it, feeding it, playing with it, with the result that the baby cried continually.

By December, the Mannings decided that they could manage on their own, and the Eskimo family returned to Southampton Island. The tent was made clean and tidy with fresh snow. Even though it meant a great deal of extra work for both of them, they were delighted to be alone for the first time.

During the winter, they made several trips with the dogs and the komatik [sled], the longest one being when they mapped 180 miles of previously unknown coast. This took them almost the whole of February, travelling over very rough terrain, in temperatures of $-35\,°$F. Pups were born to one of the dogs on this trip and had to be cared for. Food became short for them and for the dogs. Often it was hard to find the right snow at the end of the day's travel to build an igloo, a process which could take $2\,\frac{1}{2}$ hours.

The Arctic spring begins to show itself in late April and by June it bursts forth in full glory with birds, flowers, and perpetual daylight. The snow melts to slush and puddles appear everywhere. On the coast of Baffin Island, the predominant features are mud and wetness.

Spring and summer journeys were much harder than winter ones. The rough terrain was more difficult as the snow became scarce and heavy. The heat of the sun made the caribou clothing unbearably hot. In the first summer it rained every day but four during July. Late in July they were able to get the *Polecat* into the water to travel north in search of the breeding ground for the geese. The tides which ebbed over mudflats, the shifting ice, and the strong winds combined to make life on the boat an adventure.

By mid-August they were already making preparations for their second winter, although they were able to continue travel up the coast in the boat until early in October. Mrs. Manning used the time on the boat to work on new caribou garments for the coming winter. When the clothes were finished, by mid-December, the Mannings decided to make a trip to Cape Dorset for supplies, hoping to get there for Christmas, but not arriving until early in January of 1940. The first news they heard was that war had been declared in the previous September. From Dorset they continued on to Pangnirtung, without maps, and without having travelled in that part of the country before—a journey which lasted from January 11th until late in February. Pangnirtung had a Hudson's Bay post, a Church of England mission, a hospital with one nurse and one doctor, and an R.C.M.P. barracks. They enjoyed the novelty of company and lavish hospitality for five days before starting back, arriving at their camp on March 10th. They had been travelling for three months, covering hundreds of miles with only two brief breaks at Hudson's Bay posts.

With the return of spring and summer, preparations were initiated for the return to the outside. Thomas was still searching farther up the coast for the elusive nesting grounds of the geese while Mrs. Manning stayed in camp alone with one of the dogs for company. July was wonderfully fine, rain only four days, in contrast to the year before. The trip to the outside began, in a small way, on July 6th, as they headed north with the canoe, paddling it, or wading and pulling it along in the melted water close to shore, making very slow progress. By late July, the *Polecat* could be launched, to begin the painfully slow journey northward around the coast of Hudson Bay to Igloolik, sometimes hemmed in by pack ice, sometimes stayed by winds. The need to conserve what little fuel they had meant relying as much as possible on the sails. Their aim was to reach the Hudson's Bay post on the tiny island of Igloolik, at the northwest corner of Hudson Bay, to connect with a ship which would take them and their boat to the outside. Ice, fog, and gale-force winds made it a very rough trip. September 4th was clear as they passed the Fury and Hecla Strait leading through to the Arctic Ocean. Tom remarked, "Not one piece of ice in the Strait—I do wish we could go through—no one has ever before found it clear—if we had supplies, I should be awfully tempted."

They arrived at Igloolik exactly one day before the ship was due, but the ship which arrived was not the one expected, but a much smaller ship. The captain was willing to take them but not their boat. Their decision was to sail on as far south as possible toward Churchill. They left Igloolik on September 8th and travelled until freeze-up. Thomas knew there was an abandoned police barracks at Cape Fullerton, eighty miles north of Chesterfield Inlet. With the engine giving trouble, the bilge frozen, and the *Polecat* caked with ice, they squeaked into Fullerton Harbour on October 12th. They were able to make the police barracks habitable, found a bed spring, found coal, and settled into their first real house. Two white trappers arrived soon after, with police permission to use the house for the winter, so their quarters had to be shared.

By December 21st, there was enough snow for the Mannings to leave with the dog team. They reached Churchill on January 20th, the day before the train, scheduled at three-week intervals, left for the outside. They had reached Churchill very short of food, in a state of exhaustion. After a bath, a change into her "old Harris tweed suit and nice brown oxfords," and a good meal, Ella Manning felt more like herself. Thomas was ready to turn around and head North again.

Mrs. Manning has described this 2½ year adventure in a small book entitled *Igloo for the Night*.[25] Her writing is very spare and understated, chronicling their life in a matter-of-fact way, neither dwelling on nor making light of the dangers and hardships, merely stating the facts as they occurred. Few women would have accepted such a challenge and carried it off with such aplomb.

It was in the day-to-day life, apart from travel, that Ella Manning's experience differed from that of the other women travellers. For more than two years she lived without the amenities that would normally be taken for granted: communication with family or friends, fresh fruit and vegetables, a change of clothing, hot water, plumbing. To balance these deficiencies the Mannings had a freedom and independence rarely experienced in regular society. Their only obligations were to produce data for the scientific mission—and to survive. The effort required to survive mainly off the land, (clothing and food from the caribou, oil for cooking and light from the seal), filled most of their waking hours. Isolation, independence and the zest of living were the predominant ingredients of this northern experience.

*   *   *

These eight women ranged in age from their mid-twenties to their late forties. The average was closer to forty than to thirty. They were American, British and Canadian in roughly equal proportions, with the exception of Lillian Alling, a Russian. They possessed wealth and leisure in varying degrees. Some referred not at all to the cost of the expeditions while to others, the expense was a factor to be considered carefully.

Most were working women or had professions and were used to making decisions independently and carrying them through. The two non-professionals, Elizabeth Taylor and Florence Tasker, both came from well-to-do American families with the wealth and leisure for such extensive travel. Anna Jameson and Clara Vyvyan were writers who planned to use their experiences in future books. All but Lillian Alling and Elizabeth Taylor wrote books or articles as a result of their experiences. Most travelled out of interest, sociological or scientific, or just plain curiosity about a rarely visited part of the world, and most of them had the education and training to appreciate what they experienced. Anna Jameson, as well as travelling for interest, shared with Lillian Alling the need to escape from an intolerable situation.

While Florence Tasker and Ella Manning travelled in the company of their husbands, the rest with the exception of Mrs. Jameson, were unmarried at the time of their expeditions. All would acknowledge that they had depended to some degree on the assistance of men to make their journeys possible, yet in this they were no different to all the men who had made such journeys.

It is difficult to generalize about the women. Of all the women Lillian Alling, the mysterious, lonely and almost tragic figure, has the least in common with the others. With all of them she shares the characteristics of strong-mindedness, independence of thought, and perseverance which carried them past the impediments put in their paths at the beginning, through the hardships along the way, to the successful conclusions.

Possibly all but Florence Tasker would echo the words of Ella Manning, in an article written for *The Beaver*. "Would I go North again? Of course, if we can find ways and means to carry out our work. Would I advise anyone else to go? Certainly not. Whoever really wants to go and has the opportunity will not need or ask advice. But I can say this in all sincerity: if I had it to do over again, I would not hesitate, even if I knew the difficulties and discomforts that lay ahead."[26]

Women are travelling in the North in increasing numbers for their own pleasure and satisfaction. They hike across Baffin Island, they canoe down the rivers of the Barrens, they go as tourists to a remote lodge on Bathurst Inlet, or they fly on chartered flights over Axel Heiberg. No longer are they hampered by the social mores and the awkward clothing of the nineteenth century. Technology has created materials which are light, warm and wind-proof, and is constantly improving camping equipment to make travel easier.

Why do women seek to travel in the North? Exploration is no longer a valid reason with detailed aerial survey maps available for all regions. But there are still the elements of self-testing and self-discovery that come with meeting a challenge. There is the sense of adventure of going into the relatively unknown, for the immensity of the North allows it to keep a sense of mystery. Most important of all is the need, deep inside of some—men and women alike—for direct contact with wilderness: the need to walk where there are no footprints; the need to hear silence broken only by the wind, a wolf call or the cry of a long-tailed jaeger; the need to gaze to the distant horizon across a land untouched by humanity. These reasons are as compelling today as they were for those women who broke trail for all who travel North in their footsteps.

ENDNOTES

1. For two pioneering studies of fur trade women see Sylvia Van Kirk. *Many Tender Ties* (Winnipeg 1980) and Jennifer S. H. Brown, *Strangers in Blood* (Vancouver 1980).

2. A survey of the *Canadian Geographical Journal* from 1930 to the present gave no evidence of women on scientific expeditions to the North before 1947, when Dr. Moira Dunbar began her study of Arctic ice. An expedition in 1950 included two women, unnamed, but by the 1960's women were regular expedition members.

3. Anna Jameson. *Diary of an Ennuyé* (London 1826).

4. Anna Jameson. *Winter Studies and Summer Rambles in Canada* (Toronto 1965) p. 67.

5. Ibid.

6. Ibid., p. 213.

7. Ibid., pp. 255-6.

8. James Taylor Dunn. "To Edmonton in 1892", *The Beaver*, June 1950, p. 3.

9. Grace Lee Nute. "Paris to Peel's River in 1892", *The Beaver*, March 1948, p. 19.

10. Ibid., p. 22.

11. Grace Lee Nute. "Down North in 1892", *The Beaver*, June 1948, P. 43. While the articles in *The Beaver* do not give actual sources for their quotations, they mention letters as some of the sources.

12. In 1908, Agnes Deans Cameron, (1863-1912) native of Victoria, teacher, school trustee, journalist, made the same journey (still an unusual feat for a woman) in the company of her niece and a typewriter. She used the experience to write *The New North—Being some account of a woman's journey through Arctic Canada*, and launched herself in a series of public lectures across Canada and the United States in praise of the North.

13. Dillon Wallace. *The Lure of Labrador* (Reprinted St. John's, Nfld. 1977).

14. Mina Benson Hubbard. *A Woman's way through unknown Labrador* (New York 1909).

15. It is known that at the time of the publication of her book, Mrs. Hubbard lectured in the United States, in Canada, and in England where she married Harold Thornton Ellis, the son of a distinguished British member of parliament. In an interview on the C.B.C., Jean Crane of Happy Valley, Labrador, daughter of one of the men on Mrs. Hubbard's expedition, gave a vivid hearsay account of her father's recollections of the trip. She also stated that Mrs. Hubbard returned once to Northern Ontario in the 1930's and made another canoe trip with George Elson, and that she died in England in her 80th year when she walked into the path of a moving train.

16. Florence A. Tasker. "A Woman through Husky-Land", *Field and Stream*, February 1908, p. 823, and March 1908, p. 943.

17. Obituary. *New York Times*, July 15, 1937, p. 19.

18. Florence A. Tasker. "A Woman Through Husky-Land", *Field and Stream*, March 1908, p. 943.

19. Clare Coltman Vyvyan. *Arctic Adventure* (London 1961).

20. C. C. Rogers. "On the Rat River", *Canadian Geographical Journal*, January 1931, p. 48.

21. Clare Coltman Vyvyan. *Arctic Adventure* (London 1961).

22. Lillian Alling's pilgrimage was noted in Calvin Rutstrum's *The New Way of the Wilderness* (New York 1958), p. 1. He may have read the article by W.W. Bride, "Lone Adventuress", *The Beaver*, September 1943, p. 15.

23. *Dawson News*. Saturday, October 6, 1928, p. 4.

24. Reference to Tom Manning is found in the preface to *Hudson's Bay Trader*, by Lord Tweedsmuir, son of Canada's Governor General, reprinted by Nelson Foster and Scott General, Toronto 1978, and in the same preface he mentions travelling to Cape Dorset on the Nascopie with Ella Wallace. He contributed an introduction to Mrs. Manning's book.

25. Ella Wallace Manning. *Igloo for the Night*. (Toronto 1946).

26. Ella Wallace Manning. "Explorer's Wife", *The Beaver*, September 1942, p. 15.

The Written Word on Canoeing and Canoe Tripping Before 1960

Bruce W. Hodgins

In Canada, recreational canoeing is as old as Confederation.[1] Just before the turn of the century as our cities grew, such canoeing expanded and diversified. So did literature about canoeing. That branch of paddling which involved wilderness voyages, especially to the near North, gained great popularity. Men and occasionally women went "tripping" for excitement or tranquility, for escape or physical health, for fellowship, personal discovery or renewal. Soon, eager parents and devoted leaders of youth movements would be sending children and young people on canoe trips for a variety of alleged therapeutic and educational purposes.

What were the means by which these people learned how to canoe and where to canoe? Important sources of knowledge in this learning process were the detailed canoe manuals and the instruction portions of the many descriptive canoe tripping books. Even if ignored by many trippers, this literature indicates the complex evolution of approved styles of paddling, canoe tripping, cooking and wilderness lore. Furthermore, an examination of the written word on canoeing and canoe tripping, varying as that word did over the decades to mid-century, reveals a great deal concerning the ideals and attitudes of the authors and, through them, the beliefs of those persons in society who were deemed to be potential canoeists. The written word on canoeing has thus become part of our social history and even our intellectual history. Certainly these books show us something about our past ethics, our changing attitude toward outdoor recreation, the wilderness and the North, and more than a little concerning evolving middle class views about nurturing our young people in a society of increasing urbanism, complication, differentiation, and feared community breakdown.

The canoeing books can be windows on our evolving past. They show, for example, an involvement with the rise and maturation of the liberal social gospel relating to Protestant Christianity. The books indicate a growing secularization, and they touch the issue of equality for women versus the special differentiated societal role of women. The writing often relates to the conservation movement, to multiple land use controversies, and to the tardy beginnings of an environmental ethic and an ecological historiography. They expose at times an intense theoretical argument over the proper balance of safety and of high-risk adventure. By implication, they assert the importance of "group living," with regard to both child upbringing and to adolescent growth and development. Was there a place, the experts asked, for the rugged wilderness canoe trip in the nurturing of responsible urban "young ladies?" The answers were varied.[2]

This sophisticated social concern is not to be found in all the early canoeing books nor in later volumes dedicated only to descriptions of routes and procedures. Nevertheless, such works were often thorough, detailed and, in their

141

own way, indicative of significantly changing attitudes towards our lifestyle, toward our leisure time and toward the natural environment.

Most adults who went on canoe trips during this long period did so either to find fellowship or fish, for high excitement in whitewater or still peace in earshot of the wail of the loon and the crack of the beaver's tail. Most were only dimly aware of the philosophical arguments over the value of—or the reasons for—going on recreational canoe trips, trips which nearly always involved some hardship, toil and at least mild deprivation. Fewer youths, even if they read the canoe manuals, knew or cared about such things. In a sense, all children who went tripping were at first "sent"; if they enjoyed the experience, they gradually took on the cause and insisted on repeating it annually. For some it then became a way of life to trip each year. Yet the experience generally went largely unexamined. It had its own reward and its own meaning.

The quantity of recreational canoe tripping increased until for adults it reached a zenith during the prosperous summers of the late twenties. The number of adults then canoeing would probably not be surpassed until tripping's recent unprecedented expansion in the last score or so years. Throughout all these decades many remote, colourful and lengthy canoeing expeditions of adventure did take place in the far North. Yet most recreational canoe trips were paddled not in the high latitudes, but in the relatively accessible near and middle North, that is, in the southern reaches of the Canadian Shield. They took place in places which had written trip reports describing their hazards and attractions.

Serving as hosts to most of these excursions were the many rivers and streams flowing into the Ottawa River, the several Muskoka Lakes and the other lakes and rivers of the eastern Georgian Bay watershed, and also the intricate waters of the upper Trent valley. After rail access in 1905, the headwaters country of the Temagami Forest,[3] despite being almost 500 kilometers from Toronto, became for canoeists both a principal destination and a base for somewhat longer expeditions over the divide to the James Bay watershed. For these routes, reliable reports have long existed.

Most of these trips into the near North lasted a fortnight or less, with participants coming mainly from the expanding middle classes of urban Central Canada and from those of adjacent upstate New York, Ohio and New England. These innumerable voyages, rather unsung and often unrecorded, were undertaken by both novices and experts. Apart from youth trips, only occasionally did the participants employ a guide.

To be able to undertake these voyages of personal discovery, the participant, unless he or she wished to be merely a supervised passenger, or "mojo," had to know at least something about how to paddle and how to camp. Trippers were often self-taught or taught by more experienced friends, and occasionally they learned their skills at canoe clubs. After 1920, the wilderness youth camp was frequently responsible for the first canoeing experiences. But if not directly, then indirectly, the written word on how to canoe played a major role.

*   *   *

By far the most significant and revealing of the early canoe trip manuals was *Camping and Canoeing* by James Edmund Jones (Toronto, Briggs, 1903) of the Aura Lee Club of Toronto. This book grew out of a series of wilderness canoe trips undertaken by the Club, beginning in 1897, when John D. Spence was the log writer. The purpose of the book was to help those keenly interested in becoming skilled canoe campers. It did not deal with basic paddling styles. It was designed to make tripping "smooth" but not "pampered", because "the men of the North are stalwart." Thus the earliest of major Canadian canoeing manuals links canoeing with our myth or our belief in our national nordicity and its ruggedness.

The best canoe, Jones argued, was the sixteen foot "Peterborough," the pure, varnished cedar strip vessel without a canvas cover. A basswood variation was cheaper and less brittle, but it became heavier much faster.[4] Naturally the best tripping canoes were "open." Tripping light was vital because of the portages, and portaging was central to canoe tripping. Ordinary canoes should always be carried upside down and singly; carrying by two persons was dangerous on the usually uneven terrain. When portaging one should use cord to make loops to fasten in the paddles, so that the blades could act as shoulder supports. Any ordinarily muscular person could flip the canoe onto his shoulders, but a shoulder cushion would help ease the strain on long carries. Big birchbark canoes accommodating the entire party were, however, still probably preferable to small canoes when travelling in the far North with a guide, he admitted.

Jones' equipment list stressed lightness and spaciousness, and he urged the use of woollen clothes because of wool's drying speed. Pack personal gear into a dunnage bag, and keep the weight under thirty pounds, he insisted. A cap, sweater and a light raincoat were essential. "Boots, not shoes, should be worn when wading, as otherwise the ankles suffer much"; many persons, but not Jones, now were even using "'beefs' — heavy waterproof foot-gear made of beefskin." Avoid rubber boots! Flannel nightshirts and stockings were great for sleeping. A boiled mixture of pine tar, castor oil and "penny royal" was the best bug repellant, but he also advocated a tent (floorless, so ground sheets were necessary) with something like sod cloth around the edges that could be packed down tightly to keep out the mosquitoes. Everything including bed roll and food should be carried in water proof bags, made of duck or a substitute. He recognized that people in 1903 brought along a lot of tinned goods, and because carrying them on one's back was almost certain, they needed to be carefully packed in a grain sack. Spoons and jackknives were also essential; table knives and forks were not. One should use three "graniteware pots" which would "nest," but he suggested that the frying pan handles should be removable.

His first aid kit stressed bandages, "court plaster" (an adhesive tape), "arnica and witch hazel, . . . some purgative medicine and medicine for summer complaints." "If you value your self respect, carry whisky or brandy only for use as a medicine in case of emergency. The man who desires stimulants while he is living a pure and natural life in the open air ought to be ashamed of himself." Furthermore, he noted, "it is illegal as well as immoral to treat or debauch an

Indian." Avoid lanterns and "such abominations"; candles give enough light.[5]

He appeared to use a leather tump to carry everything *except* the canoe. Taking camera equipment and packing it carefully were encouraged. Axes were to begin sharp and be kept sharp. Compasses and field glasses were also necessities.

Throughout, Jones stressed early rising, early-aways, taking time to study nature, and stopping early. Mouth organs were useful, and mixed with "reading aloud" to companions made the evenings enjoyable.

Jones was very cautious about, but not opposed to, the running of rapids, if first scouted. A heavily-laden Peterborough canoe, he argued, could not shoot rapids as well as a birch bark one.

His menu stressed simple basic cooking, with emphasis on bacon, ham, spiced beef, bologna sausage, beans, rice, sugar, tins of condensed milk, flour (pancakes were central), bread, raisins and rolled oats, and especially tea, but he mentioned tinned salmon, sardines, cornstarch, lemonade, root beer "tablets," lime juice and raspberry vinegar. "Evaporated potatoes" and "evaporated apples," apricots and peaches, were now making their appearance on the market.[6] If the trip was extra long a "Dutch oven" was a very nice addition for baking bread substitutes. He described a classic reflector oven made of tin, $19 \times 12 \times 9$ inches, and open at the fire side. Freshly caught fish was for Jones a delicious and an important food supplement.

More than a third of the book was dedicated to discussing ideal canoe routes in Ontario and adjacent Quebec. He warned the reader that water levels varied and conditions changed. Good maps, four miles to the inch, were then available for the areas he described. Twenty routes were detailed and more mentioned. Five were very tame. Two of these involved the Thousand Islands and the Rideau system, one the upper Trent watershed from Coboconk to Peterborough, one the Mattawa River, and one the Ottawa. Three were medium range trips involving Algonquin Park, one of these involved paddling up from Fenelon Falls to Canoe Lake in Algonquin, via the Gull; another from Huntsville and the Oxtongue to Tea and Canoe Lake; another from Canoe Lake to South River. The difficult run on the Petawawa River was carefully outlined, including a discussion of Rollaway Rapids and Horse Race Rapids. Muskoka trips included paddling down the Severn and up the "Musquash" to Bala and then down the Moon; up the Muskoka South Branch and down its North Branch; and down the Magnetewan from Burks Falls to Byng Inlet.

Many of the Northern Ontario routes were interlocked. The canoeist was guided by the book up the Ottawa to Lake Temiskaming and newly founded Haileybury, and to the mouth of the Montreal River, the "entrance to famous Temagamingue district."[7] Indeed, the Temagami district was emphasized, even though no railway approached Lake Temagami until 1905, two years after the book appeared. He described in detail five Temagami routes.[8] Similar details were given, courtesy of Thomas Stewart, of the long route from Kipawa, Quebec, upstream and over to Grand Lake Victoria in the Ottawa headwaters and over to Lac Barriere, "Kakebonga" and the Gatineau system and down to the city of

Ottawa. The route up the Whitefish River (from Lake Huron) via Panache and Long Lake (just outside Sudbury) and over to the Wanapitei River and the CPR was also described, as were the routes north from Temiskaming to Lac Abitibi, and south from Nipissing down the French River and back up the Wanapitei River.

Jones thus included, in 1903, the majority of recreational canoe routes used today in Central and North-eastern Ontario, exclusive of most of those in the James Bay watershed. Jones concluded by urging all trippers to keep logs and to remember the closing of the 1897 Aura Lee trip report: "Stronger, heartier and more helpful we go now about our daily work by reason of the brief bright experiences of a very pleasant trip." Work and "self forgetfulness" were stressed. More central were a

> manlier heart and tougher muscles, the glory of the sunset and the freshness of the dawn, the moonlit stillness of the Lake and the sweep of the river as it flushed and gurgled among the stones. A brief return to the evidences of nature; a brief renunciation of the artificiality of business and social life; a brief enjoyment of skies and lakes and rocks and pine trees at their freshest and best. Then, with firmer grip and steadier purpose, back to the work or the waiting, back to the rush and bustle of the city . . . .[9]

In 1918 the Committee on Canadian Standard Efficiency Training of the National Council of the YMCA of Canada produced the *Manual for Tuxis Boys*. Organized in Toronto in 1907 and nationally in 1912, Tuxis was a very popular alternative movement to Scouting in Canada immediately before, during and after World War I. It exemplified dynamic and athletic liberal Christian training and education. It was the main youth wing of the social gospel. Tuxis and its *Manual* were endorsed by the appropriate bodies of the Methodist, Anglican, Presbyterian, Congregational, and Baptist Convention churches. Its originator had been Taylor Statten, the National Boys' Work Secretary and his Committee of the National Council of the YMCAs.

The 446 page *Manual* contained a major chapter on "Campcraft," half of this devoted to canoeing. The entire chapter was written by the same James Edmund Jones, and the canoeing portion was in fact a youth-oriented, abbreviated version of his book of fifteen years earlier. The pinnacle of canoeing, he noted, would be a trip up the Lady Evelyn system:

> Some day you may have the glorious experience of climbing Maple Mountain, above Lady Evelyn Lake, Temagami, up the River Namabinnagasheshingue. In the joy of your youth and vigor you will revel not only in the beauties of that tiny trail, but will even glory in the portages, more than a score, which take from stretch to stretch, past falls and ledges varying from one foot to over one hundred feet in height, your camera ever busy to record the succession of scenes in unforgettable beauty.[10]

The focus of canoeing was thus the wilderness canoe trips. Jones described the cooperative one-and-a-half trip method (saving one mile in three) of carrying equipment over a portage, again disclosing that the canoe should be portaged singly. The use of tumps for carrying dunnage was stressed, noting that some men could carry 400 pounds in this way, but admitting that 100 pounds was a heavy load. Having the boys running rapids was quite acceptable, but one should be able to see the calm at the end before attempting a run, and generally should first check from the shore. "Remember, a back eddy affords a canoe a place of safety if threatened with being carried over a fall"—a profound piece of advice usually left out of early manuals. His suggested routes added several in New Brunswick and Northwest Ontario not in the 1903 book—but none was really described. Obtaining provincial township maps was recommended, and Mitchie Co. of Toronto was recommended as the source for trip maps of most of the routes, many of which had been initially supplied to Mitchie by the author. The food list was similar to that in the earlier book, but had the therapeutic note: "Prunes—get good ones and eat often. 'KYBO'."[11]

The junior version of Tuxis, the Trail Rangers, also had a *Manual*, published in 1922. This programme was designed for boys ages 12 to 14. Its campcraft section, also written by Jones, significantly did not contain a canoeing section.

In the twenties, both Tuxis and Trail Rangers declined after the YMCA turned them over to the Churches. Meanwhile, in 1921, three years after publishing the Tuxis Manual, Taylor Statten established Camp Ahmek for boys in the wilderness of Algonquin Park. James Edmund Jones, by then a magistrate, a noted hymnologist, and a singer of comical part-songs, was for several years a part of the Ahmek staff.[12]

Two famous American canoeing manuals, which underwent several reprints, were widely used in Canada as well as in the U.S. during the twenties and thirties: Robert E. Pinkerton, *The Canoe: Its Selection, Care and Use* [1914] (New York, Macmillan, 1923) and Elton Jessup, *The Boys' Book of Canoeing: All about canoe handling, paddling, poling, sailing, and camping* (New York, Dutton, 1926).

Pinkerton stressed that recently in eastern Canada and the U.S. the recreational use of the canoe was expanding "wonderfully," as people were "losing that great distrust" formerly associated with it. He wanted to further this by making "the safe use of the canoe more universal." Pinkerton distinguished among three basic kinds of sixteen or seventeen foot tripping canoes, the traditional and "becoming scarcer" birch bark, the canvas-covered canoe which when properly made was "the best craft" and in greatest use in the U.S., and the popular cedar or basswood variety "so commonly used in Canada." The pure wooden canoe was ribbed with hardwood, while the canvas covered canoe was both planked and ribbed with cedar.[13] He basically excluded consideration of the non-tripping, covered sailing canoes, but gave a careful analysis of the advantages of various shapes and sizes of recreational canoes and paddles.

Both bow and stern functions were carefully described. He emphasized in the bow both rudders and draws. He urged short fast strokes with stress on the early part of the delivery. He noted that the sternsman gradually learned that, "by ending his stroke with a slightly outward shove, and by twisting his paddle so that the inner edge of the blade leads to the other," he steered the boat without the loss of time and effort. Pinkerton claimed that the Indian, vitally concerned with keeping his weight low, sat on his heels in a canoe which had no seat at all; the American invented and popularized the comfortable but high canoe seat; and Canadians, who used canoes more frequently than Americans, "effected a compromise" by using a "board thwart about ten inches above the bottom and kneeling with his hips resting on the thwart." Pinkerton urged use of the American seat as if it were only a thwart and sitting only for periodic relaxations.[14]

Paddling alone had its special use and attraction but when doing so in an American canoe, he argued, one should face the stern and use the bow seat as a thwart. "In nearly all Canadian canoes the centre thwart is placed ten or twelve inches off of the center and is thus perfect for singling, bow first." He stressed that for the singler, both bow and stern strokes should be used, and he introduced what is now often called the "C" stroke.

"In lake travel," he added, "the canoeist probably meets the greatest test. Rapids may be dangerous, but they decide quickly." On a lake, "white-capped and squall-swept," a "fight" may go on for hours.

For the "skilled canoeman," on the other hand, "river work probably offers the greatest attraction." Poling was basically for upstream work, and the author gave it great emphasis. "Perhaps the first thing a canoeist should learn is the power of moving water." The city man could begin by watching the "faucet in his bathroom." In shooting rapids, "it must always be remembered that the canoe must move faster than the current if there is to be steerage way." If drifting at river speed, manoeuverability could only be affected by "reaching far up to the side and pulling the canoe over with sheer strength."

So, he appears not to have been aware of the "slower-than-the-current" approach. Thus the canoe must always be kept "straight with the current" and just to the side of the great rocks. Broaching broadside on a rock was the greatest danger. Changing channels required bow draws or rudders and hence severe heavy paddling only by the sternsman. In describing downstream lining, the author did not mention the desirability of keeping the upstream end high, by means of fastening the line with a harness system under that end. Nevertheless, he did say with regard to whitewater, that "no other form of canoeing offers so much sport to the man who has mastered his craft and himself."

If using a canvas-covered canoe, one must carry "Ambroid" or "white lead" to facilitate the repair of tears; this glue plus a little piece of cedar were also used to repair a major break in a wooden canoe.[15]

In portaging recreational canoes, Pinkerton noted that the centre thwart was unfortunately rarely in the midship of the canoe; hence one should employ paddles, looped in with cord, as shoulder braces. When having your own canoe built, insist on a thwart being placed exactly midship, he urged, thus creating three sides of support for the portage. Another "old" method of portaging canoes was by also carrying a pack on the shoulders, as a support system. "Some Indians employed a fourth method and carry the canoe by a headstrap or tumpline attached to a stiff pole lashed to the middle thwart and on top of the gunwales." Yokes were coming into use, he noted, to help carry canoes over 80 pounds. If your canoe was too heavy—say over 125 pounds—then and really only then have two people to carry it, using the gunwales near the ends as shoulder supports.[16]

The best way to pack gear was probably still by the traditional Canadian method of a tumpline and duffle bags, though for shorter trips "pack harness, pack basket or pack sacks" may be good alternatives. The packsack, a Minnesota product, was becoming more widely used each year. Until a few years earlier it was unknown except in Minnesota and western Ontario,[17] and it should have a short tumpline attached to it. Another carrying contrivance was the packbox, usually wooden, carried by a traditional tumpline. He noted only once that there might, in fact, be women, in the party, who would affect the choice of the preferred carrying method. Canoeists should travel "light but right," but such a phrase was admittedly quite variable in interpretation. If portaging on the trip was not extensive, then an inflatable air mattress, which would be over nine pounds in weight could be carried. Most canoeists used a bedroll of blankets, but a few now insisted upon a "contrivance" called a sleeping bag, weighing from 16 to 30 pounds and in which body moisture was trapped, unfortunately creating coldness and dampness. Very recently, new light llama wool or camel hair bags without waterproof coverings were solving these problems, but they should be used only with a tanalite ground sheet. One very new bag on the market had brought the weight down to $3\frac{1}{2}$ pounds but the cost for such an outfit was very high—$50. For most people, the four point HBC, twelve pound wool blanket was best. Using balsam boughs under the bed was also urged. Tents should be light and easily erected; the most common were the outside ridge pole type, using forest-cut poles. Many now had tanalite floors and were made of light cotton, not heavy canvas.

Cooking equipment was little different from that used earlier by Jones and included a tin and aluminum "folding baker," but the outfit now included forks and table knives and nesting pots of aluminum alloy, though the frying pan should be steel. "All food should be carried in muslin or light duck bags." He advocated carrying only a short 20 to 24 inch sheathed axe. Food was little different from Jones, though there was greater stress on dried fruit, trip-made biscuits and "sour dough bread." He put great emphasis on appetizing and nourishing meals.

Woollen clothes, including heavy socks and trousers were stressed. One should learn to take only "one pair of light underwear to be worn every day" with a different heavier set to sleep in. A lumberjack shirt was almost a necessity. While many canoeists advocated hunting boots and carried moccasins, he thought that the simple, light high cut "shoepack of Maine and Canada" were much better. Ankle-covering footwear was essential. For Pinkerton, tripping offered the challenge of overcoming physical obstacles.[18]

Whereas the Pinkerton book was designed for adult trippers, the 1926 Jessup volume was one of the first totally dedicated to "Boys" canoeing. Yet it was written without condescension. Jessup gave the same distinctions as Pinkerton between the all-wooden (basswood or cedar) and wood-canvas canoes, noting that while a Canadian is likely to stand by the all-wood boat with its greater speed yet freight capacity, the vast majority of Americans favoured the canvas-covered which could be easily repaired and was more capable of standing "hard knocks." He too denigrated the use of seats in American canoes. Concerning wooden canoes, the wide planked "rib and batten" variety was being replaced by the narrow ribbed "longitudinal strip," "no batten" variety. Furthermore, a third variety of canoe, the extra safe but heavy sponson, with its large air chamber on each side, had its devotees. For safety, he urged standing up only to pole or to get a better view of "treacherous water" ahead. He described the safe "over-and under" method of changing positions and the need to keep the weight low. Fortunately, a tipped canoe acted as a "life preserve," he noted. Even in heavy whitewater, though the canoe "twists, thumps, and pounds," one should normally try to hold on to it.[19] He described paddling a swamped canoe and, in detail, the technique for shaking out the water from a submerged canoe.

For the bow strokes, Jessup emphasized putting the shoulders into the task. Although he described a proper "J" stroke in the stern, the name was not yet used. Draws were portrayed, but so were what he called the difficult "throw stroke"—actually rigid bow rudders. Upstream travel was emphasized by carefully describing tracking, poling, and portaging—and again single carrying was preferred, either with paddles lashed in or by using a yoke.

Jessup warned about the dangers of white-water, but he did not shy away from what might lead sometimes to "a wet, battered and bone-chilling experience." Enthusiasts would consider running whitewater worthwhile even if it led occasionally to the loss of "a boat-load of camp duffle."[20] The danger from what are now called "sweepers" was described, as was that from broaching on a boulder. He advocated heading straight downstream, though he did suggest the use of a "side push," and he warned against ever getting broadside to the current. Claiming that one should never travel at the speed of the current, he noted that travelling slower than the current was "safer" but "not always as practicable."[21] Yet ferrying and back paddling, essential manoeuvres for slower-than-the-current travel, were not even mentioned.

His equipment included the light waterproof "balloon silk or tanalite" tent without floors, not the canvas variety. For sleeping gear, only blankets and groundsheets were noted, and balsam boughs were praised. Waterproof bags, aluminum pots and steel frying pans were extolled. Tump carrying, using duffles, was described, though "grub boxes" and especially Duluth packsacks with both tumps and shoulder straps were also endorsed.

Jessup expressed no philosophy, mysticism, or religious overtones. Meanwhile, in 1915, one year after the Pemberton volume first appeared, *Maclean's* magazine printed a fascinating descriptive article which strongly urged women to participate fully in the adventures of canoeing and canoe tripping. Mrs. Emerson Hough, the author, asserted that any healthy woman could carry enough provisions to last "a considerable voyage." The woman in that early age of female self-assertion was admonished to "first study the theory of the canoe. It is like any wild or thoroughbred creature—dangerous to the inexpert but docile to its master." Yet "any woman could get into the heart of these secrets." For long trips with cool nights, "wool underclothing" was advisable, "hot khaki and canvas, especially canvas shoes with rubber soles" would be useful and for outings "sportiness, snap and colour" including the jaunty hat were in order. Hough encouraged women to become active in this most adventuresome, participatory, amateur and individualistic sport, but she still held to a certain amount of role playing. "The glory of a girl is in her tane," she announced and warned that all but the few most experienced female canoeists should avoid all whitewater and canoe sailing, especially because they might have to return "to superintend something as prosaic as a dinner."

Mosquitoes could easily be tolerated, but women should use flydope made of petroleum and citronella oil, she noted, and avoid the odorous mixture of tar and oil affected by the male contingent."[22]

Canoeing, a short book written in 1931 for the Boy Scouts of America by Waldemar Van B. Claussen, followed the Jessup pattern. "Girls" were mentioned only once and that in the introduction. Claussen noted the bad reputation of canoes as dangerous vessels and urged the careful acquisition of skills, as their use nevertheless and happily expanded. He urged kneeling and always remaining with one's canoe after an upset. Besides the recovery techniques described by

Jessup, Claussen emphasized, with pictures, the canoe-over-canoe rescue. For the first time, several strokes appear with their current names—the proper "J" stroke, pushover, backwater, sweep etc. Use of the seats was again discouraged. The usual portaging styles were described, though flipping by the carrier was not recommended.

Only the "experienced" should attempt whitewater, Claussen argued. He, therefore, only briefly considered whitewater techniques.

*   *   *

The same year, 1931, a Canadian, Richard Garwood Lewis, edited and partly wrote *Small Watercraft: How to select, handle and care for all kinds of small watercraft* (Toronto, Fullerton, 1931). Here was a Canadian book with several chapters on various aspects of canoeing and with some portions written by or adapted from the writings of the aforementioned Claussen. The volume was thoroughly endorsed by the Boy Scouts' and Girl Guides' Associations of Canada. *Small Watercraft* was a high quality little volume with excellent canoeing pictures, all depicting adult males.

The pattern was that of Claussen. Lewis very carefully outlined his "J" stroke using the proper wrist turn, somewhat awkward and strange in its motion but with "a continuous curve without any pause between the pulling back at the beginning and the pushing out at the end."[23] For single paddling he advocated the "Hook Stroke," a motion rather like the current "Canadian" stroke. He even suggested kneeling slightly off centre when singling, especially in those canoes without a keel. "Draws" and "throws" were also described, as were "climbing in," "shaking out a submerged canoe" and "canoe-over-canoe rescue." His "don'ts" included standing up, abandoning the boat if it tipped, canoeing without a preserver or cushion, and putting your hands on the gunwales. He was very cautious but permissive about "running water," noting its superlative thrill. Kneeling in such conditions and always keeping the paddle in the water were mandatory, while deviating from a predetermined route was prohibited. Alarmingly, Lewis ordered everyone "to stick with the canoe," no matter how badly it might be battered against the rocks, "because enough wood" would hold to keep one afloat. Then he noted that "a canoe is steered by strokes of paddles and not with a rudder." "It makes no difference," he claimed, "whether it is moving slower, at the same speed or faster than the current," but the vessel had to be kept pointing "straight downstream."[24] He seemed to have no consciousness of ferrying or eddy turns. In heavy current with submerged rocks, slower than the current was best, and often side slipping was essential. Lewis' portaging stressed lashed paddles and head tump, and he mentioned yokes. Beginners could use the teepee method of getting the canoe on the shoulders, while the expert should master the flip. Double carrying was strongly discouraged. Three manufacturers were recommended: the Peterborough Canoe Co., established 1879; the Canadian Canoe Co., of Peterborough, established 1893; and the Chestnut Canoe Co., of Fredericton, established 1903. Canvas-covered canoes would take more "hard bumping without splitting but will not stand as much scraping, grinding and scratching." "Therefore for long rough trips in shallow rocky streams and for carrying heavy freight the all-wood canoe is sometimes preferred," though canvas leaked less.[25] His trip equipment list was quite basic. His food was standard—bacon, ham, hard tack, rolled oats, and beans etc., no cans except for butter—but included "evaporated" fruit. Major sections on flat water racing and sailing canoes affirm the continuing possibilities of those two different variations of the sport.

*   *   *

Coincident with Lewis, there appeared a whole series of small canoeing volumes put out by Canada's Department of the Interior (and after 1936 by its successor, Mines and Resources). Its *Canoeing in Canada* (1926) written by Ernest Voorhis, quoting Archibald Lampman, praised the rugged beauty of the Canadian Shield, and promoted recreational canoe tripping. The various versions of its *Canoe Trips in Canada* were most elaborate. The 1934 edition had 61 pages and outlined standard canoe trips in each of the nine provinces. The section on Quebec even included the Rupert-Marten-Rupert trip from Mistassini to Rupert House on James Bay. The Ontario section was the longest, with 41 routes briefly outlined. The southern trips featured Algonquin Park, the Rideau Lakes and the Magnetewan, Muskoka and French Rivers. The Northeastern Ontario routes stressed the Temagami District, the Mississagi River and across the divide onto the Mattagami, Abitibi, Missanabie and Albany to James Bay. The Northwestern Ontario routes focused on the upper Albany, the Ogoki, the English and Winnipeg Rivers, and the Quetico Park area. Instruction in these booklets was very sparse, but care was urged in running rapids. The warning, "never drift into swift water" and the command to "have plenty of steering way" indicate only a faster-than-the-current approach to rapids in the 1938 edition.

*   *   *

Archie Belaney, later known as Grey Owl, famous wildlife conservationist, wrote about canoe tripping in Northern Ontario in his books, especially in *Tales of an Empty Cabin* (Toronto, 1936). In that book he vividly described Biscotasing, north-west of Sudbury, around the time of the First World War, and various canoe trips from there on the Mississagi, the Spanish and beyond. Grey Owl had first learned to canoe on Lake Temagami, and Biscotasing lay just beyond the western edge of the huge Temagami Forest. The trips were undertaken by "Rivermen" who had worked first for the fur trade and then for the CPR construction projects:

> But the old-time canoemen are very few today. They are not needed any more; and the War got a lot of them. Some have just disappeared. And the happy, careless voyageurs, gay caballeros of the White Water who whooped and laughed and shouted their way down or up unmapped rivers, and thought their day would last for ever, have gone, vanished like the snows of last year, their long-dead fires all overgrown with moss and their footsteps hidden by the fallen leaves of many an Autumn. And Bisco, its contribu-

tion to the history of the Frontier nearly closed, lost in recollection, sits musing on those ancient granite hillsides, waiting quietly, and perhaps a little sadly, for the inevitable.[26]

"I too," he claimed, "was once a Riverman, the canoe my trade, such men my boon companions." For such a man, it was only necessary "that he be able to cook his own meals, keep his canoe right side up in any water, carry a man's load, make a good camp under any circumstances, get around without becoming lost, and otherwise show that he can take care of himself and so not become a charge on the community or the object of a search party, or turn up drowned or frozen to death."[27]

Grey Owl's writing style is quick and vivid, not instructional. But we do catch his canoeing method:

So speed, speed, speed, grip the canoe ribs with your knees, drive those paddles deep, throw your weight onto them, click them on those gunnels twenty-five strokes to the minute; spurn that water in gurgling eddies behind you, bend those backs, and drive! Sternsmen, keep your eyes on the far objective, far off in the blue distance, and take your proper allowance for a side-wind don't make leeway like a greenhorn! Thus, eyes fixed ahead, watchful of everything, breath coming deeply, evenly, backs swinging freely from the hips, paddles dipping and flashing, we drive her—fifty miles a day or bust.[28]

He describes lake country. Portaging was marked by the "Pattering of moccasined feet on the narrow trail, as men trot with their canoes, one to a man or step easily along under their loads." They carried no "potatoes, eggs, caviare, nor canned lobster":

But we have flour, salt and baking powder with which to make bannock, a kind of large scone cooked over hot coals; this delicacy is of Scotch origin, having been introduced by the Hudson Bay people who were largely Scotsmen. It is also known as Indian loaf. We also have tea, sugar, white beans, which latter have a very high nutrient value, a few dried apples, and soap, matches and tobacco.[29]

On the Mississagi River itself whitewater was central. The canoes were all wood and handled well—but were driven fast:

Part of the load is desembarked at the portage, as we will run with half loads, taking only stuff that can stand a wetting. For this is a tough spot, and we will ship water, inevitably. We go to centre of the stream again, set the canoes at the proper angle for take-off. The canoes seem to leap suddenly ahead, and one after another, with a wild howling hurrah, we are into the thick of it. Huge combers, any one of which would swamp a canoe, stand reared and birling terrifically beside us, close enough to touch. The backlash from one of these smashes against the bows and we are slashed in the face by what seems to be a ton of water; we are soaked to the skin, blinded by spray—on one side is a solid wall of water, there is a thunderous roar which envelopes us like it was a tunnel, a last flying leap and we are in the still pool below, safe, wet, and thrilled to the bone. It was a short, wicked pitch, and we have saved two loads on the portage, so it paid us will to run; and for you, I think the experience was worth the wetting. We go ashore, unload and empty out, carry the remaining stuff over the portage, load up and are away again—happy with a great, new-found sense of self-reliance, and looking for more thrills. There are plenty.[30]

He cautioned everyone about the first half mile of the Twenty Mile Rapids on the lower Mississagi. "The portage is on the left. Take it, you may need it. We won't, but don't let that bother you. You only live once."

> The current, smooth as oil, deep and swift, carries us in its irrestible suction towards the dark V of deep water that marks the channel, and the canoes, driven a little faster than the current to gain steerage-way, are worked almost broadside on into this and at railroad speed, one after another, are flung like chips into this raging inferno of water—God.... To fail means death. The bowsmen throw themselves forward, sideways, backward, the sternsmen sometimes standing, sometimes crouching in the bottom, reaching forward or behind, the paddles of both cutting the water like knives, their blades beneath the surface for half-a-dozen strokes.[31]

In 1938 Grey Owl died. With the immediate revelation of his English origins and thus the fact that he had in a sense perpetuated a gigantic hoax, his literary reputation was severely tarnished. For more than twenty years his writings and movies went into eclipse. Yet in so many ways Grey Owl had captured the spirit of contemporary canoe tripping, especially for Northeastern Ontario and Northwestern Quebec. With his conservationist ethic he had deeply influenced many of today's older adult trippers.

Meanwhile Ronald H. Perry was becoming the chief recreational canoeing authority for most youth camping. Back in 1917, Taylor Statten had made his acquaintance with Ron Perry, a young lad attending an Ontario Boys Conference.[32] Thus began a very long association which would result in the establishment of Perry as the major author and publicist of the new Algonquin Park canoeing style, one oriented toward children and youths, in considerable conflict with the earlier advocacy of Lewis and the continuing tradition of Keewaydin[33]

and other Lake Temagami youth camps. Taylor Statten established Camp Ahmek on Canoe Lake in 1921, and in 1923 Perry joined its counselling staff and taught canoeing. Perry, off summer, became the master in charge of the Junior School at Pickering College and later headmaster at Ashbury College in Ottawa. By the late fifties he left Ahmek to operate Camp Kawabi. In 1948, Ron Perry first published the sixty page *The Canoe and You* (Toronto, Dent). The book contained a forward by Taylor Statten. Very quickly it became a best seller in the Ontario youth camp circuit, becoming *the* authority. The Lewis volume seems to have lost all influence. Perry's book secured endorsement by the Canadian Red Cross, the Canadian Camping Association, the National Camp Training Centre (where Perry was then Associate Director), and the Training Department of the Boy Scouts of Canada.[34] In his preface Perry lamented how little the summer resorts had done for canoeing, and claimed how much youth camps, with their focus on teaching, had accomplished.

The Canoe and You was a short, authoritative, clear enunciation of polished basic canoeing, aesthetically presented, containing very helpful line drawings, with almost all figures looking like healthy male teenagers (except one showing a young girl and one a stylized Indian brave). Thousands of young people in Ontario and beyond grew up directly or indirectly on its wisdom. Linked with the teaching of Algonquin canoeists such as Omer Stringer, Perry's principles still form the basis of much of Algonquin Park, Haliburton and Muskoka youth camp canoeing.

Following a very brief survey of the history of the canoe, Perry mentioned quite negatively the new style aluminum, plywood, sectional and plastic varieties. After devoting only one paragraph to the traditional Canadian all-wooden model with its problem of increasing weight from moisture absorption but its strength when bashed by rocks, he focused on his beloved canvas-covered variety, especially the sixteen footer, then by far the most popular in both the U.S. and Canada. The transition was complete. The Canadian distinctiveness was gone. Safety was paramount.

Safety was packaged in six "DON'TS," which included "Don't stand up in a canoe," "Don't shoot rapids," and "Don't abandon the canoe if you upset."[35] Here were the three items which he and his disciples considered axiomatic and obvious, which earlier manuals did not usually assert, and which nearly all present day authorities would reject. Perry did allow that the shooting of rapids by the most experienced adults might perhaps be attempted, but "never by amateurs or young people." He warned of the most serious consequences.

Prior swimming skills were essential for all canoeing, he asserted, and the procedures to follow after an upset were carefully explained, along with "shaking out" in deep water, climbing in, paddling a submerged canoe, canoe-over-canoe rescue, and rescuing a person from the water. If weather was rough or if the paddler could not shake out the water, he was still to remain permanently with his buoyant canoe, no matter how long, until he drifted to shore or was rescued by a boat or a helicopter. Apparently Perry did not foresee drifting over a falls or perishing from exposure. The threat of cold water is nowhere even considered. Yet for most of the summer, even in the middle North, hypothermia is a serious threat. Furthermore, life jackets played absolutely no role in Perry's canoeing. The canoe itself served as the life jacket.

The core of the book is devoted to the description of proper paddling style and to bow and stern strokes—including the "J", draw, sweep, backwater, pushaway, sculling, "Indian," bow draw, cross bow draw, bow rudder, and cross bow rudder. The proper "J" is carefully explained, allowing contact with the gunwale; the faulty push-rudder variety is ridiculed and christened the "Goon stroke," typical of "summer resorters" and four out of five "self-taught paddlers." Paddling both in the kneeling position, "knees wide apart," and "sitting on the heels" are explained.[36] While reviewers praised the book, it was noted that his dogmatism would be challenged along with his focus on "DON'TS" and his prohibition of ever sitting on the seats. In 1948 the book sold 716 copies.[37]

Perry concluded his book with a suggested set of "canoeing standards." The deep-water "shake-out" was reserved for Master Canoeist candidates and was "not required for girls."[38] For this very top award, the candidate only had to have tripped 100 miles! Slightly modified these standards were soon accepted by dozens of youth camps. They also formed the basis both for the first canoe instructors' course in 1954 (led that year by Professor Kirk Whipper on Toronto Island for the Ontario Camping Association) and also the more elaborate set of standards which the OCA itself temporarily adopted.[39]

In 1953 Perry published a popular supplementary volume entitled *Canoe Trip Camping* (Toronto, Dent). In it he described the food lists, menus and equipment requirements which he had been sorting out since the early thirties.[40] In the foreword to this volume, Perry's friend Mark Robinson, who for 29 years had been ranger and then superintendent of Algonquin Park, wrongly claimed that the volume was the "first publication" ever to select "the canoe trip as a special type of camping." In this book Perry again argued that the summer camp was "the training centre for canoe trip camping." Though tourists generally were attracted to the unsurpassed charms of Canada, the youth camp had "taken on the job of developing better citizens," and canoe tripping was an integral part of this. *Canoe Trip Camping* stressed good, sound, mature and thoughtful leadership rather than merely "how to" information. For this, knowledge of safety procedures, training in first aid, and skills in swimming were essential. His excellent chapter on first aid acknowledged his indebtedness to Dr. Harry Ebbs. Trip leaders and their participants were admonished to "avoid" shooting rapids or "wearing boots" in canoes.[41] Even seventeen year old boys should not be allowed to carry loads over 50 pounds—and girls none over 40 pounds.

In portaging techniques Perry noted the "popular variation" of using a head tump to help with the carry, but he did not, as earlier writers had, deprecate the double carry. The campcraft section stressed basic axemanship. His cooking systems included the longitudinal fire with green logs serving as a grill; the "double crane" style in which pots were hung from various notched sticks of diverse lengths suspended by means of a short branch-hook on each stick, looped over a long horizontal pole held in place by two forked upright stakes; and the single pot style, whereby the pot is looped directly over a sloping pole secured with stone counter weights and a forked fulcrum stick. A reflector oven was mentioned only once as a possible supplementary piece of equipment, but neither its appearance nor use were described.[42] Food menus were wholesome and basic, and he introduced dehydrated vegetables, especially carrots and apple flakes, and prepackaged desserts. Nevertheless, there was a fairly heavy concentration on canned goods. In tenting, silk was preferred over canvas, because of the former's durability, light weight and waterproof retention. Most of his tents had floors. Sleeping bags were recommended, as were woollen clothes. Latrines and little garbage pits were recommended for "permanent or semi-permanent camps," but not for overnight stands when, nevertheless, "campers must be told the hygenic and scenic importance of covering refuse," and should be made to "adhere to a distance rule when answering the call of nature."[43]

Throughout, Perry emphasized the central role of the experienced, well-equipped summer youth camp in establishing good canoe tripping practices. In fact, he implied that there was little place for recreational canoe tripping outside the organized camp framework, though he did mention adult tripping. "The change from dependence on modern conveniences to a reliance on one's skill and judgement seems to sharpen the appreciation for all the little, but important things of life—food tastes better, clothes are more comfortable, nature takes on a new meaning and living becomes exhilarating."[44]

Although Perry's emphasis was clearly on boys' canoeing, he did recognize the existence of girls' camps. Mary G. Hamilton, in *The Call of Algonquin: a Biography of a Summer Camp* (Toronto, Ryerson, 1958), described a quality girls' camp in the Perry mould. Today the camp would certainly be regarded as self-consciously sexist. In 1925 Hamilton had founded Tanamakoon in Algonquin Park, and she directed it until 1953. Previously, she had been a physical education teacher at the Margaret Eaton School and from 1926 its Principal. In 1924 she explored Algonquin looking for a permanent camp site. She noted in her book that Wapomeo, Taylor Statten's girls' camp, had been established that same year in the Park, that Northway Lodge, an American girls' camp on Cache Lake, had been founded by Fannie Case of Rochester as early as 1906, making it the oldest girls' camp on record in Canada. She admitted that her 1924 trip had been her first experience in carrying a canoe. Then and there she resolved that at her camp "no one but a guide accustomed to the task would carry one," definitely not a girl, and that she would strive for feather-weight equipment.[45]

Most of the girls at Tanamakoon, if they could swim, went on a short canoe trip, but not before July 15 because of the insects. Normally there were eight campers, one female CIT, one female counsellor, and two male guides, with four canoes—occasionally four campers, one counsellor and one male guide. The male guides "portaged the canoes and extra packs," were "responsible for the site, tent and fires."[46] Tanamakoon tripping under Mary Hamilton suited what was becoming the Perry style.

Indeed, by the mid-fifties, at least as far as the written word was concerned, the impact of Ron Perry and his two books represented a major shift in focus away from a canoe tripping style which had emphasized wilderness, high adventure and physical challenge, especially for adults and maturing youths. They indicate a strong tendency toward protected canoeing and cautious canoe tripping which emphasized group dynamics and was especially designed for children and youths, not adults.

A successful literary counter offensive would eventually come, led first in the sixties by Eric Morse and soon including Heb Evans, Ned Franks, J. W. Davidson, John Rugge, Bill Mason and others. It would take some time before this new wave was ascendant. By then, film and video tape would play a role along side the written word.[47]

*   *   *

It was 1956 before the American Red Cross produced its first canoe manual, simply called *Canoeing*. Canoeing had been a small part of its National Aquatic Schools since the early twenties and a major part since 1948. For some reason, however, the book did not seem to exercise much influence in Ontario or Quebec tripping circles, not even where the Canadian Red Cross was powerful. *Canoeing* was a very thorough and sophisticated volume, and it did not shy away from whitewater. It was not in the Perry mold. Yet even in whitewater, only one of the canoeists in the many hundreds of pictures wore a life vest. Three whitewater speeds were accepted. In "moderate water" the speed of the current was seen as appropriate. But heavy, turbulent water dictated a speed much slower than the current to prevent the canoe from burying into large waves and to give the needed time to observe this water and select the best course. Faster than the current was only wise in very easy moderate, familiar rapids. Yet the canoe was to be held for all three methods "in line with the current." If upset, one was to hold on to the craft upstream, the book instructed. Furthermore, the swimmer was told to keep his feet up and float down on his back and to let go of the canoe if the going was too "turbulent."[48] Less than two pages were, however, given over to backpaddling techniques in white water. Ferrying and eddying out were not mentioned, nor was leaning downstream. Of the hundreds of good pictures printed in the book, in only one, a war canoe race, did women appear.[49] Although a significant book in the U.S., it had little Canadian impact. Canoeing seemed to be for children and their leaders, and Perry seemed to reign supreme, at least outside of Temagami. The adult world awaited the written word from Eric Morse and his voyageurs.

*   *   *

Through the meanderings of this stream-like story of our canoeing literature runs the silhouetted form of the tiny little open vessel itself. It remains a most appropriate symbol for historic Canada at work and play. The craft thrusts and glides over quiet ponds, turbulent lakes and roaring rivers and is flipped and hauled through dense forest portages.[50]

Since the 1880s, the canoe trip has been an important part of our recreational history. As the manuals and the books on canoe routes indicate, its style and technique often changed. But it always involved a voyage into the wilderness, and a re-entry into the urban world. The late Prof. W. L. Morton, himself a skilled canoeist, repeatedly argued that "this alternate penetration of the wilderness and return to civilization is the basic rhythm of Canadian life."[51]

Historically the recreational canoe trip and the written word about it seem to have united us mystically with the nordicity of our national past. Symbolically, even psychologically and spiritually, many trippers associated themselves with the heroic quest journeys of epic literature and mythology. The more reflective came gradually to recognize, however, that "the exploration of the wilderness becomes a voyage into the interior of the self."[52] Wilderness and the canoe thus have been and remain, not a denial of sophisticated culture, but an integral part of it.[53] The canoeing books are thus an important part of our national literature.

ENDNOTES

1. See especially Jamie Benidickson "Recreational Canoeing in Ontario Before the First World War," in *Canadian Journal of History of Sport and Physical Education*, IX (Dec. 1978), pp. 41-57; and his "Paddling for Pleasure: Recreational Canoeing as a Canadian Way of Life," in John S. Marsh and Geoffrey Wall, eds. *Recreational Land Use: Perspectives on its Evolution in Canada*. Note also John Bonfitto, "The Golden Times," and "The Dark Ages," *Canoe*, Sept. 1980 and Feb. 1981 and Eric Evans, "Debunking the 'Golden Age'," *Canoe*, June 1982; and C.E.S. Franks, "White Water Canoeing as an aspect of Canadian Socio-Economic History" and "The Revival," in his *The Canoe and White Water* (Toronto, 1977), pp. 53-68.

2. Note Diana Pederson, "On the Trail of the Great Quest: the YMCA and the Launching of the Canadian Girls in Training, 1919-1921," paper presented to the Canadian Historical Association in Ottawa, June 1982; and David MacLeod, "A Live Vaccine: the YMCA and Male Adolescence in the United States and Canada, 1870-1920," in *Histoire Sociale/Social History*, XI (May, 1978), 5-25.

3. See especially Bruce Hodgins and Jamie Benidickson, "Resource Management Conflict in the Temagami Forest, 1898-1914," *Historical Papers 1978* (Canadian Historical Association, Ottawa, 1979), and the latter's "Temagami and the Northern Ontario Tourist Frontier," *Laurentian University Review*, XI (February, 1979), pp. 43-69. Note also the chapter on Temagami by the author in this volume.

4. Jones, pp. 5-9. John Marsh has shown this author an earlier American Canoe Manual first published in 1885: C. Bowyer Vaux, *Canoe Handling* (3rd ed. New York, Forest and Stream, 1901). Aimed at an American audience, it stressed closed-boat canoe sailing and double-blade paddling; it has only one short paragraph on rapids and only a brief discussion of the "Canadian canoe," propelled by a single blade paddle. American sources also frequently refer to a classic work on outdoor living by Horace Kephart entitled *Camping and Woodcraft* (New York, 1917).

5. Ibid., pp. 25-41.

6. Ibid., pp. 61-88.

7. Ibid., p. 119.

8. Ibid., pp. 132 and 141-43.

9. Ibid., pp. 149-50.

10. *Manual of Tuxis Boys*, p. 191.

11. Ibid., p. 187.

12. C.A.M. Edwards, *Taylor Statten: A Biography* (Toronto, 1960), pp. 85-119. For a critical analysis of the Tuxis movement etc., see David MacLeod, "A Live Vaccine: the YMCA and Male Adolescence in the United States and Canada, 1870-1920," in *Histoire Sociale/Social History* XI (May, 1978), pp. 5-25.

13. Pinkerton, pp. 14-18.

14. Ibid., pp. 52-59.

15. Ibid., pp. 65-96.

16. Ibid., pp. 99-102.

17. Ibid., p. 111.

18. Ibid., pp. 123-162.

19. Jessup, p. 37, earlier quotations, pp. 8-35.

20. Ibid., p. 95.

21. Ibid., p. 110.

22. "Canoeing for Girls" August, 1915. The byline implies that the article was a reprint from the *Ladies Home Journal*.

23. Lewis, p. 21. 24. Ibid., p. 20-26.

25. Ibid., p. 36.

26. Grey Owl, p. 171.

27. Ibid., pp. 172-73.

28. Ibid., pp. 182-83.

29. Ibid., pp. 184-86.

30. Ibid., pp. 206-207.

31. Ibid., pp. 219-220.

32. Edwards, *Taylor Statten*, p. 56.

33. See, for example, Brian Back, *The Keewaydin Way: A Portrait: 1896-1983* (Temagami 1983). Note also the works of Heb Evans noted below and the chapter in this book by the current author, on Temagami-based canoe trips.

34. Dust jacket of the *Canoe and You*. Also note, in the Trent University Archives, the Ron Perry Papers, Review in the *Scout Leader*, December 1948. In 1982 the Perry Papers and the Perry Collection were donated to the Trent Archives (to be linked with Ontario Camping Association Papers) through the efforts of Dr. Harry Ebbs (son-in-law of Taylor Statten) who joined the Ahmek staff one year after Ron Perry, that is in 1924.

35. Perry, *Canoe and You*, p. 31.

36. Ibid., pp. 24-28.

37. Perry Papers, clipping of Sidney Cooper's review in the *Beaver* of June 1949, and receipts from the publisher.

38. Perry, *Canoe and You*, p. 61.

39. Perry, *Canoeing for Beginners* (New York, Toronto, Associated Press and Welch). In the seventies, the OCA canoe standards were folded into the first drafts of those being prepared by the Canadian Recreational Canoeing Association.

40. As the Perry Papers make clear.

41. Perry, *Canoe Trip Camping*, pp. 133-170.

42. Ibid., pp. 22, 32-35, and 77.

43. Ibid., p. 86.

44. Ibid., p. 119.

45. Hamilton, p. 11. She also noted that the private Camp Pathfinder and most other boys' camps in Algonquin were all American.

46. Ibid.

47. Ibid., p. 132.

48. G. Heberton Evans, *Canoeing Wilderness Waters* (New York: Barnes, 1976; for years Evans was the chief "Bay Tripper" for Keewaydin on Lake Temagami); C. E. S. Franks, *The Canoe and White Water*, (Toronto, UTP, 1977); James West Davidson and John Rugge, *The Complete Wilderness Paddler* (New York, Knopf, 1976), and Bill Mason, *Path of the Paddle: an Illustrated Guide to the Art of Canoeing* (Toronto, Van Nostrand and Reinhold, 1980). This is not to imply that rugged adult tripping itself ceased, as the accounts of Blair Fraser and the writings of men such as Sigurd F. Olson and Eric Morse attest. See for example, Olson, *The Lonely Land* (New York, Knopf, 1961) and Morse, *Fur Trade Canoe Routes of Canada: Then and Now* (Ottawa, 1969), plus Morse's many articles in the *Canadian Geographic* and elsewhere.

49. *Canoeing* (1956), pp.358-60.

50. Ibid., p. 304.

51. *The Canadian Identity* (Toronto, UTP, 1961), p. 5.

52. William James, "The Canoe Trip as Religious Quest," in *Sciences Religieuses/Studies in Religion*, 10 (Spring 1981), pp.151-66, quotation p. 159; see also a revised version in this volume. For an extended analysis of another expression of the role of the quest journey in our mythology see Keith Walden, *Visions of Order: The Canadian Mounties in Symbol and Myth* (Toronto, Butterworths, 1982), especially pp. 101-17 which deal with the Mounties' trek west. Both James and Walden make great use of Joseph Campbell *The Hero with a Thousand Faces* (New York, Meridian, 1956).

53. John Wadland, "Wilderness and Culture," *Park News*, 19 (Summer, 1982), pp. 12-13; see also a revised version in this volume.

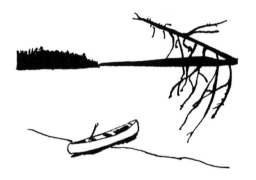

"Idleness, Water and a Canoe": Canadian Recreational Paddling Between the Wars

Jamie Benidickson

"The ingredients of a holiday in Canada," Howe Martyn informed readers of the *Queen's Quarterly* in the Spring of 1940, "are idleness, water and a canoe."[1] The statement reflects the important place that Canada's traditional watercraft had secured in summer recreation after the decline of the fur trade. Although the origins of Canadian recreational canoeing may be traced from at least the mid-nineteenth century, the focus here is on the interwar years, the two decades immediately preceding Howe Martyn's remark. The period spanning the 1920s and 1930s was a transitional era of gradual but noticeable development in all aspects of recreational canoeing.

Before the First World War, recreational canoeing in Canada encompassed a wide range of activities and pastimes.[2] Fishermen and hunters used the canoe in conjunction with their sporting pleasures. After the 1870s, organized canoe clubs featured canoe sailing, races and regattas. Wilderness canoe travel enjoyed considerable popularity, often associated with northern resort lodges or the developing youth camps of the early twentieth century.* When holiday paddling revived during the 1920s and 1930s after an interlude occasioned by the war, it was the wilderness and camping tradition which continued to attract interest and participation. With a few notable exceptions, the organized canoe club was of limited significance, although flatwater racing enjoyed a certain prominence associated to some degree with the success of Francis Amyot in the 1936 Berlin Olympics. Canoe sailing had lost much of its earlier appeal and the role of the canoe in fishing and hunting was somewhat diminished by the advent of new forms of transportation offering access to favoured locations remote from congested cities.

For the harried urban dweller, recreational canoeing's promise of quiet enjoyment of the natural world persisted through the 1920s and 1930s. The writing of Grey Owl and the work of Tom Thomson and other artists undoubtedly contributed to this continued trend, perhaps enhancing appreciation of the landscape itself and the natural environment as part of the nation's heritage. Commercial interests — notably the railways — continued to promote canoe vacations but were now actively joined in this effort by the federal government, whose range of publicity material is truly remarkable. Considerable diversification in canoe design and style occurred in the interwar years, but the most

---

* See Bruce Hodgins' article, "The Lure of the Temagami-Based Canoe Trip", elsewhere in this volume.

notable features of the period, in relation to canoe building, were the virtual displacement of the all-wood canoe by the wood and canvas model and the consolidation of a major part of the Canadian canoe manufacturing industry. Instructional materials on canoeing and campcraft together with improvements in equipment and outfitting arrangements probably all played a role in stimulating the interest in canoe holidays that Howe Martyn described.

*   *   *

The flourishing interest in Canadian landscape painting associated with Tom Thomson and the Group of Seven enhanced the significance of the canoe as an important symbol and image of Canadian life. Direct representations of the canoe, such as J. E. H. MacDonald's painting of "The Beaver Dam," or "The Red Canoe," were infrequent — but the canoe's role in the evolution of the new Canadian style of art was widely acknowledged.[3] Tom Thomson's life — and his death in Canoe Lake in July, 1917 — were central.

"Tom Thomson and Algonquin Park are virtually synonymous from 1913 until Thomson's untimely death in 1917," J. Russel Harper recently wrote, and this impression is confirmed by writings on the artist's life and work which appeared shortly after his death and continued into the 1930s and 1940s.[4] The titles of these volumes often emphasized the linkage of the artist to the landscape and the importance of the canoe in Thomson's life. Blodwen Davies produced *Paddle and Palatte: The Story of Tom Thomson* (Ryerson, 1930), and in *A Study of Tom Thomson: The Story of a Man Who Looked for Beauty and Truth in the Wilderness* (Ryerson, 1937) the artist "was celebrated as a canoeman, although to be a competent canoeman is no distinction in Canada where a canoe constitutes the only means of transportation over such large areas."[5] The cairn in his memory at Canoe Lake served as a continuing reminder of the links between the Canadian landscape, artists, and the canoe.

For A. Y. Jackson, too, the canoe provided access to the scenery depicted in so many well-known paintings and sketches. Jackson remarked in his autobiography, that "camping and canoeing have been my favourite pastimes and though I never was an expert like Thomson or MacIver, I managed to get around."[6] Many of Jackson's sketching trips among the Georgian Bay islands were solo expeditions, but he canoed as well with Dr. James M. MacCallum, "patron saint to the Group of Seven" and McCallum's sons. The many other canoeing companions Jackson mentions included Barker Fairley of the University of Toronto, also an artist of great accomplishment. Jackson's trips were often in the Georgian Bay and Muskoka district, but the 1922 expedition down the well-known Mississagi route from Biscotasing was undertaken because of MacCallum's wish to follow Tom Thomson's earlier travels.[7]

The literary career of another prominent paddler was also closely associated with the Mississagi, for in 1912 Archie Belaney (Grey Owl) worked as a ranger for the Ontario Department of Lands and Forests in the Mississauga Forest Reserve. There he met the characters who were to appear years later as "The

Rivermen" in *Tales of an Empty Cabin*. These men, who earned their livings on the water, were professional rather than recreational canoeists — the twentieth century descendants of the voyageurs:

> How I loved them, with their trousers baggy at the knees from long hours, and days, and months of kneeling — no, not in prayer, but in a canoe . . . . How I loved them for their sharp, barbed, gritty humour, their unparalleled skill in profanity, their easy-going generosity. For these were no kitchen-garden woodsmen or carpet knights, but hard-bitten bush-wackers, nurtured in hardship, who lived precariously by first principles, and who at no time called a shovel an agricultural implement . . . .
>
> White man, red-skin and half-breed, they belonged to that fraternity of freemen of the earth whose creed it is that all men are born equal, and that it is up to a man to stay that way. For in this society, the manner of a man's speech, where he comes from, his religion or even his name are matters of small moment and are nobody's business but his own.[8]

Perhaps not models towards which the urban recreational paddler would naturally aspire, "the rivermen" nevertheless played a role in sustaining the canoeing tradition in Canadian life. Grey Owl's work, from the 1931 publication of his first book, *Men of the Last Frontier*, greatly contributed to popular awareness of the historic and continuing importance of the canoe as an integral feature of the central Canadian landscape. The narrative emphasis on paddling as the skill that made the wilderness accessible was reinforced by numerous photographs of rivermen in the rapids or on a portage. The same message was transmitted to a wider audience through Grey Owl's film work, such as the 1937 production based on material from *Tales of an Empty Cabin*.[9]

The relationship between canoeing and artistic or literary activity during the interwar era supplemented, rather than replaced, the longstanding attractions of recreational paddling. Thus, during the 1920s and 1930s canoeing continued to offer many forms of personal satisfaction. Canoeists would explain their enthusiasm for recreational paddling by referring to the thrill of challenge and adventure, or the refinement of skills and the exercise of ingenuity, or by reflecting on a sense of comradeship with fellow paddlers. Others might speak of their feelings of spiritual, mental or psychological well-being derived from the experience of the outdoors and the natural environment:

> The carefree, take-it-easy life on a Canadian canoe trip is a splendid tonic for worn nerves and minds numbed by cares of office, mart or study.[10]

Such sentiments were openly expressed from the 1880s onward and are still heard today.[11] Despite this overall similarity, the interwar years may be distinguished for a slight shift suggested by an apparent decline in emphasis on the canoe trip as an activity for fishermen, hunters and sportsmen, and a greater tendency to regard canoeing as a means of seeing nature, contemplating scenery and experiencing the landscape. From these "passive" pleasures of recreational canoeing, which focus on the experience of canoeing for its own sake and the appreciation of landscape in art and photography, it is possible to discern the emergence of a tradition of autonomy in recreational paddling. That is, it is now possible to see the popular canoeing holiday as pleasurable and worthwhile itself, apart from any incidental benefit that could result from character development, physical fitness, and improvement that would aid one in the urban struggle, and apart from the triumph over nature represented by the fisherman's "string of beauties" or the hunter's trophy.

As early as 1883 *The American Canoeist* speculated that "photography is such a delightful accompaniment to canoeing that it will probably become a common amusement among our brothers of the paddle";[12] but turn-of-the-century sportsmen's magazines such as *Field and Stream*, *Forest and Outdoors* or *Rod and Gun* provide little evidence of a trend in that direction. Instead, canoeing stories from these periodicals are generally oriented toward the trials and successes of the hunter and fisherman. By the 1920s, a modest shift had taken place and the camera appeared to be gaining acceptance as a means of capturing game. A party of canoeists in the Georgian Bay district reported an encounter with a deer:

> We had soon a sight worth remembering and it had been more fun shooting that deer with a camera than a rifle, as we had stalked him across the open lake in broad daylight.[13]

A few years later, an extensive review of canoe trip outfitting in *Rod and Gun* devoted far more attention to camera equipment, film packaging, developing and printing than to fishing and hunting gear.[14]

Several factors may help to explain the disintegration of earlier linkages between hunting and fishing and the canoe. Improved commercial provisioning may have reduced the vacation paddler's dependence on rod and gun to supplement food needs; or easier access for outboards may have reduced the fisherman/hunter's need for the canoe. Women and children may have been found more frequently in canoeing parties. Perhaps more effective fish and game regulation and enforcement may have controlled off-season activity, but it is also possible that the sensibilities of the interwar recreational paddler were changing and appreciation of the environment was taking a new form.

The railways contributed to the widespread awareness of the attractions of the outdoors. Eager to promote passenger traffic, they continued to advertise canoeing holidays throughout the 1920s and 1930s, as they had done before the war. The *Sport and Recreation Bulletin* of the Canadian Pacific Railway provided route descriptions which were actually relied upon by some canoeists as late as the 1940s.[15] The Temiskaming and Northern Ontario Railway, with its colourful brochures produced by the provincial government, prominently featured canoeing in photographs and cover designs. More closely tailored to the needs of canoeists, however, was the lengthy pamphlet on *Canoe Trips and Nature Photography* issued by the Canadian National Railways. This brochure appealed initially to the adventurer with an introductory assault on travel packages and routine:

> There are types of outdoorsmen and vacation seekers to whom "ready-made" voyages or "ready-made" anything savor so much of the timetable and follow-the-leader as to suggest neither sport, recreation, nor any form of personal happiness. Crowds and clatter distress them. "Organized" recreation leaves them speechless. The very name of sightseeing by bus loads puts their emotions in a jumble. "Perfect cuisine" and "dancing pavilion" meet with an audible yawn, and any claim that sport has been so primped and polished as to make it possible to spend a long summer without soiling their laundered ducks brings hardly the reaction of a lifted eyebrow. To many men and women equally — the call of the "regularized" vacation is not much more than a monotonous repetition of the office and the trolley car if it does not supply some sharp and inspiring contrast, if it fails to draw freely upon the instinct for muscular adventure and for the allurement of strange places.[16]

Canoe Trips and Nature Photography described about thirty routes across the country combining the "'big stuff' requiring five or six weeks or more, with the maximum of novelty and daring" and "the less exciting canoe trips where every evening ends at a modern hotel and a four-course meal". The Ontario trips, for example, covered the range from travel on the Rideau Canal and Trent Waterway, to James Bay trips along the Mattagami, Missinaibi, Abitibi and Albany Rivers.

The only Manitoba route mentioned was a 644-mile return trip from The Pas to Fort Nelson or York Factory on Hudson Bay. Clearly, in the railway's view, recreational canoeists prepared for serious northern wilderness travel existed in substantial numbers, in both Canada and the United States. Significantly, nature photography was accorded rather prominent recognition, as indicated by the pamphlet title.

A notable feature of interwar recreational canoe travel was the active involvement of the federal government in the promotion of wilderness trips and camping. Under the aegis of the Department of the Interior, numerous pamphlets were produced recommending canoe vacations and outlining available options. *Canoeing in Canada* appears to have been aimed at the non-Canadian canoeist in an effort to introduce the "unlimited choice" provided by this country's river and lake routes which railways had brought "within easy access". The Canadian shield country's attractions were enthusiastically proclaimed:

> This entire region is by nature adapted to the needs of the voyageur who travels by canoe. Large sections are not suitable for agriculture and here nature remains in its primitive condition. One may follow the streams for a long summer outing and never see a village or dwelling, and yet civilization lies so close at hand that return is easily possible. The unevenness of surface presents everchanging and picturesque views of

distant heights covered with forest. Waterfalls and rapids, large and small, lakes of
singular beauty hidden in the forest, islands covered with pine and spruce trees, surprise
one day by day.[17]

Having lauded the landscape, the pamphlet turned to flatter the potential tourist
with the suggestion that "the modern canoeist is the replica of the historic
voyageur and pioneer".[18]

Lest the thought of a voyageur's existence in the 20th century appear
more as a deterrent than an attraction, *Canoeing in Canada* was quick to point out
the conventional benefits of a summer in the wilds: "The priceless rewards for all
his toil are steady nerves and hardened muscles, self-reliance and resourcefulness,
and that self-poise which faces all emergencies".[19] A. E. Elias, who wrote *Canoeing in Canada* for the Natural Resources Intelligence Service of the Department of
the Interior, developed the same theme in a companion volume, *Camping in
Canada*, which was also circulated in 1925:

> The camper learns to mould himself into conformity with the existing conditions,
> entering into the harmony of nature, and in the process develops his own individuality.
> Difficulties, unexpected emergencies and sudden changes will test his power of self-
> control and stimulate his mental acumen. After facing the forces of nature and discov-
> ering the value of a stout heart, one returns to city life a stronger and healthier man.[20]

The government's efforts were refined in subsequent years so that increasingly
detailed information was distributed to canoeists. By 1930 the National Development Bureau was distributing a series of titles including *Canoe Routes to Hudson
Bay*, *Canoe Trips in Canada*, *Canoe Trips in Ontario*, *Canoe Trips in the Maritime
Provinces*, *Canoe Trips in the Western Provinces* and *Canoe Trips in Quebec*. The
latter pamphlet was also available in French. The 1934 edition of *Canoe Trips in
Canada* ran to 60 pages and listed numerous canoe routes in each of the provinces
and the Yukon Territory, where a trip from Fort McPherson via the Rat River and
McDougall Pass to the Bell and Porcupine Rivers and down these to Fort Yukon
was recommended. After the tourist had selected a specific route or region,
detailed descriptions and accompanying charts could be provided by the National
Parks of Canada branch of the Department of the Interior. This rather striking
federal initiative is further evidence of an official belief in the existence of
significant numbers of canoe trippers in the 1920s and 1930s and of the enthusiasm of several public servants for the canoe vacation.[21]

The appearance of canoe advertisements in prominent national magazines, as well as the traditional sportsman's journals like *Rod and Gun in Canada*
and *Forest and Outdoors*, also suggests that the appeal of the canoe holiday might
have been widening. The Canadian Canoe Company of Peterborough and the
Lakefield Canoe Company advertised in *Maclean's* in the 1920s.[22] The T. Eaton
Company used *Saturday Night* to promote canoe sales, leading off its text with the
exhortation, "Whatever else is lacking, there must be a canoe". A 16-foot, cedar-
plank craft "covered with special grade canvas" was "specially fitted for the rocky
lakes and rivers of Muskoka and further north". The prices of this canoe, at

$69.50, and a similar model in painted basswood at $59.50, were well above pre-war levels.[23] Another *Saturday Night* article of the early 1920s drew attention to the limitless vacation possibilities of northern Ontario and northern Quebec:

> Rivers, many of them mighty streams, which for generations have served as highways to adventurers, fur traders and trappers bound to and from Hudson Bay, are almost beyond compute in number, the country being grid-ironed by them. Wonderfully interesting canoe trips, either extended or limited, are available. Take, for example, the six routes to Moose Factory, all of which find their way into Moose River about 30 miles south of Moose Factory on James Bay.[24]

*   *   *

Changes were also evident in canoe building during this period. In the years preceding the First World War, the birchbark canoe was displaced as a recreational craft by cedar, basswood and butternut canoes manufactured by a plethora of small canoe companies. Some canvas-covered models appeared, and sailing canoes enjoyed a brief period of popularity in Canada although their use was more widespread in the United States. During the 1920s, evolution in canoe design and manufacturing practices continued, often in response to technological changes associated with other forms of transportation. There was some experimentation with new construction materials and, on the manufacturing side, a tendency toward consolidation may be noted.

James Edmund Jones, author of the 1903 guidebook and instructional manual, *Camping and Canoeing*, reported in 1920 on his experience with a six-man galvanized iron canoe. This vessel, 20 feet in length, complete with air bulkheads at each end, proved more satisfactory than Jones and his companions had anticipated, but was not destined for commercial production or popular acceptance.[25] An earlier experiment with metal canoes, using aluminum in the 1890s, had also proved short-lived because of corrosion and deterioration, although the light weight of the product was expected to ensure its eventual appeal. A 17 foot, 33 lb. aluminum canoe was commercially available in the United States in the 1930s from Frank E. Beers of Los Angeles, and the Aluminum Company of America developed prototypes in the same period.[26] Jones' iron canoe lacked the lightness of aluminum, a difficulty which was ingeniously circumvented by a design feature which allowed the 20 foot model to be packaged in two 70 pound sections. Other adaptations of this sectional approach to canoe building soon appeared.

Wartime advances in aviation which the Ontario government adopted for civilian use greatly facilitated surveillance of the province's vast forest regions and fire-fighting in remote districts. Nevertheless, rangers were still required to travel by canoe along the northern waterways and the early aircraft, which did not take off easily, were often incapable of transporting these vessels into the wilderness interior. This problem was met in the 1920s by the construction of sectional canoes, the parts of which could be fitted inside one another for convenient shipment in a small plane. These compact canoes were manufactured for the

Department of Lands and Forests in Sault Ste. Marie, where the Ontario Provincial Air Service was based after 1924.[27] The Chestnut Company's Labrador model was also designed to conform to the existing limits and possibilities of air travel:

> A feature of this canoe is that it has been well constructed with a straight top so that it will lash to the underbody of a hydroplane, cabin type. The ends or hoods of the canoe are detachable and can be secured inside the hull for transport.[28]

Convenience or compactness was apparently desired by at least some recreational canoeists, for experiments were also made with collapsible canvas models.* These were attractive because of the comparative ease with which they could be transported, particularly in the increasingly popular automobile and by train. One observer described the folding canvas canoe as "specially designed for people who are willing to try anything once" and told this story of a camper in one of Ontario's Forest Reserves:

> The ranger on duty examined his permit and fishing license, and then asked, "Where is your canoe?"
> "Right here", replied the camper, touching with his toe a long cylindrical bundle that lay beside his bed roll. "It's a folding canvas canoe that weighs only twelve pounds and folds into a bundle, as you see, forty-eight inches long and six inches thick. It can be put together in half an hour without tools and folds up in ten minutes."
> "Oh!" said the ranger, and I must give him credit for the fact that there was not the slightest trace of scepticism in his tone or manner. Like most woodsmen, he was always most considerate of other people's feelings, no matter what he might think of them. He showed the camper the canoe landing just above the falls and even helped him to carry his outfit from the station platform.
> "Would you like me to help you put your canoe together?" he asked politely.
> "Oh, no, thank you. I watched the man that sold it to me put it together in the store and I know just how it goes."
> "Quite", replied the ranger in exactly the same manner and tone of voice as before.
> The camper unfastened the bundle and opened out the canoe and its framework. He apologized for having to borrow a screwdriver to loosen a screw that had been fastened too tightly and then borrowed a monkey wrench to loosen a bolt that seemed to jam a little. He managed to get the frame set up all but one end which did not seem to fit as well as it should. When he forced it, the other end came apart again, so the ranger held it in place for him. Two small bolts were missing at one joint, so the camper borrowed some wire and a pair of pliers and wired it firmly together. The ranger began to take more interest in what to him was an interesting problem, and I came in toward the end of the struggle and helped a little myself. By noon, four hours later, the canoe was completely set up and ready to be launched. We carried back to the ranger's shack, the Hudson's Bay Store and the sectionmen's toolhouse a monkey wrench, two screwdrivers, a pair of pliers, a claw hammer, a ball pene hammer, a cold chisel, a platelayer's sledgehammer and what remained of a coil of fence wire.
> "Of course", he said, "this is the first time I have ever put it together myself. Next time I ought to be able to do it inside the half-hour easily."
> The ranger and I were politely silent.

---

* Indeed, the Catalogue of the Ontario Canoe Company for 1886 advertises a "folding canoe".

If this was not enough to cast doubt on the virtues of the collapsible canvas model, the story's conclusion eliminates all uncertainty:

> The canoe was soon well out in the current, and while it was doing its best it must have felt that it had fallen down badly in failing to assemble itself in the allotted half-hour, for it suddenly proceeded to fold up all by itself, without tools or assistance of any sort, and made a complete job of it with nine minutes and fifty seconds to spare out of the ten minutes guaranteed in the advertisement.[29]

Another technological development to alter canoe design significantly during the interwar years was the outboard motor. Ozark Ripley sought to persuade readers of *Forest and Outdoors* that, despite the uncertain performance of early models, the outboard in 1928 was a useful and reliable asset for canoeists:

> Nowadays, when a fellow wants to make a trip into the faraway places, going by train or auto, he can take this little indispensable, certain performer with him, store it under his berth, strap it to his car and, when he arrives, stick it on in a few minutes to most any kind boat or canoe and get going without any further perfunctory or subsequent arrangements.[30]

Johnson, Evinrude, Elto, Caille and Lockwood motors were all available in the 1920s.[31] Engine manufacturers offered a bracket by which the outboard motor could be attached to a canoe. This arrangement was considered to be "fairly satisfactory, although the thrust of the motor is not directly behind and in line with the centre of the canoe". The square-ended canoe with a transom for mounting a small motor was also introduced and, on occasion, described as the outboard canoe. One centre of manufacturing for this craft was the Canadian Canoe Company plant in Peterborough where the Outboard Marine Company of Canada produced motors. The Peterborough Canoe Company was actually a distributor for the Canadian Johnson Motor Company, Ltd.[32]

The all-wood models of an earlier period did not disappear but, for wilderness travel, canoeists were now commonly urged to use the canvas-covered model which combined greater protection and strength with design features adapted to rough country. "The standard guide or tourist models of most manufacturers are designed to meet the varying conditions of travel in the north woods and are almost always the most satisfactory in the long run." Readers of the May, 1927 edition of *Illustrated Canadian Forest and Outdoors* were advised:

> When new and dry, a canvas-covered canoe is usually lighter than an all-wooden canoe and, being easier to keep watertight, it usually retains its lightness for a longer time. If it does get thoroughly waterlogged, it becomes a veritable backbreaker on the portages. Repairs are easily and quickly made. Small punctures can be stopped with a daub of hot pitch, ironed out with a heated knife blade. Larger cuts or tears require patches . . . . Being constructed somewhat like a basket, the canvas-covered canoe is flexible and will stand some very hard knocks that would split the planks of an all-wood canoe.

Yet the all-wood canoe was thought to withstand more "scraping, grinding and scratching" than the canvas model and was, therefore, sometimes preferred for shallow rocky streams or for spring and fall travel where thin, hard ice might be encountered.[33] It appears, though, that during the interwar years, and probably by 1930, the canvas-covered canoe completed its rise to market dominance.

In the early 1920s the organization of canoe manufacturing in Canada entered a period of transformation. The network of small builders, often individual craftsmen, which existed prior to the First World War was replaced by an environment dominated by a few major firms — including the Chestnut Canoe Company of Fredericton, New Brunswick, and the Peterborough Canoe Company. The latter was already the product of an earlier consolidation of small firms when it entered into an arrangement with the Chestnut interests. In 1923 Peterborough and Chestnut agreed to the formation of Canadian Watercraft Limited, a holding company which owned the two firms. Canadian Watercraft then purchased the Canadian Canoe Company in 1928. However, despite the consolidation of ownership, Peterborough, Chestnut and the Canadian Canoe operation continued to manufacture under their own names throughout the 1930s. Not all the smaller companies disappeared, of course; for example, the famous Lorretville "Huron" canoe continued to be available from Gagnon and Jobidon in Quebec.[34]

*   *   *

Of further interest is the manner in which canoeing and wilderness travel skills were acquired or transmitted from experienced paddlers to novices. Some vacationists learned paddling in the school of hard knocks. A. Y. Jackson, for example, told this story of an early encounter with the waterways around Georgian Bay:

> My companion was a very cheerful, careless fellow, as inexperienced as I . . . We were paddling against some swift water at a bend in the river. Westengard was paddling bow, rather indolently, and the current caught the bow, swung it sideways, and over we went. We swam around getting all our stuff ashore, retrieving the canoe, and getting it righted. As we were thus engaged another party came down the river. We tried to look unconcerned, as though this was normal practice with us, but they were not fooled. A few miles further up-river, at a portage, we decided to camp and dry our stuff. We made a big fire and unpacked everything.[35]

But manuals, guidebooks, and other sources of instruction were being produced for the purpose of avoiding such mishaps.

Since at least the turn of the century at the time of Robert E. Pinkerton's article "The Canoe-Half Stolen", which appeared in *Outing* magazine, it was recognized that paddling techniques had been neglected when canoe design was adopted from the Indians.[36] Few twentieth-century paddlers would have enjoyed the opportunity afforded young Archie Belaney to learn from Indian canoemen the paddling skills which contributed to his transformation to Grey Owl.[37]

Some paddlers learned canoeing skills as fire-rangers with a government forest service, although the ranks of rangers and canoemen were thinned by the war. Often the new recruits were students, summering on the job in various northern districts:

The danger period of fires is three months in the summer, coinciding nicely with vacations from Canadian universities. Youth and lack of continuity were no disadvantages. There was real work to be done, of commercial value, and small cash income above expenses to be earned. It was outdoor life twenty-four hours a day, full of vigorous exercise without strain, as healthy as could be found. Vast areas had to be closely watched, giving employment on a considerable scale. Beyond all this, there was extraordinary experience to be gained, in uninterrupted, isolated months in the wilderness practically spent in a canoe.[38]

Perhaps the attraction of this form of summer vacation was conveyed to some by works such as Richard Garwood Lewis' *The Romance of Fire Ranging*. Youth camps and the surviving canoe clubs were other sources of instruction. Information was also to be found in a few early manuals and such outdoor magazines as *Rod and Gun in Canada*, *The Illustrated Canadian Forest and Outdoors*, and *Field and Stream*.

Whitewater skills were an important aspect of the wilderness canoeist's knowledge and experience, if the surviving written record is any indication. The editors of *Camping in Canada* refer to "the breathtaking dash through the white water of wild rapids". A. Y. Jackson shot rapids with Dr. MacCallum on the Mississagi. *Saturday Night* reminded fishermen that the Nipigon country also offered "rapids to shoot, taxing the dexterity of the most expert to guide the canoe through the maddened, boiling waters without a spill", and numerous individual trip accounts treat rapids as a more or less standard aspect of most expeditions.[39] Robert E. Pinkerton published the novel *White Water* in 1925 with many references to Ontario and to river work:

White water lad, ain't you? Go to it, son, while you can. White water. I know. Never portage unless you have to, and then take a chance. Only . . .[40]

Again, though, Grey Owl developed the theme of challenge, risk and adventure most effectively:

The current has much increased in volume and power. Rapid succeeds rapid in quick succession. Most of them we run, some full loaded, others with half loads, saving a lot of work on portages. A few are more in the nature of low waterfalls, or else too filled with stones, and are impossible. There is a marvellously picturesque cataract, running through a chasm in a series of chutes and sudden drops, that is worth the trouble of going off the portage to see. This spot is known as Hell's Gate. The old rapid is too dangerous to run with any load, and the canoes go down empty. No useful purpose is served in attempting these places, it being done only for the excitement to be got out of it. In such spots, brother, we leave you on the shore, and I think that the skill and dare-deviltry, the utter disregard for personal danger with which a good canoeman flings (there is no other word) a good canoe from place to place through a piece of water in which it seems impossible that anything could live, will furnish you with a spectacle that you will be a long time forgetting. And you may sometimes, too, remember the narrow plot that is a grave, surrounded by a picket fence, at one of them. A man was drowned here a few years ago, an old, experienced trapper, who made perhaps this only one mistake in all his life. Some rivers have their private graveyards, to which they add from time to time. But Mississauga is not considered dangerous; there are portages round all bad places. We are only running them for the fun of it.[41]

Despite Grey Owl's enthusiasm for the whitewater challenge, the approach of a typical recreational paddler was not likely to be one of reckless abandon. Thus, we would naturally expect to find some concern about the process of skill development and interest in instructional materials as they became available.

One of the more comprehensive instructional canoeing manuals of the interwar period observed that "there is nothing to compare with the thrill of running a fast rapid"; nevertheless, the author advised paddlers not to run rapids for fun "unless you are an expert or are paddling with one".[42] Instructional literature stressed the importance of studying the rapids before a descent. Richard Garwood Lewis, in an article which appeared in a summer 1929 issue of *Forest and Outdoors* noted the usefulness of standing at the top of a set of rapids for a good view of the route:

> Under ordinary circumstances only a fool stands up in a canoe, but you seldom see a northern Indian start to run any rapid without first standing up in his canoe to take a mental snapshot of the channel just before he enters the swift water.[43]

In *Small Watercraft*, the same author was emphatic that one should "never under any circumstances" run an unfamiliar rapid without first checking its entire course from the shore.[44] The stricter advice of the later work may be explained by the fact that the intended audience of the instructional manual included beginners and children, while *Forest and Outdoors* readers presumably had some experience on the water. In any event, suggestions for reading the water to identify obstacles and to select a safe course through were seldom very fully elaborated.

Speed and steering in rapids were subjects of particular interest. The significance of the canoe's speed relative to the current was recognized as an important influence on control. The *Boy's Book of Canoeing* advised:

> In order to pick your way, you must travel either faster or slower than the current. The slower speed is the safer of the two although not always as practicable . . .
>
> In many instances, you can check your speed as needed by backpaddling with vigorous "shove back" strokes. In extremely swift water, however, paddles haven't the power to hold you back. Therefore, your only alternative in such conditions is in getting steerage way by travelling faster than the current.[45]

Essentially the same message was given to readers of Lewis' *Small Watercraft*, a manual approved by the Canadian Boy Scouts and Girl Guides Association as a handbook for those seeking merit badges.[46] The principles of steering in fast water were sufficiently understood in the 1920s that Lewis could write in his whitewater article: "In order to avoid an obstacle it is necessary to actually drag the canoe sideways into a part of the stream which is passing the obstacle unhindered." In *Small Watercraft* he remarked simply that "a canoe is steered by strokes of paddles and not with a rudder".[47] In both publications he explained the combined use of draws and pries for travelling sideways in the current, although the adult readers of *Forest and Outdoors* seem to have been given a more comprehensive description. Similar recommendations on speed and steering were to be found in American canoeing literature dating back to World War I, and the information presumably crossed the boundary without interference.

Warren Miller, who served for several years as editor of *Field and Stream*, acknowledged in a 1918 publication that opinion was divided on the issue of speed in rapids. But his own no doubt influential preference for the slow style was presented emphatically: "In swift water full of rocks and snags the principle to aim at is to keep the canoe going slower than the water is flowing".[48]

John W. Worthington went beyond his contemporaries in recognizing that "a canoe, like the well-known pin, may be pointed one way and headed another". Most other commentators remained committed to the view that the canoe should always be aligned with the current. Jessup in *The Boy's Book of Canoeing* was somewhat ambiguous on this point, but on balance held the traditional view. Lewis, however, was insistent that one must "always try to keep the bow pointing straight down- stream", and this instruction was repeated for some time.[49] Yet this is probably the key difference between interwar advice on technique and present practices. In other respects — backpaddling, draws and pries around obstructions, and stabilizing strokes — interwar paddlers understood the open canoeist's basic whitewater skills as widely known today. And Worthington unquestionably described eddy manoeuvers and endorsed the principle of the downstream ferry without using modern terminology.

Published explanations of the kind illustrated here demonstrated a lively concern for the further refinement and dissemination of skills. They also suggest some sense of responsibility or community of interest linking more experienced paddlers with novices. If developments in Canadian art and literature helped to sustain the "spiritual" tradition of canoeing during the interwar era, the relatively informal instructional publications on paddling encouraged and facilitated physical access by urban Canadians to the country's waterways.

*   *   *

Trip preparation and outfitting are other aspects of canoeing that have always been crucial for the success and enjoyment of a paddling holiday. Forgotten items are not easily replaced and the typical camper's enthusiasm for opening cans with a tent peg and an axe is decidedly limited. The increasing availability of advice on packing, provisioning, campfire cooking and equipment during the interwar years suggests that canoeists in significant numbers were outfitting their own expeditions. This trend may be contrasted with the period before World War I when commercial outfitting by suppliers such as Michie's of Toronto or by camps, resort hotels and fur trade posts appeared to be common practice. Foods packaged and preserved for wilderness use and lightweight equipment, such as tents and sleeping bags, were not yet generally available. Instead, canoeists had to assemble their camping kit and supplies with a view to the serviceability of items rarely designed with canoe camping and portages specifically in mind. Thus, when the Department of the Interior offered the reminder that "the ideal canoe outfit is light and compact", it was only able to suggest that "these features are usually attained by avoiding duplicate articles and non-essentials".[50]

An *Outing* publication dating from 1912 made the same point somewhat more firmly:

> Even though the weight of some of them may be insignificant, the weight of each additional claptrap makes one more thing to look after. There are a thousand and one claptraps, indeed, that outfitters offer, but which do not possess sufficient advantage to pay for the car and labour of transportation, and my advice is, leave them out, one and all.[51]

This manual and some of the other pioneering and prewar literature on campcraft and trail skills for vacationers were rapidly supplemented or supplanted by other works in the field.[52]

Most campcraft authors assessed clothing, equipment and gear, but information of this nature was also available from commercial suppliers. *Michie's Tourist Topics* and Eaton's summer catalogues were probably important sources in this regard. In the United States, Leon L. Bean, having introduced his popular "Maine Hunting Shoe" to the market in 1912, was active in mail-order camp outfitting and consulting. C. P. Storey's "Outfitting for the Long Canoe Trip", from *Rod and Gun in Canada*, is an example of commentary directed specifically toward the needs of the recreational paddler.[53] Most canoeing manuals also contained advice on camping and wilderness skills, including equipment lists.

Every aspect of camping practice and procedure was debated and discussed at length in the outdoor literature circulating during the interwar years. Pack design, footwear, the sleeping bag versus the blanket kit, tent styles and materials, "bifurcated" garments for women, the dreaded mosquito and his ally the black fly, aluminum reflecter ovens and any number of illumination devices all divided opinion and raised controversy. Developments concerning tents and insect repellants illustrate some of the changes of the interwar years.

In *Campcraft: Modern Practice and Equipment* Warren Miller compared tenting with cottage or cabin life, explaining his preference for the former:

> The principal function of a tent is to make a real "woodser" of you. A shack or a log cabin, located in the heart of the woods, will shelter you from the elements and put you in reasonable touch with the sights and sounds and smells of the wilderness, but you are not of it, not in the real heart of the wild life, nor will a year in a cabin be as beneficial to your health as thirty days in a tent.[54]

The tent dwellers themselves still faced many choices and, as Dillon Wallace earlier observed, "personal likes and prejudices have much to do with the form of tent chosen". Many styles were offered in a variety of materials from duck or drill to balloon silk, also referred to as tanalite. The commercial options were much debated. A tent could also be made at home. That the latter option might be attractive in certain circumstances is suggested by C. P. Storey. After recounting an unfortunately damp experience on a canoe trip-honeymoon, he warned others of the "numerous freak tents" on the market: "Some of these tents are made to sell, not to give comfort and protection to the tired camper who is caught out in a heavy rainstorm".[55] In Canada, though, Woods tents were a highly regarded and popular choice of shelter among canoeists and campers. Opinion strongly favoured mosquito netting or the less-expensive alternative of cheesecloth, for it was readily admitted that insects were prevalent, bothersome and unpleasant.

"The curse of the Canadian wilds in the summer are mosquitoes, black flies and their relations", lamented one popular account, while a Nova Scotia paddler named the mosquito, along with sunburn, as the "only two foes . . . to be dreaded by the summer camper in this province". R. G. Lewis felt that the annual expeditions of veteran canoeists were made into a "martyrs' pilgrimage" because "mosquitoes sting them, black flies and bull dogs bite them, and no-see-ums burn them with a thousand fires".[56] An Ontario Department of Mines report contained this grim account of mosquito damage from the survivors of a survey and exploration trip in the Abitibi region:

> It is impossible to convey an adequate idea of the suffering which we were obliged to endure from their attacks, and no application of oil or salve to our hands and faces seemed to have any effect in keeping them off.

The same expedition also reported considerable inconvenience occasioned by the black flies' habit of "congregating in large numbers in soup, gravy and other articles of diet". The prospects for relief appeared limited, yet commentators offered some hope in the suggestion that insect pests "have practically passed away when August arrives" or by advising that the insect "will not, as a rule, attack one while on the water", and reporting that "after midnight the mosquito seemed to betake himself to repose". Another veteran advised wilderness travellers to camp on high ground "where there will be a night breeze to blow off the mosquitoes". The Department of Mines commentary even ventured the opinion that "it is altogether probable that as the country becomes cleared and drained and the soil cultivated, they will largely disappear and life will then be as tolerable in this region as in the older parts of the Province".[57] So much for prophesy.

If netting was needed at night, something else was required for daytime activity. Repellants were typically of a do-it-yourself variety. William Hume Blake recommended to readers of his *In a Fishing Country* that a repellant should be pungent and should have enough body that it would not dry off quickly. One option was a 20:1 mix of crude petroleum and oil of citronella. "As the strong odor of citronella becomes exceedingly trying if it is used constantly", some woodsmen counselled that eucalyptus be carried along as an alternative. Another veteran was cautious in his recommendation on citronella for he concluded that some "brands" of mosquito "seem to prefer it to any other drink". Blake himself offered this notable combination:

> An excellent mixture for one who is not pernickety about his complexion is pine tar, three ounces; castor oil, two ounces; penny royal, one ounce; simmered over a slow fire; but there is a choice for all tastes within the general formula.

Wallace had previously offered his followers the same formula, attributing its origins to Nessmuk the renowned American canoeist and woodsman, and encouraging its adoption with this commendation:

> . . . it is claimed for this mixture that the dead will rise and flee from its compounded odor as they would flee from external torment! It certainly should ward off such little creatures as black flies and mosquitoes.

Another Wallace recipe featured oil of tar (three parts), sweet oil (three parts), oil of pennyroyal (one part), and carbolic acid (three percent), though he seemed unconvinced that this potion would prove more effective than the custom — which he attributed to the Indians — of rubbing salt pork rind on exposed surfaces. Readers of the Canadian National's *Canoe Trips and Nature Photography* manual were introduced to a mixture of 30 percent salol, 30 percent camphor and 40 percent heavy petrolatum (jelly) which was said to have no objectionable odour.[58] One wonders about the effects of these concoctions on their user and whether any of them are commercially available today.[59]

Relief for the camper whose repellant defences had failed or were neglected also tended to emphasize the home-made remedies or improvised solutions. In a comment on "Canoeists and Mosquitoes", the *American Canoeist* seemed to endorse a suggestion put forward in *Edinburgh's Medical Journal*, that itching and pain could generally be eliminated by rubbing the affected area with moist soap and allowing the lather to dry on the skin. William Hume Blake offered:

> . . . a remedy handed down by generations of fishermen — 8v sovereign against pain, itching and swelling of all poisoned stings — is acetate of lead, three drachms; carbolic acid, four drachms; tincture of opium, four drachms; rosewater, four ounces.[60]

*   *   *

The wilderness and camping tradition, rather than canoe sailing and canoe club paddling, were central to the revival of recreational canoeing in Canada that followed the First World War. In one respect, the recreational wilderness paddler of the 1920s and 1930s simply preserved an historic association between canoeists and the landscape, adapted from the Indians and maintained through the exploits of explorers and fur traders, or the last expeditions of woodsmen, geologists and anglers. Shifts from birchbark to wood and canvas, from railway advertising of canoe vacations to active government promotion of wilderness holidays, and the emergence of an extensive literature on canoe technique may all be regarded as evolutionary changes in the history of a popular summer pastime. Yet these same developments and other transitional events of the interwar years may also be viewed as elements in a more complex and fundamental transformation of the canoeist's world and place in Canadian life.

An apparent decline has been noted in prewar emphasis on the canoe trip as an ancillary activity for fishermen, hunters and sportsmen. There is evidence in its place of a greater tendency to regard canoeing as a means of seeing nature, contemplating scenery and experiencing the landscape:

> Domination is not the mode of the canoe. In its red and green painted canvas, replacing the dust-colored birch bark, in its playful action on the water, there is a frivolous

appearance. For the pleasure of life in the harsh Canadian environment this is not regretable.[61]

Thus it appears that at the conclusion of the interwar era, the contemplative pleasures of paddling in harmony with nature were becoming dominant. Recreational paddlers have continued to emphasize this aspect of their activity and for many subsequent wilderness canoeists, a commitment to conservation and the environment has been considered axiomatic. But the independence of recreational paddling from the fur trade tradition of direct resource exploitation was in some respects deceptive.

If the trophy-seeking hunter and limitless fisherman were less evident in the ranks of canoeists, paddlers had by no means desentangled themselves from general social developments. In transportation, the outboard, the automobile and the airplane were increasingly part of the canoeist's equipment and support system. The energy intensive aluminum canoe was on the horizon, together with manufactured camping gear — Wallace's claptrap — ad infinitum. Some canoeists find the aluminum paddler's commitment to landscape preservation somewhat contradictory. Rivers are dammed to produce the hydro electricity required for the production of aluminum, yet the free flowing natural waterway remains the ideal canoeing environment. This dilemma which troubled the consciences of many paddlers as the environmental movement emerged to prominence in the 1970s was not the only later recreational canoeing controversy whose roots developed in the interwar period.

The expansion of canoeing literature during the 1920s and 1930s certainly broadened access to information and technique, and arguably contributed to the democratization and expansion of canoeing itself. At the same time, however, the basis for conventional standards and guidelines was laid. Some have found in the development of guidelines and manuals — particularly when these are adopted or endorsed by organized groups in the camping movement, the schools or government agencies — the unpleasant prospect of regimentation and standardization or even the eventual possibility of skill-based licensing systems to control physical access to the wilderness. Again, recreational canoeing's interwar evolution contributed to later controversy and debate amongst canoeists concerning risk vs. security and individual freedom vs. social responsibility and control. Paddlers, of course, were not alone in facing such dilemmas.

Although summer between the wars was a good deal more complicated than "idleness, water and a canoe", paddling for pleasure continued to play a role in Canadians' experience of the landscape as it does today.

ENDNOTES

1. Howe Martyn, "The Canadian Canoe", *Queen's Quarterly* (Spring 1940) p. 147.

2. These are discussed at greater length in previous work by the present author. See "Recreational Canoeing in Ontario before the First World War", *Canadian Journal of the History of Sport* IX (December 1978) pp. 41-57 and "Paddling for Pleasure: Recreational Canoeing as a Canadian Way of Life" in J. S. Marsh and G. Wall eds. *Recreational Land Use: Perspectives on its Evolution in Canada* (Toronto 1982).

3. A convenient survey of the national movement in Canadian art during this era may be found in Ramsey Cook, "Landscape Painting and National Sentiment in Canada" in *The Maple Leaf Forever* (Toronto 1977) pp. 158-179.

4. John Russel Harper, *Painting in Canada* (2nd). Albert H. Robson in *Tom Thomson: Painter of Our North Country* (Ryerson 1951) recounts Thomson's canoe travel in Algonquin Park and the Mississagi Forest Reserve.

5. Blodwen Davies, *A Study of Tom Thomson: The Story of a Man Who Looked for Beauty and for Truth in the Wilderness* (Toronto 1937) p. 51.

6. A. Y. Jackson, *A Painter's Country: The Autobiography of A. Y. Jackson* (Toronto 1958; memorial edition 1976) p. 91.

7. Ibid., p. 87.

8. Grey Owl, *Tales of an Empty Cabin* p. 172.

9. Lovatt Dickson, *Wilderness Man: The Strange Story of Grey Owl* (London 1975).

10. *Canoeing in Canada* (Ottawa 1934) p. 61.

11. See Benidickson, "Recreational Canoeing in Ontario Before the First World War".

12. *American Canoeist* (March 1883) p. 17.

13. L. C. T. Beveridge, "Blazing a New Canoe Trail" in *Illustrated Canadian Forest and Outdoors* (November 1923) p. 700.

14. C. P. Storey, "Outfitting for the Long Canoe Trip", *Rod and Gun* (March 1927) pp. 595-597, 629-632.

15. Robert D. Price, "Mississaugi, A White Water River", *Appalachia* (June 1946) p. 486.

16. Canadian National Railways, *Canoe Trips and Nature Photography* (1928) p. 3.

17. A. E. Elias, *Canoeing in Canada* (Ottawa 1925).

18. Ibid.

19. Ibid.

20. A. E. Elias, *Camping in Canada* (Ottawa 1925) pp. 8-9.

21. The Department of the Interior reported in the weekly magazine *Canada*, 29 December 1928 at page 391 that requests for information on canoe trips were common, and that "chain selling" was having a great impact. "When one party has successfully navigated a chain of Canada's rivers and lakes and experienced the thrill of shooting rapids, many other parties follow".

22. *Maclean's Magazine*, 1 April 1923, p. 40 and 15 April 1923, p. 9.

23. *Saturday Night*, 27 May 1922, p. 36.

24. "The New North — A Sportsman's Paradise", *Saturday Night*, 15 July 1922, p. 12.

25. James Edmund Jones, "A Cruise in a Galvanized Iron Canoe", *Rod and Gun* (August 1920) pp. 249-251.

26. *Forest and Stream* (24 September 1891) pp. 196-197; Thomas D. Cabot, "Tin Canoes", *Appalachia* (June 1936) pp. 115-116.

27. R.S. Lambert and Paul Pross, *Renewing Nature's Wealth* (Toronto 1967) pp. 234-245.

28. William G. Luscombe and Louis J. Bird, *Canoeing* (London 1936, 1948) p. 30. In *Canoes and Canoeing* (1937), British canoe builder and author also advocates the use of sectional canoes.

29. R.G. Lewis, "Advice on Canadian Canoes", *Illustrated Canadian Forest and Outdoors* (May 1927) p. 252. On the construction of collapsible canoes, see W. R. Stewart, "Letter", *Rod and Gun* (February 1927) p. 564.

30. Ozark Ripley, "The Evolution of Outboard Motoring", *Illustrated Canadian Forest and Outdoors* (April 1928) pp. 224-226.

31. Ibid.

32. R. G. Lewis, "Paddle Your Own Canoe", *Illustrated Canadian Forest and Outdoors* (June 1930) p. 344; *Rod and Gun* (June 1928) p. 35, advertisement.

33. S. E. Sangster, "By Paddle and Portage", *Forest and Outdoors* (August 1938) p. 230; Lewis, "Paddle Your Own Canoe", p. 344; Lewis, "Advice on Canadian Canoes", *Illustrated Canadian Forest and Outdoors* (May 1927) p. 251.

34. *The Chestnut Canoe Company Limited Papers*, Minutes of Directors' Meeting 16 July 1923, New Brunswick Provincial Archives; Mary Strickland Rogers, "The Peterborough Canoe"; Francis H. Love, "Peterborough . . . Canoe Capital of the World", *Forest and Outdoors* (September 1949) pp. 6-7, 22; *Rod and Gun* (June 1928) p. 65.

35. Jackson, *A Painter's Country* p. 84.

36. Robert E. Pinkerton, "The Canoe-Half Stolen", *Outing* (May 1913) pp. 159-163.

37. Lovat Dickson, *Half Breed: The Story of Grey Owl* (London 1939) pp. 97-99.

38. Martyn, "The Canadian Canoe" p. 153.

39. *Camping in Canada* (Ottawa 1939) p. 3; Jackson, *A Painter's Country* p. 88; "Real Sport for the Angler", *Saturday Night* (August 16, 1924) p. 12.

40. Robert E. Pinkerton, *White Water: A Novel* (Chicago 1925) p. 19.

41. Grey owl, *Tales of an Empty Cabin* p. 207.

42. Richard Garwood Lewis, *Small Watercraft* (Toronto n.d.) p. 27.

43. Richard Garwood Lewis, "Riding the 'White Water'", *Illustrated Canadian Forest and Outdoors* (August 1929) p. 466.

44. Lewis, *Small Watercraft* p. 25.

45. Elton Jessup, *The Boys' Book of Canoeing* (New York 1926) p. 110.

46. "Contrary to the common belief, it is not necessary or even advisable when running with the current that the speed of the canoe should always exceed that of the water in order to keep steerage way . . . .If the current is slow and obstacles can be seen well ahead the canoe can be paddled faster than the current and steered around obstacles as in still water. In faster water or where there may be submerged rocks or snages, the slower the canoe is travelling, the better." Lewis, *Small Watercraft* p. 26.

47. Lewis, "Riding the 'White Water'" p. 466; Lewis, *Small Watercraft* p. 26.

48. Warren H. Miller, *Camping Out* (New York 1918) p. 88. A particularly impressive discussion of "Quick-Water Canoeing" by John W. Worthington in *Appalachia* (June 1929) p. 271 similarly explained:

> The object in downstream work, is not to drive the canoe; the water furnishes all the power needed for mere propulsion. Time is required, more time than the river is disposed to give . . . The canoeman . . . may push or pull laterally either end of the canoe or the whole canoe . . . The drawing strokes are the more used and usually the more effective . . . One seems to take hold of a piece of water and pull himself toward it.

Luscombe and Bird in their major English canoeing book which first appeared in the interwar period also regarded backpaddling as the standard North American practice for white water work:

> The moment he (the canoeist) approaches heavy water he definitely backwaters so as to check the headlong plunge of the canoe and give the bow ample time to rise easily and steadily on the crest of the wave, then slide down into the trough slowly, and rise again to

the second wave, and so on. Over there many of the fast streams are so dotted with exposed rocks that a straight course through white water is impossible, and the technique of holding back, therefore, not only enables the canoeist to come through dry, but also allows him to draw the canoe sideways, either to starboard or port, as often as may be necessary to dodge the rocks which may be in the course.

49. Worthington, "Quick-Water Canoeing" p. 272; Jessup, *The Boys' Book of Canoeing* pp. 106-107; Lewis, *Small Watercraft* p. 26. In 1950, S. C. Ells stated that "the sole duty of the man at the stern is to ensure that so far as may be possible the centre line of the canoe does not deviate from the direction of the current". See "White Water", *Canadian Geographical Journal* (April 1950) p. 183.

50. Department of the Interior, *Canoe Trips in Canada* (Ottawa 1934) p. 59.

51. Dillon Wallace, *Packing and Portaging* (Outing Publishing 1912) p. 20.

52. Warren H. Miller, *Campcraft: Modern Practice and Equipment* (New York 1915); Miller, *Camping Out* (1918); Miller, *The Sportsman's Workshop* (1921); Harriet I. Carter, *Camping, A Biography* (1942). Horace Kephart's classic *Camping and Woodcraft* appeared in 1917. Warren H. Miller produced a series of books on various aspects of camp life. By 1942 a modest bibliography on camping could list some twenty titles under the general campcraft heading. Subclassifications greatly extended the range of references. Under outdoor cooking, for example, one could consult Cora, Rose and Bob Brown's *Outdoor Cooking* (1940), Elton Jessup's *Camp Grub* (1924), Kephart's *Camp Cooking* (1935) or J.A. Wilder's *Jack-Knife Cookery* (1929). Naturally, the general campcraft books dealt with food, cooking and camp-fires; there were specialized articles as well.

53. *The L. L. Bean Guide to the Outdoors*; C.P. Storey, "Outfitting for the Long Canoe Trip", *Rod and Gun* (March 1927) pp. 595-597, 629-632; George Bowering, *Protective Footwear* (Toronto 1978).

54. Miller, *Campcraft: Modern Practice and Equipment* p. 26.

55. Dillon Wallace, *Packing and Portaging* p. 15; Storey, "Outfitting for the Long Canoe Trip" p. 596. See also Aritha Van Herk, *The Tent Peg* (Toronto 1981).

56. "Canoeing in Canada", in *Canada Today, 1913* (London and Toronto 1913) p. 71; Lewis, "Paddle Your Own Canoe" p. 156.

57. Ontario Bureau of Mines *Annual Report, 1903*, Vol. 13, Pt. 1, pp. 127-128; Martyn, "The Canadian Canoe" p. 156.

58. William Hume Blake, *In a Fishing Country* (Toronto 1922) p. 247; Storey, "Outfitting for the Long Canoe Trip" p. 631; Wallace, *Packing and Portaging* pp. 26-27; *Canoe Trips and Nature Photography*.

59. See R. E. Gosselin et al., *Clinical Toxicology of Commercial Products* (London 1976).

60. *American Canoeist* (May 1983) p. 56; Blake, *In a Fishing Country* p. 247.

61. Howe Martyn, "The Canadian Canoe", *Queen's Quarterly* (Spring 1940).

The Nastawgan:
Traditional Routes of Travel
in the Temagami District*

Craig Macdonald

Nastawgan is a word still in common usage amongst the older, native-speaking Indians of Northeastern Ontario. *Nastawgan* are the ways or the routes for travel through the land of the Temagami district in Northeastern Ontario, just south of the height-of-land.

Before the advent of roads and railways, waterways provided the principal routes for travel and communication over much of the shield country of Northeastern Ontario, including the Temagami and Lady Evelyn watersheds. It was much easier to travel on the waterways than to traverse the rugged, rocky and densely forested terrain. Waterways were used not only in the summer for canoe travel but also in the winter for travel by snowshoe and toboggan. In many instances, the winter routes of travel varied little from those used in the summer.

A trail network based on waterways provided a wealth of natural campsite locations as well as access to fisheries which furnished a major portion of the summer diet for early residents. Unlike land based trails, full exposure to biting insects was limited to campsites and portages. *Onigum* or canoe portage trails were maintained to by-pass unnavigable portions of the route: rapids, falls, heights-of-land between waterways and floatwood jams known to fur trade canoemen as "embarrasses."

Bon-ka-nah or special winter trails over land were equally important. In winter, the chief obstacles to snowshoe travel were and still are open water and unsafe ice, found where moving water resists the formation of ice. Sometimes the Algonquin Indians simply extended the trail at the ends of portages in order to reach calmer water with sufficiently thick ice for safe travel. Rivers with strong current extending continuously over long distances posed a greater challenge, especially where there was no space for travel along the shorelines. In such cases they made longer *bon-ka-nah*. *Bon-ka-nah* were also constructed specifically as shortcuts to reduce the length of winter travel routes.

Although *onigum* (portages) and *bon-ka-nah* (winter trails) were part of the

---

*The material for this article has been derived as part of a detailed on-going study covering Northwestern Quebec and Northeastern Ontario. Sources include archival map collections, survey records, and especially personal field inspections. Particularly useful were interviews with many of the elders of the Temeaugama Anishinabay on Bear Island and elders of adacent Indian bands, some of whom are now deceased. This invaluable resource has provided deep insight largely unobtainable from the written record.

nastawgan, there were advantages to using waterways for both winter and summer travel in preference to the land trails. Probably the most important advantage was the ease of transport for equipment and supplies. Before the arrival of Europeans, the native population did not have horses or cattle to serve as beasts of burden. Without the use of the wheel, summer land transport was limited to dog travois, dog packs and to what a person could drag or carry. On lengthy land routes this imposed severe weight restrictions.

Canoes, on the other hand, permitted extraordinary loads of equipment and supplies to be transported even on the most difficult routes. For every mile of travel only a fraction was covered by portage. Because of the relatively small portion of the total distance requiring portaging, several trips could be made over each portage without significantly slowing progress. As long as the cargo could be subdivided into units which could be carried, large loads were transported with relative ease. Another advantage was the limited maintenance required to keep the routes passable. On the water portions, maintenance was restricted to cutting out fallen trees which obstructed travel on narrow creeks. The portages or *onigum* themselves received maintenance similar to that of any land trail, but being short they were relatively easy. Most work consisted of breaking down obstructing branches and sometimes marking the route by blazing trees with an axe. Fallen trees blocking portages were rarely removed, especially if cutting was involved. Either a few branches were knocked off so one should step over the tree, or the trail was simply re-routed around the obstacles.

Onigum passing over wet areas received greater attention. Logs were layed on the ground to improve footing. In some instances, *metigo-mikana* was used to replace simple logs for traversing wet areas. Unlike the corduroy of the pioneers, *metigo-mikana* was laid longitudinally in the direction of travel so that a minimum of cutting was required for construction. The walkway was often 3 poles wide, connected by cross stringers which provided lateral stability. Cedar was the preferred building material. Joints were often notched and secured by spruce root.

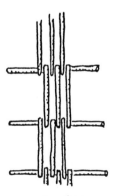

metigo-mikana
(separation in walkway members exaggerated to show construction details)

pioneer corduroy for wheeled traffic

In the winter, use of frozen waterways meant limited trail maintenance and relative ease of transport. Travel on frozen lakes proved much easier than on trails over rugged terrain. Not only did the lakes provide a level surface for pulling toboggans and sleighs, but the wind-packed snow frequently encountered on lakes was more easily travelled than the deep, soft, mid-winter snows common to sheltered land trails. A man in good physical condition could pull over frozen lakes a load of 90lb. on a toboggan all day without tiring. On the uneven terrain of many land-based trails, this would prove an exhausting if not impossible task. *Onigum* constituted such a small portion of the total distance that the deep unpacked snow of these portage trails could be profitably broken by snowshoe in advance of bringing across the load without too much loss of time. If the load still proved unmanageable, it was broken up and dragged across in portions.

Depending on weather conditions, as much as three months of the year was poor for travel along water routes. Freeze-up and break-up have always been a most difficult time for wilderness travel in the Canadian North. For a period during freeze-up, the open season for canoe navigation could be extended by making arduous land detours around shallow lakes which had already frozen. Otherwise, the traveller could use a canoe-sleigh to transport the canoe across the ice. If the ice was not too thick, it could be broken with a paddle or axe to reach open water. *Barres d'abordage* or canoe shoes could also be added to the outside of the canoe's hull to protect it from ice damage, but soon even this became impossible. Travel on the water routes was usually suspended until the ice thickened sufficiently to support at least the weight of a man.

Even now most experienced wilderness travellers consider spring break-up to be the most unsafe time to travel, because of the unpredictable strength of the ice. Sometimes, however, the period between travel on ice and travel on open water can be as little as two days. Traditionally, travel on weakening ice-plates was accomplished by the ingenious employment of the canoe-sleigh. A canoe was secured in an upright position on top of the sleigh and the travellers walked along the surface of the ice holding on to the ends of the canoe. Often two or three dogs were harnessed to assist with the pulling of the load. If the ice gave way, the travellers quickly jumped into the ends of the canoe, preferably before getting wet and thus very cold. The sleigh would then be untied from the bottom of the canoe and placed inside. The cycle would be completed by running the canoe up on solid ice and reloading. As this type of travel was slow and dangerous, it was usually undertaken only in times of extreme necessity.

Utilising a water system for winter transport required good knowledge of travelling on ice. Lakes with large water inflows in proportion to their total surface area were the most hazardous. These lakes are prone to water level fluctuations which stress and weaken the ice plate along the shoreline and encourage the development of surface slush and air holes. Furthermore, the ice surrounding inflows can be dangerously thin, not unlike ice in other areas with current, such as narrows or obstructing shoals. Underwater springs whose water is several degrees above freezing create an additional hazard. As a result, well defined routes of travel were sometimes established on the most dangerous lakes.

If the route was to be followed frequently, the designated snowshoe path was often marked at regular intervals with evergreen boughs. This was done in anticipation of the packed trail becoming obscured by drifting or new fallen snow. Even if covered with new snow, a packed trail provided a firmer base for sledding and snowshoeing. Since the packed trail was elevated above the surface of the ice there was less chance of encountering slush that would freeze onto the snowshoes and the running surfaces of the sleighs.

Slush was a problem. Slush is often created by heavy snowfalls depressing the surface of the ice so that water seeps up through cracks in the ice to flood the lower layers of snow. When insulated from the cold by additional layers of snow above, the slush sometimes persists for weeks before it eventually freezes. By packing down a trail on snowshoes, the upper layers of compressed snow lose their insulating value, thus permitting the underlying slush to freeze. During windy weather, the trail was often packed down to a double width so that the track did not fill with drifting snow before the slush had a chance to freeze. If such an effort was made to secure passage, the trail was often marked with boughs for possible re-use later that winter. Such track preparation and marking naturally reduced the daily distance which could be travelled hauling sleighs, unless people were sent ahead of the main party to do this work. Usually an hour lead time was needed to freeze the surface of the slush sufficiently for passage with sleighs and toboggans.

For the *bon-ka-nah* or land trail portions, extensive use encouraged an increase in the amount of trail maintenance undertaken. This included trail marking by blazing trees, and greater efforts to remove wind falls and overhanging limbs.

Since side sloping trails were very difficult to negotiate with toboggans and seighs, the surface of the trail was often levelled with a snow shovel at the worst locations. Levelling was especially needed where the trail traversed the sides of hills. Shovels were also used to fill in the hollows along the trail if heavy freighting was to be undertaken.

Seepage of ground water was another problem. Since water coming from below the ground is several degrees above 0°C, it resists freezing even in very cold air temperatures. Rivulets of ground water cannot easily be detected when they flow under the surface of the snow. However, when a winter trail was packed down, the flow of water often melted away the entire layer of snow with a few hours. To repair the trail at these locations, it was common to cut evergreen boughs and place them over a series of sticks laid in the washout, thus creating an insulating mattress of vegetation. Snow was then shovelled over the boughs and packed down with snowshoes to freeze and create a snow bridge. The warm water could then pass under the trail through the sticks and boughs without melting away the surface of the trail or the snow bridge.

Occasionally, it was necessary to construct simple bridges or ramps. The bridges were used for spanning open creeks or sharp gullies while the ramps were made to facilitate scaling of abrupt rock ledges along the trail that could not be bypassed. Most ramps would take the form of a ladder with two outer, spanning poles connected by a series of cross rungs. The larger structures were rarely "brushed" with boughs. Instead the sleighs and toboggans were hauled up over the bare wood rungs. This permitted snow to pass through the structure, thus preventing a build-up which would allow the sleighs and toboggans to slip off the side of the span. These trail improvements were always undertaken only to the extent warranted by normal use. Travellers put in the minimum of work needed to keep the routes passable throughout the winter.

Some exceptions to this generalization did develop in the Temagami district. After contact with Europeans some routes were significantly upgraded for winter freighting by employees of the Hudson's Bay Company.

Up until the 1940s, over 75 well maintained *bon-ka-nah* existed in the Lake Temagami area. Macominising (Bear Island), Wa-wee-ay-gaming (Round Lake), Shkim-ska-jeeshing (Florence Lake), Abondiackong (Roasting Stick), Non-wakaming (Diamond Lake) were major intersections in this system of winter trails. Depending on the nature of the local topography and waterways, the *bon-ka-nah* ranged from a few hundred meters to many kilometers in length. Often the shorter *bon-ka-nah* formed links between a chain of ponds used only for winter travel. For example, the winter route from Maymeen-koba (Willow Island Lake) to Ka-bah-zip-kitay-begaw (Katherine Lake) followed a series of small ponds and connecting *bon-ka-nah* lying between the two branches of the Manja-may-gos Zeebi (Lady Evelyn River).

It took detailed knowledge of the terrain to determine the best location for many of the longer *bon-ka-nah*. Much evidence survives of the skillful use of swamps and geological faults in order to keep the trails direct and to minimize climbing. An outstanding example of using geological faults for easy passage through hilly terrain can be found today in a long fault which runs from Scarecrow Lake adjacent to Ishputina Ridge, the highest elevation in Ontario, cross country through Florence, Diamond, Jackpine, Net Lakes and the Ottertail River to Lake Temiskaming. No less than 14 *bon-ka-nah* are located along this great fault.

The *onigum* and *bon-ka-nah* of the Temagami district total over 1,300 in number. But inter-related network of summer and winter trails represents only a small portion of a larger system of *nastawgan* that until a few generations ago covered most of the Precambrian Shield country of eastern Canada. They defined the way of the wilderness traveller. Fortunately, the *nastawgan* of the Temagami district have remained in a largely unaltered condition. These ancient wilderness routes represent an important remnant of Canada's cultural heritage.

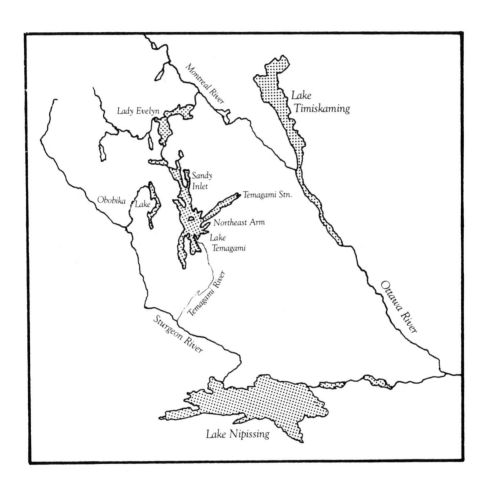

Lake
Timiskaming

Montreal River

Lady Evelyn

Sandy
Inlet

Temagami Stn.

Obobika Lake

Northeast Arm

Lake
Temagami

Ottawa River

Temagami River

Sturgeon River

Lake Nipissing

The Lure of the Temagami-based Canoe Trip

Bruce W. Hodgins

The Temagami experience has long attracted both youths and adults. Beginning in the late nineties of the last century and vastly expanding after the arrival of rail service in 1905, Lake Temagami became a major centre for men and women seeking canoe tripping adventure. After 1903 the Lake also became a principal base for a rugged type of organized youth camping, camping which was canoe-oriented, organized by both Canadians and Americans.

In 1901 Ontario established the Temagami Forest Reserve in the pre-Cambrian headwaters country of its northland. In 1903 the province dramatically enlarged the Reserve to just under six thousand square miles. Ontario designated the Forest, then the largest pinery in Eastern Canada, as an area to be nurtured under the best conservationist-oriented principles, so that it might sustain a perpetual yield of lumber. Secondarily, the Forest was dedicated to wilderness and semi-wilderness recreation.[1] While widespread lumbering was postponed in most parts of the Forest until the mid-twenties and while forestry practices failed decisively to achieve conservational goals,[2] the awesome, pristine beauty of its waterways, its rocky and wooded shores and its rugged hillsides survived, protected by shoreline reserves and, on Lake Temagami itself, by a broad skyline preserve and a policy of no mainland development beyond the emerging village.

This great Forest, some 500 kilometres north of Toronto, straddled the three great divides of Northeastern Ontario. Most of Lake Temagami flowed southward to Georgian Bay, down the challenging Temagami River to the Sturgeon, Lake Nipissing and the French. Yet Lake Temagami also had a small northern outlet whereby water flowed into the Lady Evelyn system which became the focus of one of the main concentrations of canoe tripping activity within the Forest. The Lady Evelyn was technically a part of the Ottawa valley; it emptied into the Montreal River which in turn flowed into Lake Temiskaming. Finally, to the northwest, the Temagami Forest crossed into the James Bay portion of the Arctic watershed and contained the headwaters of various tributaries of the Moose.

In 1926, road access on the primitive Ferguson Highway brought more canoeists to the Temagami-Lady Evelyn wilderness. But still it was probably the boys' canoe camps, beginning back in 1903, and later the girls' and co-ed camps which gave particular canoeing fame to the district. These youth camps later resisted many of the trends of organized camping farther south, trends taking place during the thirties, forties and fifties toward a more placid, more "child centred," in-camp focus. The Temagami camps helped keep alive for young people a tradition of wilderness travel.

*　　*　　*

The ubiquitous and controversial colonizing priest, Father Charles Alfred Paradis (1848–1926), seems to have initiated Temagami's role as a canoe tripping haven. Paradis claimed that he and three other young Ottawa clerics in 1880 (before their ordination) had become the first tourists to visit Lake Temagami when they paddled from Mattawa to Temiskaming, up the Matabitchuan and over to Lake Temagami, for fishing and general holidaying on Rabbit Nose Island.[3] Later, after he had established around 1891 his strange little orphan-farm mission at Sandy Inlet on Temagami's North Arm, Paradis often took time out to go on major canoe trips with journalists and railway publicists, often acting as their guide.

His most famous guided trip was that of 1898, which was belatedly written up and published with pictures in the April and May 1905 issues of *Rod and Gun in Canada*.[4] The group centred around L. O. Armstrong, the CPR's chief colonization officer who anonymously wrote it up for *Rod and Gun*. "Lake Temagami," he noted, was "shaped like a chrysanthemum, whose pistil is Bear Island, and whose petals, extending in every direction, enable us . . . to travel several hundreds of miles without visiting the same spot twice." The group rallied in Mattawa and took the new CPR spur line to the village of Temiskaming in Quebec. The group included the presidents of two American fishing clubs, a senior Montreal newspaperman, a senior railway official, and a professional photographer. From Temiskaming the participants took a steamer to the new little village of Haileybury where they were met by eight Indians with four birch bark canoes. The gear was transported in a wagon the six miles southwest to Sharp Lake, while the participants and Indians walked. They paddled and portaged to the Montreal River, proceeded upstream to Matawpika Falls, crossed into Lady Evelyn Lake and then Diamond. From Diamond the group portaged over the Sharp Rock Portage into Lake Temagami by its then northern outlet. Often during a short evening fish, the group caught as many bass as the 16 of them could eat, and they instituted a "heavy penalty" on anyone who killed more than could be consumed. On Lake Temagami, the trippers paddled onto the main part of the North Arm, back up Ferguson Bay to stay at Paradis' retreat for the night.

The next day they reached the Hudson's Bay post at Bear Island, purchased supplies, repaired their leaky canoes and pushed on to Island Bay. They camped "on a beautiful sandy point to the west of High Rock Island." It was a memorable night.

> We drank to sweethearts and wives, we smoked to the glory of God, . . . we had a regular broker's exchange of stories, and altogether spent many profitable hours before turning in to our very comfortable camps. The photograph of our Camp is very beautiful, but not nearly as fine as the camp itself—the magnificent coloring of the red pine, the bark of the trees, the green of the needles, and the perennial blue of the water, the whole making a combination which photography can reproduce only very imperfectly. W left Timagami by Timagami River, and found the fishing both above and below Timagami Falls better than anywhere else in the Lake.

Writing in 1905, Armstrong believed that the new railway and the publicity given earlier trips would "enable the best classes of people to enjoy" travelling around Lake Temagami:

> When I say 'best classes,' I mean those who will protect the fish and game, and by their sportsman-like behaviour add a charm if that be possible, to that far northern country. . . . Great is the number of those who are showing a hunger and a thirst for the thrilling excitements of exploring the unknown. This phenomenal condition though remarkable, is easy enough to explain. The marvellous growth of the American cities, the destruction of everything that is natural, and its replacement by the artificial, the pressure of population in the Eastern and even the Middle States, have reduced the wild regions south of the boundary line to such an extent that the lovers of the wild find it increasingly difficult, if not impossible, to gratify their tastes for life in the woods and wilds and turn longing eyes to the north. Canada has room eough in her illimitable stretches of forest, with lakes, streams, and mountains, extending practically from ocean to ocean, for all who may come. In addition to her other attractions, Canada can give space enough to make playgrounds for the world.

*   *   *

Already Archibald Lampman, the Ottawa poet and civil servant, had made the area famous with his poem *Lake Temagami*, "Set with a thousand islands, crowned with pines." Indeed, Duncan Campbell Scott in 1900 claimed that Lampman's heavy exertions on his 1896 canoe trip to Temagami upstream from Nipissing and then east from Temagami via the Matabitchuan to Temiskaming, had severely damaged his already weak heart, leading to Lampman's early death at the age of 37.[5]

In the spring of 1899, preceding the establishment of the Temagami Forest, the responsible Ontario cabinet minister, James M. Gibson (then styled the Commissioner of Crown Lands), his dynamic Assistant Commissioner Aubrey White, and Thomas Southworth, then Director of the Bureau of Forestry, all canoe tripped extensively through Lady Evelyn and Temagami Lakes, along with fire rangers and six guides. They had arrived by steamer at newly founded Haileybury, and had been carried by wagon to Bay Lake on the Montreal River where the canoe trip began. After sojourning a Bear Island, they left via the Northeast Arm, and the Matabitchuan River back to Lake Temiskaming.[6] Gibson wrote his close friend E. H. Bronson, the Ottawa Valley lumber baron who had large holdings on the west side of Temiskaming, that he should visit Temagami (he never did). The canoe trip, wrote Gibson, had been "one of the most enjoyable" trips of his life, and he thanked Bronson for first promoting the concept of the Temagami country as a Forest Reserve.[7] In July 1899, *Rod and Gun* asserted that the chief result of that high powered canoe trip would be the early establishment of a special and extra large forest and recreational reserve. It was.

Beginning in 1894, *Forest and Stream* ran a series of articles on northern canoeing featuring several Temagami routes. Other magazines followed. Thus, even before the arrival of rail, Temagami was well known to canoeing enthusiasts. Indeed, in 1903, James Edmund Jones in a major work entitled *Camping and Canoeing* described five major Temagami based wilderness canoe routes. One went from Lake Wanapitei to Lake Temagami via Lake Maskinonge, the Sturgeon, and Manitou Lake. A second, outlined with portage information, went down the Temagami River to the CPR at Sturgeon Falls; the third up the Montreal to Lady Evelyn Lake, south to Lake Temagami and down the Matabitchuan back to Lake Temiskaming. From Lady Evelyn one could ascend the exquisite Namabinnagasheshingue or Trout Streams flowing down "from the mountains." This stream, alternately beginning to be called the Lady Evelyn River, was "a route to the great Northland"; with its "eighty foot fall" (presumably Helen's Falls), it was "a paradise for photographers." With information supplied not by Jones but by George M. Kelly, the volume described in complex detail the route up the Sturgeon River to Apex Lake and over to Smoothwater Lake, then either east down the full Lady Evelyn River or north down the Montreal River.[8]

In 1900 the Ontario government commissioned a massive land survey of Northern Ontario. The surveyors and biologists explored the region, moving about by canoe. Its Party No. 3 covered the Temagami-Lady Evelyn-Smoothwater-Sturgeon waterways in the finest detail. Never before or since, in one summer, was so much of Temagami and its environs examined and reported upon by one team. Their descriptions of water courses, portages, fauna, flora and rocks appeared the next year in the *Report of the Survey of Northern Ontario, 1900*. The report was a treasure house of vital information for canoe trippers.

Blueberries

But it was 1905 before trippers could reach Lake Temagami other than by a long upstream canoe trip from either the CPR line by Sturgeon Falls or from Lake Temiskaming, via Haileybury and the Montreal River or up the Matabitchuan. That year the Temiskaming and Northern Ontario Railway (TNOR) passed by the Northeast Arm of Lake Temagami, thus putting the Lake within a day's train ride of Toronto. The same year, silver was discovered along the TNOR construction line nearby what became Cobalt, and the great Northern Ontario mining boom was on. Publicity for "New Ontario" was intense, and the Temagami area basked in reflected glory. It soon became the major Ontario playground for many executives and northern business developers, and this in turn attracted many more up from Toronto, Cleveland, and Rochester. Between 1905 and 1910, *Rod and Gun*, in particular, featured many stories on the delights of Temagami and Lady Evelyn canoe tripping—trips which were superior, it argued, to the much tamer Algonquin and other southern canoe haunts. Famous Canadians were soon paddling the Temagami waters in the canoe wake of Archibald Lampman. They included the novelist Ralph Connor, the poet Duncan Campbell Scott, and the artist C. W. Jeffreys.[9] No canoeing dark age this!

*   *   *

On August 21, 1904, even before the TNOR was officially opened, three Cleveland men, A. R. Horr, C. E. Sanders and Willie Bill Whiting secured a lift on a construction train to what became Temagami station. The next day they boarded a little steam-driven boat to Bear Island. Here they picked up three guides, Pete Beaucage, Mike Restoul and Mike Beaucage, and canoed north, up past Sharp Rock Inlet over to Nonwakoming (Diamond Lake) and to Lady Evelyn Lake (still often called Monzkaananing), where they passed a Grand Trunk party, photographing promotional scenes, and then another group of Cleveland friends which include Robert "the King" Newcomb and F. N. Cobb. The two groups followed the Wakimika-Obabika loop back to Bear Island, whereupon the Horr party continued to the south, passed Temagami Falls, Cross Lake and down the full Temagami River, with its many rapids and chutes, to the lower Sturgeon, until stopped by log jams eight miles from the rough wagon road in from the Sturgeon Falls CPR station. This was the first of a series of canoe trips undertaken by the Horr-Newcombe connection which was soon jocularly being called the Canadian Camp Fire Club of Cleveland.[10]

The next year Horr, Sanders, Cobb and Whiting tripped far up the Sturgeon River with five Indian guides, including Frank Commanada, and a cook. This time they disembarked the CPR at Wahnapitae just east of Sudbury and were hauled with their three or four Peterborough canoes, first by wagon and then by boat, across Lake Wanapitei to its north shore where canoeing began. The route headed north on the Chiniguchi system to Dewdney and Stauffer lakes and over to the Sturgeon. Then they ascended it with great tracking difficulty, up to Kettle Falls, the highest point in the valley ever reached by Americans, they reasoned. There they turned around, shot numerous rapids till they reached

Obabika Creek which they ascended;—"two miles of the hardest kind of paddle exercise against a vicious current that sapped the strength from the ancient arms." Via Wawiagama and Obabika, they reached Lake Temagami, purchased supplies from Harry Woods of the Hudson's Bay post on Bear Island, turned south into Gull and Emerald and to the lower Sturgeon, down it past the mouth of the Temagami River and to the same wagon road by Sturgeon Falls, used the year before. The experience is preserved by dozens of quality photographs mounted in a handsomely published album.[11] Whiting said he knew "how Wallace and Hubbard" felt and that it was "Labrador next year."

Although that was not to be, Horr and Adrian G. Newcomb did trip to James Bay in 1908. In one big all-wooden canoe, Horr and Newcomb, with Bear Island Indian guides Presque Petrant and William Peshabo (the latter as sternsman) disembarked the CPR at Missinaibi Station far northwest of Sudbury, and paddled down the Missinaibi, with its many rapids, and the Moose to Moose Factory and out onto the Bay. Then they returned up the Moose, Abitibi, and Frederick House Rivers back over the divide to Matachewan and Montreal River and south to Temagami, Bear Island and "King" Newcomb's Red Pines Island.

Fifteen year later, in 1919, Horr and Cobb took R. B. Newcomb and W. C. "Wild Cat" Boyle on a nostalgic return trip to the area. Another large and handsome annotated album survives. From Lake Temagami in seventeen foot Peterboroughs they went down the Obabika and briefly up the Sturgeon to the Yorston (apparently not yet called that), up it to its source at Bluesucker Lake and over to Florence in the headwaters country of the Lady Evelyn. They then descended its South Branch, Main Branch and South Channel, over to Diamond and Temagami. Beautiful photographs of the various falls are included in the album, as are many action shots in calm water and in rapids.[12]

Around 1905, at the beginning of his prolific writing career, the American George T. Marsh canoe-tripped through the Temagami country and far beyond. In 1908 he linked the various waterways of Northern Ontario and Northern Quebec in a haunting poem, "The Old Canoe," recently put to music. At one point, the song asks:

> When the sunset gilds the timbered hills that guard Temagami,
> And the moon beams play on far James Bay by the brink of the frozen sea,
> In phantom guise my spirit flies as the dream-blades dip and swing,
> Where the water flow from the Long Ago in the spell of the beckoning spring.
> Do the cow-moose call on the Montreal when the first frost bites the air,
> And the mist unfold from the red and gold that the autumn ridges wear?
> Do the white falls roar as they did of yore on the Lady Evelyn,
> And the square-tail leap from the black pool deep where the pictured rocks begin?[13]

Then in 1911, Marsh, Thomas Horr and "a half-breed Cree named Charlie," used their Temagami experience by proceeding by rail far to the northwest, to a point sixty miles south of Lac Seul. From there, near the Manitoba border, they began a three month canoe trip involving the full Albany River, all the way to Fort Albany on James Bay; the route then involved a coastal paddle to Moose

Factory. There they abandoned their "almost shattered" small Old Town canoes from Maine, obtained a new large Peterborough, dismissed the drunken Charlie, and with two local Crees ascended the Abitibi. It was October before they reached the new east-west National Transcontinental rail line, still under construction. Thus, their "days of hardship and delight in the silent places ended."[14]

*   *   *

By 1905, when the TNOR officially opened, Lake Temagami already had two boys' camps devoted to quality wilderness canoe tripping; the Canadian-owned Camp Temagami and the American-owned Keewaydin, both established in 1903. Until 1905 it required a week long canoe trip merely to reach the two camps. A. L. Cochrane, the owner of Camp Temagami, had operated for two seasons in the Muskoka area. Cochrane was a drill and physical education instructor at Upper Canada College, the source for many of his campers. He had the Temagami experience endorsed by UCC's headmaster Sir George Parkin. Cochrane also founded the Royal Life Saving Society of Canada, and swimming and life saving skills held a major place in the in-camp routine. "But nothing," his 1905 brochure stressed, "is so fascinating to the adventuresome spirit of a boy as a [canoe] trip." Camp Temagami stressed the value of fine tuned physical education in the out-of-doors, a program in which vigorous canoe trips played a significant role.

Keewaydin had operated in Maine since 1893. A. A. Gregg Clarke directed Keewaydin which was owned by an American company of educators singularly dedicated to the challenging canoe trip as a character-building exercise which would create American leaders. Keewaydin ran the more adventuresome trips, with virtually no in-camp program. Its ivy league owners, who were linked to various New England prep schools, had "in a bark canoe found" Lake Temagami in 1902 with the help of Mattawa Indians and Métis guides. "The trip in," being by way of the Matabitchuan River, henceforth was commemorated by a long song which included the refrain: "Otta, Ottawa, Temiskaming, Matta, Matta, Mattabitchouan, Waboos, Waba, Mokwa Sagaigan and fair Temagami."[15] By 1904 they were operating on their permanent North Arm Devil's Island site with 66 campers and staff; by 1906 Keewaydin had 131 participants, and by 1914, the number was 226.[16] The Mattawa natives for decades "guided" the more ambitious Keewaydin sections. But "guiding" did not mean conducted tours. The guide was merely a leader responsible for the route, for the on-water decisions, and for providing advanced campcraft skills. Counselling was the responsibility of the trip's American staffmen. The Mattawa men introduced late nineteenth century Temiskaming-Abitibi-Kipawa fur trade packing, portaging and paddling techniques. Mastering difficult rapids was, to them, in integral part of all canoemanship. The head tump was basic to the carrying of both gear and canoe. On Keewaydin trips food and cooking utensils were carried in a wanagan—a wooden box strapped up with a tump. The now famous (or infamous) wanagan (spelled "wannigan" by Keewaydin) seems to have come to Northern Ontario from early

New Brunswick lumbering usages, via Maine and the Keewaydin origins.[17] Outside ridgepole tents without floors, plus clothes and bedding were all carried in a duffle or in a canvas-covered bed roll, also wrapped up by a tump or secured on top of the wanagan. The trip was expected to be efficiently organized but difficult. Soon, Keewaydin sections were following the many remote Indian and fur trade routes of Northeastern Ontario.

In 1911, after several years of planning, Keewaydin launched its first trip from Lake Temagami over the divide and down the Abitibi and the Moose Rivers to Moose Factory and James Bay.[18] The "Bay trip" immediately became a tradition. In the early years the routes to the Bay, besides the Abitibi, included the Mattagami, Kapaskasing, Missinaibi and Abitibi. All trips involved a good deal of white water. The upstream return paddle was particularly difficult; it usually involved ascending the Abitibi River to the Frederick House River, ascending that river to its source, then crossing the divide to Matachewan and paddling down the Montreal River. The 1915 camp brochure explained that the six week "extremely hard" Bay trip would "go every foot of the way by paddle and portage" and would be open only to the hardiest of canoe veterans, who would first have to prove themselves on a two week trip up the Lady Evelyn to Florence Lake and down the Sturgeon. On that 1915 Bay trip, they proceeded below Moose Factory and reached Charlton Island (as they had in 1914) on a small powered sloop which had their canoes strapped on the side; they then journeyed on a freight ship northeast to the Belcher Islands in Hudson Bay. It was September 22 before they had paddled upstream and were back at Keewaydin. Except for brief wartime interludes, Keewaydin's Bay trip tradition survives, now on very remote northern rivers, but without the arduous upstream return paddle.

In the decades which followed 1903, thousands of American boys, first through Keewaydin, and hundreds of Canadian boys, first through Camp Temagami, experienced several summers of quality wilderness canoe tripping in Northern Ontario and adjacent Northwestern Quebec. In 1930, another American, Homer C. Grafton, established Camp Wigwasati in the Southwest Arm of Lake Temagami. Grafton had seen YMCA service in Japan, and he placed a firm emphasis on social gospel Christianity, but increasingly the canoe trip became central to the program. Campers tended to come from the upstate New York, Michigan and Ohio.[19] In 1931, Ed Archibald established a second Canadian-owned camp, called Wanapitei, on Lake Temagami at Paradis' old Sandy Inlet site; one of its patrons was General Sir Arthur Currie.[20] Each of the new operations was distinctive in its own way, but to a large degree each followed in the traditions of its national precursor. Then in 1933 Camp Wabun was established by seven American staff rebels from Keewaydin, men who re-emphasized the value of the especially rugged canoe trip, but they still kept most of the Keewaydin style and Mattawa native link.[21] It was about 1940 before a camp for girls was established on Temagami, Cayuga, owned by Henry Woodman, a Quaker science teacher from Baltimore, and his Métis wife Margaret from Temagami. Cayuga had numerous staff links with Keewaydin; it focused on the quality canoe trip and had a Mattawa native as chief tripping guide.[22]

Thus, before Algonquin and Haliburton had become synonymous with Canadian youth camping, Lake Temagami had deep, abiding and different camping traditions. Canoe tripping, not an elaborate in-camp program, became the focus. River work, rapids and hard portages, with Temagami as a base for trips much farther to the north, was the emphasis. The Temagami youth camps would permanently plant their mark on canoe tripping throughout Northern Ontario, even though the Keewaydin and Wabun people would keep themselves rather aloof from most leaders in the Canadian youth camping movement.

*   *   *

Youths from the canoe camps were far from being the only people to trip extensively in the Temagami country. Increasingly, private parties made the area their destination for adventuresome but reasonably safe and, after 1905, readily accessible canoe tripping. While small groups of male friends were definitely most common, expeditions were often made up of three or four young adult couples—one couple generally being married, and acting as "chaperone" to the others, often unmarried. Sometimes, instead, it was a family group—led by a father who may have been a former camper at a Temagami youth camp. Canoes were usually made in Peterborough; initially they were all-wood, but by the thirties almost exclusively canvas-covered. They were usually rented either in the village of Temagami, which grew up around the train station at the head of the Northeast Arm, or from the Hudson's Bay Company on Bear Island, reached by steamer, the *Belle of Temagami*. Sometimes the trips were guided, especially if fishing was a central goal, usually by a Bear Island Indian or a Temagami Métis. More often the groups travelled on their own. The Forest had dozens of Rangers, portages were increasingly well-marked—often by a simple board nailed to a tree, usually with the yardage painted on the board. Reasonably good tripping maps were readily available. The opening in 1927 of the Ferguson Highway from North Bay past Temagami to New Liskeard even further increased Temagami's canoeing popularity.

Most of these private adult parties were not looking for whitewater. The goal was what they perceived as deep wilderness. We might call it a quest for nordicity. The quest involved a search for stillness, beauty, wildlife, fishing, and companionship.

One such "adult" trip, in August 1921, provided a link between Temagami tripping and the then evolving Algonquin-style youth camping. In 1906, when Taylor Statten was still a young Boy's Work Secretary for the Toronto Y.M.C.A. and one year after he had become the first Director of the Y.M.C.A. Camp Couchiching, he had gone on a short Temagami canoe trip with his assistant Wallace Forgie and several others. Then, fifteen years later, just weeks after Taylor Statten had established Camp Ahmek in Algonquin Park, he allowed his twelve year old daughter Adele (the future Director of Wapameo, the Taylor Statten camp for girls), to canoe around Temagami with six adults, including the

same Wally Forgie, by then working for the "Y" in Calgary and married to Taylor
Statten's sister-in-law Alice Page. The trip contained at least one Ahmek staff
person, Ace Milks and Ace's fiancée Florence Scott (who was Statten's "Y"
secretary). A detailed illustrated and humorous account of their canoe trip survives.[23] Ace and his friend began on the GTR's line, formerly Booth's Canada
Atlantic, in Ottawa, and seven hours later picked up young Adele ("Couchie")
and her aunt at Joe Lake in the Park. They later switched to the main northbound
line at Scotia Junction. Two came north by overnight train from Toronto, and
Forgie joined the group a day later in Temagami, by southbound train from the
West. They rented canoes in the village, naturally took no guide, canoed to Bear
Island and north over Sharp Rock to Diamond and Lady Evelyn Lake, and back to
Diamond and around the classic Wakimiki-Obabika Loop to Temagami.

They fished, swam, portaged, swatted mosquitoes, sang, played cards,
looked at the moon, and endured lots of rain and sunshine. They took turns, both
males and females (except Adele), at being skipper—and loved it. The women
were generally "khaki-clad" in knee breeches, and are pictured carrying their bed
rolls and gear with the aid of a head-tump. The menu seemed to stress Aunt
Jemima pancakes, porridge, fresh fish, "creamed chicken and peas," corn, raisins,
bully beef, honey, chocolate and lots of tea. "To those not acquainted with the
joys of canoeing," ran the report, "it might be remarked that there is really no joy
like unto the joy of getting thoroughly soaked in a fine driving rain. To have your
clothes plastered tight against you and feel the rain drops splash upon your
dripping hat is mere nothing when you think that probably the bread-bag is
floating in a growing puddle, and that each loaf will probably be well covered with
mud before its appearance at a subsequent meal." At the Sharp Rock portage they
met a "party of Yankees" who showed some concern for "folks who travel that
country without a guide but they were actually quite harmless."

For each of four years, between 1926 and 1929 Dr. Hubert Brown and his
wife, first alone, then with relatives, and finally with his young children, took
similar canoe trips in the Temagami area. Brown, as a young Toronto medical
student, had been a rare Canadian on the staff of Keewaydin for about three years,
probably 1909 to 1911. In those days, he had taken many pictures of the camp and
of tripping far up the Lady Evelyn and beyond. Fortunately, his album survives.[24]
When he returned privately in 1926 to trip with his wife, he kept meticulous
notes which also survive, notes on every conceivable detail of his tripping.[25] They
give an unsurpassed picture of private canoeing in Temagami during those years.

The nineteen day, "Obabika" trip of September 1926 cost the Browns a
total of $88.72, including train with berths and meals ($60.00), boat from
Keewaydin ($10.20) and their trip food ($15.00). They carried two wanagans,
weighing when full 78 and 92 pounds respectively; the clothes and tent bag
weighed 41½ pounds and the blankets 45 pounds. Brown was deeply impressed
with the newly marketed powdered milk (KLIM) which he used instead of evaporated milk. Food was standard and basic, avoiding cans and using dried fruit. The
cooking outfit featured pots, frying pans, pannakins, and reflector oven, and

equipment included canvas patching and tump lines. They used blankets, quilts and woolen pajamas, but no sleeping bags. He took flannel shirts, light underwear, a sweater and wool socks, while she took a "camping skirt," sweater, burbery, knitted shirts, light stockings and heavy socks. The route from Keewaydin was over the Devil's Bay portage and on into Obabika, south to Emerald, back to Obabika, with various day excursions from there, then around the route's loop to Diamond, Sharp Rock, Sandy Inlet (and Paradis' ruins), and back to Keewaydin.

In 1927 they took with them Robert's brother and sister-in-law. They began paddling at Bear Island, went through KoKoKo Lake, past Keewaydin to Sandy Inlet and on into Anima Nippissing; then they followed a very hard creek route via Harris and Shallow to Eagle, Turner, Whitefish, Diamond and the loop to Obabika, back to Lake Temagami. Hubert and his wife then went off to a five night base camp at Wasacsinagami.

The August 1928 trip included their five young children and an assistant. Six of them drove in the family car north up the new Ferguson Highway. They made it in one day, leaving Toronto at 5:30 a.m. and reaching Temagami at 5:00 p.m., averaging about 30 miles per hour. Their two canvas-covered canoes and much of their gear went by train. The morning after they arrived, they hired a launch ($25.00 each way) and were taken to Sandy Inlet where they made their base camp for almost a month. From there they took canoe jaunts and hikes, plus an overnight with Hubert and three of the children (one boy and two girls) to Jackpine Lake. At Sandy Inlet, the main problem was wind. The month cost $275.00, including $90 worth of new equipment and $93 worth of food. Before leaving, they undertook a major cleanup of the entire beach area—finding more than 337 "tins."

The base camp experience was repeated in 1929. This time all of the family went on a three day side trip to Whitefish and Turner Lakes and a four day side trip to Whitewater and Diabese Lakes. On one portage the eldest son fell, and Dr. Brown had to apply six stitches—"never squealed." Back in Temagami, the kids "gorged" on beefsteak, and Brown concluded that this indicated a "meat deficiency." "A whole month is too long without meat." Yet they had taken canned sardines, caught good fish and had 7½ pounds of "cooked, sealed" ham, 9½ pounds of side bacon and a small amount of back bacon.

From 1927 to 1930, my own parents canoe tripped with relatives and friends in the Temagami Forest. Their experiences were somewhat similar to those of the Browns, though no children were included and they were not equipped as well as the Keewaydin-oriented Browns.[26] The Hodgins trip of 1927 was their second major canoe trip, having honeymooned for two weeks in Algonquin Park the year before. Taking three days to reach Temagami, by automobile, they skirted muskeg along the Ferguson Highway, where workers were driving down poles on top of a car which had been abandoned in the seemingly bottomless mud. There was no pavement outside the towns on their entire route from Kitchener. The two couples in the party took the *Belle* to Bear Island where they rented canoes and headed north. Their eight-day trip involved he Diamond-

Obabika circle route. The next year eight of them began north of Temagami (where they rented canoes), at Latchford, and paddled up the Montreal into Lady Evelyn Lake, Diamond and back to Temagami. Often they slept under the stars on juniper bushes, much to the astonishment of a shivering southern American group which they met. In 1929 they rented canoes from Smith at Temagami, paddled the entire Lake Temagami to Diamond and more or less repeated their 1928 trip in reverse. Then in 1930 ten of them rented canoes in Temagami, but began in Rabbit Lake to the east. The group included my uncle and aunt on the second part of their honeymoon. My mother was five months pregnant with this author himself! The route was a difficult one, with dozens of portages, northwest to Mountain Lake and Anima Nippissing, down to Sandy Inlet and the Paradis ruins, into KoKoKo and back to the village. On Mountain Lake they claim to have killed a rattlesnake,[27] coiled at the foot of the bed of the sleeping "honey-mooners." Throughout, they used basic food similar to that of the Browns, but they relied more heavily on canned goods. They used Canadian-made Woods packsacks with tumps, rather than wanagans. Sleeping on ground sheets, they used large blanket pins with bedding folded to simulate sleeping bags.

Private adult canoe tripping on the Temagami waterways continued throughout the thirties, apparently on a slightly reduced scale. In 1934 Ruth Terborg and three other young women drove a car from New York City to Temagami and undertook, on their own, a fairly extensive canoe trip not dissimilar from those undertaken by the Statten group or the Brown family. The Terborg venture was the first all female canoe trip recorded in the area. Relying heavily on Horace Kephart's *Woodcraft for Women*, they paddled off from Bear Island "in a flutter of bifurcated garments." Throughout the trip, the women singly portaged their own canoes.[28]

*   *   *

The Second World War had a much greater effect than had the Depression in curtailing canoe trips. After 1945, however, rigorous canoe trips organized by the Temagami youth camps, again involving extensive river travel, revived much faster than did adult trips organized privately. Keewaydin revived its Bay trip tradition in 1948, with a voyage in Northern Quebec from Oskaleneo, Chibougamau and Mistassini down the remote Rupert River to Rupert House, a trip previously undertaken by the camp in 1934 and 1939. In 1951, by repeating the Bay trip of 1931, Keewaydin began annually to send an expedition all they way from Temagami, northeastward into Quebec, over the divide, and down the extremely difficult Harricanaw River to James Bay and then along the coast to Moosonee.[29] Meanwhile, Wabun Northwoods (a Cleveland YMCA camp based in Temagami), Camp Temagami and Wanapitei all initiated their own James Bay canoe trips. Wanapitei's first Bay trip was in 1961, led by the author.

For the older Canadian and American youths, Lake Temagami had become primarily a base, near to conveniences and to civilization. The fast-flowing rivers much farther to the north were their waterways. For most private adult trippers, particularly those who were not veterans of the youth camps, Lake Temagami itself and the hundreds of lakes and streams connected to it were their "wilderness" destination.

Each group, adult or youth, experienced or novice, whether it used Temagami as a base or as a destination, was searching for its own northland. Indeed, most individuals who tripped and returned again to trip were involved in their own personal voyage of discovery, seeking their own mythical northland. Often the young canoeists sang a song about this quest, set to the tune of "Road to the Isles," a song which began, "It's the far northland that's calling me away, as I set forth with my pack and take the road. It's the tang of the pine and balsam on the breeze that brings me to the waterways once more." Temagami was not, of course, truly in the far North—despite what campers from the United States or even from Toronto may have thought. But for canoe trippers, old and young, it lay in that mystical far North of the mind. To the canoe trippers Temagami answered their quest for nordicity.

ENDNOTES

1. Bruce W. Hodgins, Jamie Benidickson and Peter Gillis, "The Ontario and Quebec Experiments with Forest Reserves, 1883–1930," *Journal of Forest History*, 26 (January 1982), 20-33. In 1964, the "Temagami Forest" ceased formally to exist when Ontario abolished all such surviving provincial forests.

2. Bruce Hodgins and Jamie Benidickson, "Resource Management Conflict in the Temagami Forest, 1898–1914," *Historical Papers 1978* (Canadian Historical Association, Ottawa, 1979), and the latter's "Temagami and the Northern Ontario Tourist Frontier," *Laurentian University Review*, IX (February 1979, 43-69).

3. Bruce W. Hodgins, *Paradis of Temagami* (Cobalt 1976), pp. 2-3. The first canoe trip to Lake Temagami by a Euro-Canadian not connected with the fur trade was probably that by the surveyor David Taylor; see Bruce W. Hodgins, "1837: To Temagami by Canoe from Near Toronto," *Temagami Times*, July 1978.

4. See the 1905 *Rod and Gun* article; note also, Bruce W. Hodgins, "Canoe Tripping Lake Temagami in 1898," in the *Temagami Experience*, July 1978, from which the following account is basically taken.

5. *The Poems of Archibald Lampman* (Toronto 1900), pp. xix-xx.

6. PAC, MG 19, D13, *Temagami Journal*, 1894-1903, various references, 1899, 1900 and 1901.

7. PAC, MG 28, Bronson Company Papers, 18 October 1899.

8. Note pp. 119, 132 and 141-43. For more details on *Camping and Canoeing* (Toronto 1903) note the present author's piece on "The Written Word" in this volume.

9. For the influence of Temgami and the symbol of "Keewaydin," the northwest wind, in the work of C. W. Jeffreys, see Robert Stacey's three articles on Jeffreys in *Northward Journal: A Quarterly of Northern Arts*, 20 (June 1981, 5-50, especially 27-29. In general, note Jamie Benidickson, "Temagami and the Northern Ontario Tourist Frontier," *Laurentian University Review*, IX (Feb. 1979), 43-69. For Scott, see Pelham Edgar, "Travelling with a Poet," in his *Across my Path* (Toronto 1952). For Connor, see Charles W. Gordon, *Postscripts to Adventure: the Autobiography of Ralph Connor* (New York 1938), especially "The Canoe Trip," pp. 45-64, and "On the Wanapitei," pp. 65-71.

10. Horr Collection owned by Dora Young of Ooshke, Island 672, loaned in 1982 to the Temagami Historical Association for possible reproduction, TLA Archives, Temagami; and *Nizheshin Kabashwin (Good Camping Places) in Temagami Forest Reserve* (ltd. ed., Cleveland Books, 1904).

11. Horr Collection, Willie Bill Whiting, *Up the Sturgeon*, (six copies, Cleveland Books, 1905).

12. Horr Collection, W. C. Boyle, "Ramblings of the Boyle" (1919).

13. *Scribner's Magazine*, 44 (October 1908), 447, reprinted in the Frontispiece of his first of eleven novels, *Toilers of the Trails* (Philadelphia 1921).

14. "The Albany Trail to James Bay," *Scribner's Magazine*, 51 (April 1912), 433-48.

15. A. T. Fenn, *The Story of Keewaydin: 50 Years at Dunmore, 1910–1959* (n.p. 1959), p. 5. Note also Brian Back, *The Keewaydin Way: A Portrait: 1893-1983* (Temagami 1983).

16. Fenn, p. 6.

17. For this information on the wanagan, the author would like to thank Brian Back, author of *The Keewaydin Way*. On it, note pp. 64-65 and 187.

18. Ed Ruge, "The First Hudson Bay Trip," from the *Keewaydin Kicker*, 1911, reprinted in Back, *The Keewaydin Way*, pp. 81-88.

19. TLA Archives, Grafton Papers.

20. 1932 Brochure.

21. Brochures and interviews with Richard Lewis III, Wabun's current Director. See also Back, *The Keewaydin Way*, pp. 120-22.

22. Interviews with Margaret Woodman and Bella White spread over many years.

23. Trent University Archives, OCA Papers, "Seven Smiling Seraphs or Tenting Tentatively in 'Temagami'," courtesy of Adele Statten Ebbs.

24. Owned by his daughter, Mrs. Joan Hillary of Lakefield, and on loan to the Trent University Archives.

25. Originals held by Mrs. Joan Hillary, but typescript, copy of logs and equipment lists, etc. are in Trent University Archives.

26. From interviews with Stanley and Laura Belle Hodgins, 1981 and 1982.

27. Rattlesnakes are extremely rare in Temagami, which is north of their range.

28. Ruth E. Terborg, "Timagami for Women," *Appalachia*, June 1936, pp. 2-9. The author is indebted to Jamie Benidickson who discovered this article. Concerning female canoeing, also note both the article by Gweneth Hoyle in this volume and Emerson Hough, "Canoeing for Girls," *Maclean's*, August 1915, pp. 73-74.

29. Back, *The Keewaydin Way*, pp. 170-171. One of the most remarkable features of this book is the listing from documentary sources, of all major trips taken by Keewaydin from 1893 to 1982; see "Pioneering Expeditions," pp. 168-75. This listing is followed by a "Glossary," pp. 176-188, of canoeing terms, place names and Ojibwa-Cree words frequently used by experienced Temagami-based canoe trippers.

Kawartha Lakes Regattas

Jean Murray Cole

Cheering crowds lined the shore as the sleek canoes raced headlong through the water, each with twelve glistening paddles dipped in unison by its crew of Indian women:

> The Indians on the shore ran backwards and forwards on the beach, exciting . . . [the paddlers] to exertion by loud cries, leaping into the air, whooping and clapping their hands; and when at length the first canoe dashed up to the landing-place, it was as if all had gone at once distracted and stark mad. The men, throwing themselves into the water, carried the winners out in their arms, who were laughing and panting for breath.[1]

Thus Anna Jameson described the race she witnessed on Manitoulin Island in August 1837 on her Northern Ontario tour when 3,700 Indians, some from as far as 500 miles away, were encamped for the annual distribution of "presents" from the British government. The gala gathering included a grand council of 75 Chiefs, among them Mississauga, with speeches, consultations, drumming, dancing, and a canoe race one evening at sunset paddled by women only, each crew with "one man to steer."

For generations the Indians had contested skills in their sleek birchbark canoes. Fur traders and early settlers soon joined in the sport. French Canadian voyageurs, who took great pride in their prowess as paddlers, frequently engaged in races to break the monotony of their long journeys carrying furs and supplies back and forth along the western waterways. By the early 1820s these informal races had led to more structured competitions staged on the St. Lawrence and Ottawa Rivers when voyageurs, Indians and settlers vied for the honours.[2]

Of the Indians' skill with the paddle, John Langton wrote from Fenelon Falls in 1834, "I decidedly have not yet acquired the true Indian twist of the wrist," but, he allowed, "I am a very tolerable hand and can face a heavy swell or stem a rapid much to my satisfaction."[3] In the next few years he and the group of sociable bachelors who were taking up land in the area organized regattas for their amusement on Cameron Lake. John's sister, Anne, reported on the excitement they generated in July 1839:

> I take credit to myself for getting through twelve days' journal without once writing the word regatta, a sound which must vibrate on the air of these lakes some hundred and fifty times a day. On Cameron's Lake it has been the topic for the last three months. We are only just getting drawn in. The Regatta together with the steamboat at the Falls standing still, and the ship-carpenters being unemployed, has led to the building of several new boats, and very much increased our navy.[4]

Some years later, when Samuel Strickland's "agricultural school" for young English gentlemen proposing to become settlers was a feature of the Lakefield scene, their newspaper, the "Katchewanooka Herald", gave an account of an exciting race in June 1856 "between S. Strickland's boat 'The Roaring Billy' and F. H. D'Arcy's canoe 'La Belle Katarine', the 'Billy' to be pulled by E. Leigh and H. Pearse, 'The Katarine' to be paddled by R. Strickland and F. Barlee."[5]

The regattas, of which these are examples, clearly represent a move on the part of Canadian settlers to emulate their wilderness-travelling predecessors, in what can be interpreted as a part of their quest for an element of the wilderness experience.

*   *   *

The first Peterborough regatta is said to have been held in 1857, when John Edwards raced in a canvas-covered, wood-frame canoe—the inspiration for J. S. Stephenson's design of his lightweight, basswood canoe, the forerunner of the famed "Peterborough canoe."[6]

In September 1859, the Peterborough Examiner reported complete results of a two-day regatta held on Little Lake, when separate events were held for Indians and Whites, with the Indians favouring birch canoes and the white men paddling log canoes. The segregation was necessary because, pitted against each other in a paddling race, the Indians would invariably win. The names of F. H. D'Arcy, H. Pearse and R. Strickland reappear in the results of this meet. Six races were scheduled for each day. At the end of the second day a special race for Indian women was won by Betty Crow, with Mrs. R. B. Morgan second. In one of two private matches H. Crow with his canoe "Sinclair" defeated T. Irons in "Lance." They then traded canoes but finished in the same order. Challenger D'Arcy beat R. Strickland in their private race. Others who placed in races at that two-day meet included George Strickland, H. Caddy, Daniel Herald (the Gore's Landing boat-builder), H. Rogers, H. Calcutt and J. Walsh.[7]

Regattas were very much a fixture of summer life in the Kawarthas from very early days. Records show that the same names reappear as winners generation after generation. The Crow family, whose members continue to compete and win at local regattas and long-distance races to this day, won three firsts in the 1859 regatta, and featured again in an account of a regatta held at Idylwyld on Rice Lake in August 1880. On that occasion "Jerry and Robert Crow paddled against G. Toboco and D. Whootong [Whetung] of Chemong. The race was loudly applauded by the spectators and considered one of the best ever paddled on the lake."[8] Within a decade Daniel Whetung, of Curve Lake, was organizing his own regattas at the Indian Village, with prizes ranging from sets of silver knives and forks to shirts and shoes.[9]

Meets such as those held at Idylwyld were equally spectator events. The *Golden Eye* excursion boat brought a large number of visitors from Peterborough, who partook of an early dinner at Mr. Calcutt's hotel before the races began at three o'clock in the afternoon. Local Indians—J. Howard of Hiawatha and G. Toboco of Chemong Lake—took part in the first match, won by Howard who had "a much lighter and better canoe." The featured race of the day for the "Champion Cup" was a great disappointment. Jarvis, of Hamilton, and Dunspaugh, of

Toronto, appeared to be in collusion, with the latter seeming "to lose all interest in the race . . . allowing the competitor to win by about a quarter of a mile."[10] Earlier that same summer another regatta was held at Idylwyld, this one sponsored by the Peterborough Boat Club,[11] and several other meets were mentioned in the newspaper including the "annual regatta" held at Savigney's "a short distance from town" on September 1.[12]

The waterway provided a summer playground. Excursion boat operators were quick to see an opportunity for developing more business, some of them organizing regattas themselves, notably Henry Calcutt on Rice Lake. With lots of excitement for competitor and spectator alike, these outings were a popular feature of life during the last decades of the 19th century. The Sturgeon Point regatta in 1878 was attended by 2,000 people,[13] and the Chemong Park regatta in 1883 attracted a large enough crowd to generate the $7,000 in bets which changed hands over a sculling race between J. Mercer and J. E. McIntyre.[14]

By this time the Peterborough Rowing Club had been formed (1871). Already its members had distinguished themselves by placing second in the Dominion Regatta held at Lachine, Quebec, in July 1879,[15] and first at a regatta held in Barrie the same year, competing against the Toronto Argonaut Rowing Club and the Hamilton Leanders.[16] The Rowing Club members were also the canoe enthusiasts, and it was this involvement that prevented a Peterborough delegation from attending the first congress of the American Canoe Association at Lake George, New York, in 1880.[17] The invitation was refused because a Peterborough crew made up of A. J. Belcher, W. P. Shaw, G. C. Rogers, and E. B. Rogers, with E. B. Edwards and C. Show as spares, were attending the first regatta of the Amateur Oarsmen's Association at the Argonaut Club in Toronto.[18] In spite of this absence, Canadians fared well at the A.C.A. meet. Thomas Henry Wallace, of Gore's Landing, won both the men's single paddling race (with a single-bladed paddle and undecked canoe, something of a novelty to the Americans) as well as the special "Rushton Race" with the prize a Rushton-built canoe. The latter, according to a journalist's report, he won "while nonchalantly smoking his pipe and pausing to scoop up a drink of water."[19] It was apparent that the Canadian style of canoe was faster than the Americans' heavier decked cruising style, and it prompted one of the members to write later, "I think such canoes as Wallace's should be a distinct class."[20]

In 1881 the Peterborough contingent joined other A.C.A. members at Lake George and the following year E. B. Edwards, a young Peterborough lawyer, was elected Commodore. He invited the group to meet at Stoney Lake in 1883.[21] To accommodate the 400 campers who took part in the Congress, Edwards and his law partner George M. Roger (later County Judge for Northumberland and Durham) purchased the 96-acre Juniper Island, 10-acre Otter Island and another smaller island nearby, all Crown lands in Stoney Lake.[22]

*   *   *

Returning from church, Otter Island, Stoney Lake.

A.C.A. Regatta, 1883.

This was the regatta to surpass them all. Invitations went out to canoeists far and near, informing them that the two-week camp was planned for August 10 to 24, 1883, with regatta events to take place on Tuesday, Wednesday and Thursday of the second week. Arrangements were made to have supplies forwarded to the camp site. Local farmers were alerted to supply fresh milk, butter, eggs, and vegetables. Of course, fish would be available for the taking.[23] Large advertisements appeared in the Peterborough newspaper urging readers to "prepare for the meet at Stoney Lake" and offering a selection of "tents, flags, folding camp beds, chairs, tables, etc." Andrew McNeill, tailor and clothier, promised "any conceivable camp luxury."[24]

A.C.A. members from New York, Cincinnatti, Rochester, Philadelphia, and many other centres went north to join their Canadian friends at the remote wilderness setting. Even to Torontonians, Stoney Lake was the North, albeit only 100 miles away. They all made their way to Peterborough, where they boarded a train (with their canoes) for Lakefield. From there they could take the steamer *The Fairy* or paddle the 12 miles through Katchewanooka and Clear Lakes to the Juniper Island campsite, effectively setting the mood for their two-week flight from the civilized world.[25]

To the Americans it was an exotic adventure—the clear unsullied water and the rugged granite islands of Stoney Lake, unpopulated as yet by invading cottagers, provided the perfect rough-hewn setting—a taste of the North.

On the appointed weekend the crowds began to assemble, coming from as far afield as Maine and Colorado, with many New Yorkers and Ohioans among the group. Commodore Hugh Neilson of the Toronto Canoe Club and five fellow members were among the first arrivals. Seven members of the Knickerbocker Club of New York were a day late, delayed by saw logs at Young's Point. The first week was one of camaraderie, visiting back and forth among the campsites on the three islands, excursions to local points of interest such as the visit to the art gallery across the lake. Another day a party paddled over to the east shore and climbed Blue Mountain. Fishing and duck shooting were popular pastimes, augmenting the camp larders. Wives and daughters of the members were segregated at a separate camp site known as "Squaw Point" and when a male camper ventured to set forth on their territory one day, he was promptly called before a "Court" and fined—to the tune of a box of chocolates for each lady, according to one report. As the Peterborough *Examiner* of August 23, 1883, reported: "It appears that the ladies' camp is sacred ground, not to be lightly profaned, and kept guarded with ORIENTAL EXCLUSIVENESS."

Although there were eight "lady members" (six of whose canoes were named) listed in the 1883 *American Canoe Association Book*, the official organ of the association, there were no ladies' races on the program. Presumably their role was to stand by the sidelines and cheer. It appears that wives, daughters and lady friends were all segregated from the male participants who set up their own campsites with names such as the "Syndicate Camp" of the Peterborough contingent, whose hospitality became legendary, and the "Knickerbocker" campsite of the New Yorkers. Communal gatherings took place on Juniper Island, where a large marquee was set up and meetings and prize-givings took place. It is said that "girling" was much indulged in; there is no doubt that many a courtship was furthered by attendance at American Canoe Association regattas.

Church services were held on Sundays, complete with a choir. Rev. R. H. Neide, an Episcopalian clergyman from Canajoharie, N.Y., whose two sons were founding members of the A.C.A. conducted the service on the first Sunday, with Rev. J. C. French, a Presbyterian from Jersey City, preaching the sermon. Evenings were spent around the camp fire singing and story-telling. On one memorable night an illuminated procession of sixty-five canoes, all lit with Chinese lanterns, made its way around Otter Island, starting at the ladies' camp and returning to Juniper for the day's prize-giving.[26]

According to the *Examiner*, there was "a motly assemblage of canoes . . . every builder in Canada being represented, but English's canoes and those made by the Ontario Canoe Company take the lead." Dr. C. A. Neide, of Schuylerville, N.Y., the secretary of the Association, brought his Rob Roy canoe, in which he had cruised a total of 3,800 miles since the 1882 meet at Lake George. Another curiosity was the "antique birch bark canoe" belonging to Lieutenant-Colonel Kensington from the Royal Military College in Kingston, "which is an object of general observation amongst its more stylish and nobby companion craft."[27]

The rule was that members must paddle or sail their own canoes, and exchanging canoes "for racing purposes" was not allowed. According to all accounts there were craft of every description on hand. Many campers brought their canoes purely for pleasure; not all of the 300 canoes at the camp were entered in the official races.

At the 1883 regatta there were races for juniors and seniors, the former being those "who have never won an Association prize in sailing or paddling" and the latter an open class for "all who choose to enter." At the annual meeting that year members agreed to abolish these two classes and to substitute for "juniors" sailing and paddling races for "Novices" who had not been sailing or paddling a canoe for longer than one year. This annual meeting also defined more clearly the various classes of canoes. Paddling canoes were described: Class 1—length not over 18 feet, beam not under 24 inches; Class 2—length 15 feet, beam 26 inches; Class 3—length 17 feet, beam 28 inches; Class 4—length 15 feet, beam 30 inches. For sailing canoes Class A was described as not over 15 feet in length, beam not over 28 inches; Class B as length 17 feet, beam 28½ inches. Open canoes "without rudders" were allowed one foot extra in length.

The program included paddling races in various categories, sailing races, limited weight sailing races (Class A 120 lbs., Class B 150 lbs.), combined sailing and paddling, double paddling (two men, canoes not over 16 feet), sailing no ballast and full ballast, a portage race (paddle ¼ mile, ½ mile under sail, portage ⅛ mile, paddle ¼ mile), and "upset" races. Canadians performed well, winning more than their share of the honours, especially in paddling.[28]

It was a gala event, long remembered in the Peterborough area. Within a few years of its taking place cottages began to spring up on the beautiful islands of Stoney Lake. Commodore Edwards and Judge Roger both built on Juniper Island. They sold neighbouring Otter Island to a Toronto friend, Thomas S. Cole, and the third smaller island, Little Otter, to George Hilliard, a Peterborough lumber merchant.[29] Within a decade many summer homes had been built on the lake. Holiday residents made the journey by train to Lakefield and boat to their own steamer docks with family and friends, baggage and supplies to last an entire summer.

The 1883 American Canoe Association Regatta formalized the tradition in the Kawarthas. Canadian members continued to compete (and win) in the A.C.A. meets which were held in succeeding years at Grindstone Island, near Gananoque on the St. Lawrence River.[30] They also formed a Northern Division of the American Canoe Association and arranged meets closer to home.[31] Stoney Lake was the site of their regatta again in 1887, and in 1891 a meet was held at nearby Pigeon Lake.

Thus began the tradition, carried on by cottagers today, of canoe regattas in the Kawartha region, which linked participants to the early northern voyageurs.

ENDNOTES

1. Anna Jameson, *Winter Studies and Summer Rambles in Canada*, V III, (London 1838), pp. 288-9.

2. E.C. Guillet, *Early Life in Upper Canada*, (Toronto 1933), p. 304.

3. John Langton, *Early Days in Upper Canada*, (Toronto 1926), p. 55.

4. Anne Langton, *A Gentlewoman in Upper Canada*, (Toronto 1950), p. 119.

5. Trent University Archives, Guillet Papers, 13-74-003/1/4.

6. James Bonfitto, "The Golden Times," *Canoe* Magazine, August/September 1980, p. 18.

7. Peterborough *Examiner*, September 15, 1859.

8. Ibid., August 26, 1880.

9. Ibid., August 30, 1887.

10. Ibid., August 26, 1880.

11. Ibid., June 24, 1880.

12. Ibid., July 22, 1880.

13. John Marsh, "Early Tourism in the Kawarthas" in Cole, A.O.C. (ed.), *Kawartha Heritage*, (Peterborough 1981), p. 46.

14. *Examiner*, September 10, 1883.

15. Ibid., August 11, 1879.

16. Ibid.

17. Atwood Manley, *Rushton and His Times in American Canoeing* (Syracuse 1968), p. 63.

18. *Examiner*, August 5, 1880.

19. Manley, pp. 63-4.

20. Ibid., p. 65.

21. American Canoe Association Book, 1883.

22. Land patents, Registry office, Peterborough County Building.

23. American Canoe Association Book, 1883.

24. *Examiner*, August 16, 1883.

25. American Canoe Association Book, 1883.

26. *Examiner*, August 16 and August 23, 1883.

27. Ibid.

28. American Canoe Association Book, 1883.

29. Land records, Registry office, Peterborough County Building.

30. Manley, op.cit., p. 105; Borg, R. (ed.), *Peterborough Land of Shining Waters* (Peterborough 1967), p. 438.

31. *Examiner*, August 5 and August 12, 1887; July 18, 1891.

The Heritage of Peterborough Canoes*
John Marsh

The Peterborough area of Ontario lies about fifty kilometres north of Port Hope on Lake Ontario, immediately south of the Canadian Shield and Kawartha Lakes. Lake Ontario and the Kawartha Lakes are linked by the Trent River, Rice Lake and the Otonabee River which flows through Peterborough. Long inhabited by Indians, the area was first settled by Europeans in the early 1800s when individuals and government-organized groups of settlers, primarily from Ireland, England and Scotland, took up land to establish farms and villages.[1] Initially, access to the area was usually gained by travelling overland, north from Cobourg on Lake Ontario, to Rice Lake, thence up the Otonabee River to Scott's Plains where the town of Peterborough developed around rapids and a mill site at the junction of the Otonabee River, Jackson Creek and Little Lake. From Peterborough, the Kawartha Lakes were reached by portaging northwest to Chemong Lake or by continuing up the Otonabee River, past what is now the village of Lakefield, to Katchiwano, Clear and Stoney Lakes. These routes were long used by the Indians in their birchbark canoes. Until township roads were built, the new settlers likewise found the rivers and lakes most suitable for travel, trade and recreation.

Catharine Parr Traill, an early settler from England who became famous for her writings and nature studies, came north to Peterborough in 1832 by steamboat and scow.[2] Once settled on a farmstead near Lakefield, she and her family made frequent use of canoes on nearby lakes and rivers. When describing a visit to a local Indian encampment she noted:

> our nearest path would have been through the bush, but the ground was so encumbered by fallen trees that we agreed to go in a canoe. Our light bark skimmed gaily over the calm waters, beneath the overhanging shade of cedars, hemlock and balsams . . .[3]

She later recalled:

> I had the honour of being paddled home by Mrs. Peter in a new canoe, just launched, and really the motion was delightful, seated on the bottom of the little bark on a few light hemlock bows, I enjoyed my voyage home exceedingly.[4]

A sister of Catharine Parr Traill, Susanna Moodie, who also became a famous writer, settled on Upper Katchiwano Lake in 1834. Soon thereafter, she recalled:

> My husband had purchased a very light cedar canoe, to which he attached a keel and a sail, and most of our leisure hours, directly the snow melted, were spent upon the water . . . . I learned the use of the paddle and became quite a proficient in the gentle craft.[5]

---

* This study was inspired and greatly facilitated by the comments and writings of Donald Cameron, Dave Nichols, Roger Tilden, Bruce Hodgins and Kirk Wipper; their help is much appreciated.

Not only did settlers immediately use canoes for travel and fishing, very soon their potential for recreation and sporting competition was recognized. Similarly, by the mid-nineteenth century, tourists attracted to the area by its scenery, steamboat routes, hotels and cottage sites, were also making widespread recreational use of canoes on the lakes and rivers of the Peterborough area.[6]

From the first Kawartha regatta in 1835, this type of canoeing activity grew in local popularity through the century,* to such an extent that in 1885, between June 11 and August 7, there were no less than 13 regattas held on Chemong Lake alone.[7]

Settlers could obtain birchbark and dugout canoes from the Indians or make the craft themselves. For example, Samuel Strickland, a brother of Catharine Parr Traill, describes a "dangerous adventure" and unfortunate drowning that occurred while he was crossing the flooded Otonabee River in Peterborough in "a small log canoe, about twelve feet in length by thirty inches at its greatest breadth."[8] As the nineteenth century progressed, however, settlers and tourists increased in number, and the demand for more canoes with more sophisticated designs likewise increased. By the 1850s a small canoe building industry had been established in the Peterborough area. This industry survives to the present. The Peterborough Canoe Company and "Peterborough Canoe" became nationally, perhaps even globally, renowned. An examination of the initiation and development of this industry and a discussion of the character and use of "Peterborough Canoes" reveals an interesting aspect of regional history, establishing the significance of the Peterborough area and the "Peterborough Canoe" in Canada's canoe heritage.

*   *   *

The date and origin of the first canoe, other than a birchbark or dugout, to be constructed in the Peterborough area are uncertain, but records suggest that a John Stephenson of Ashburnham (now the eastern section of Peterborough) and a Tom Gordon of Lakefield were likely the first to build plank and rib canoes.[9] Apparently, Stephenson was inspired by observing a regatta on Little Lake in 1857, and by the hardship of portaging a dugout, to build a lighter more streamlined canoe, which he did in 1858. Gordon's son, Gilbert Gordon, supported this view but suggested that Tom Gordon was the first person in the area to manufacture for sale a plank and rib canoe.[10]

John Stephenson, with a partner named Graigie, operated a water-powered lumber planing mill on the east bank of the Otonabee River, immediately north of what is now the Hunter Street bridge in Peterborough. His canoes were likely built there or in a shop behind his house on Burnham Street.

Initially, Stephenson used three wide, cedar or basswood tongue and groove boards for each side "with a flush batten of elm scored in a way to give it a

---

* On Kawartha Lakes canoe regattas see the article by Jean Cole appearing elsewhere in this volume.

grip on the adjoining planks to which it was attached."[11] Later, as wood for wide boards became less readily available, Stephenson used four boards to each side of the canoe. It is unclear whether Stephenson or Gordon invented the flush batten. To facilitate construction, Stephenson did invent two devices which he patented; a new type of mould on which to build the canoe, and a paddle-making machine. The mould featured iron ribs which served to bend the nails as they were driven through the planks and ribs. The paddle-making machine, built with the assistance of a master mechanic named Wilson, was unfortunately burned in a fire at Rye's Boat House in 1943. An example of one of Stephenson's canoes has been preserved at the Centennial Museum and Archives in Peterborough.

Stephenson's business prospered. In 1870 he incorporated as the Ontario Canoe Company. In 1879 the entrepreneur, Lt. Col. J. Z. Rogers, acquired the assets and patents of the company, including the factory at Hunter and Cobourg Streets, near the railway station in Ashburnham, which continued in operation until destroyed by fire in 1892.[12]

Tom Gordon, born in 1833, was a boat builder in Lakefield all his working life. He produced everything from canoes to rowboats, motor boats and steam-boats, such as the "Golden City". Having begun business around 1858, he combined forces with a member of the Strickland family already in the boat business, and in 1860 the Lakefield Canoe Works was established. After several name changes and incorporation it became the Lakefield Canoe Company in 1904.

Gordon was an innovator who produced many new designs and tech-niques for canoe building. His numerous patterns and moulds have been handed down as prized possessions to more recent builders—some are still in use today. Gordon's early canoes, like Stephenson's, were wide board, rib and batten models without keels or steam-curved bow and stern posts.[13] A Gordon canoe purchased in 1890, still in existence, is described in each finely crafted detail:

> It is slim, 29 inches inside width, and 15 feet 8 inches in length. The planking is basswood, wide board. In fact only 3 to a side. The joints between planks are covered by zinc strips whose edges are turned down and pressed into the edges of the adjoining planks: in effect a metallic flush batten. Because of the need to support the slim metal strip the ribs are close together as in a modern cedarstrip; about 2 inch centres. There is no keelson or keel.[14]

With the progressive introduction of narrower planks, closer ribs, moulds, pat-terns and ship-lap joints the stage was set for production of the cedarstrip canoe we know today. Gordon was primarily responsible for its introduction.[15] Narrow cedar strips were more easily fitted together than broad planks. They provided greater strength. When contrasting shades of wood, or other woods such as walnut or butternut were used, a sleek craft of beauty and efficiency resulted. By the time Gordon died in 1916 such cedarstrip canoes had become widely renowned and popular. Another important figure in the history of canoe construc-tion in the Peterborough area is William English, son of John English who was listed in the 1851 census as a blacksmith and builder of wagons and sleighs.

Presumably William English saw a demand for canoes and drew on the experience of his father when he established a canoe building shop on Charlotte Street, near the present post office, in 1861. Assessment rolls for 1873 indicate that English had moved his works to the bank of the Otonabee River at Sherbrooke and Water Streets. However, a listing in the 1889 J.R. Stratton Directory suggests a return to the original site:

> English Canoe Factory at 182 Charlotte Street, a pioneer canoe factory of Canada or the world in its special line, basswood canoes of all kinds, etc.[16]

Little further information has been found on the English canoe works, although Gilbert Gordon suggested that the canoes produced were of very high quality, an opinion supported by the fact that they won numerous medals at exhibitions.[17]

In addition to the canoe works established in the mid-nineteenth century in Peterborough and Lakefield, another began at this time, further south, on Rice Lake. Daniel Herald, who came from Ireland via the United States, opened a canoe works at Gore's Landing, along with a man named Hutchinson, in 1862. Subsequent generations of Heralds, with other partners, continued the business, changing its name to "Herald and McBride Company" in 1870, "Herald Bros. Builders of Rice Lake Boats" in 1890 and "Rice Lake Canoe Company" in 1919.

Again the first canoes were plank, rib and batten models, while later ones were distinguished by a torpedo-shaped plank or "spoiler", running half the length of the canoe between the lowest two boards.[18] One unique product was "Herald's Patent Cedar Canoe", an example of which has been preserved in the Kanawa Museum in Haliburton. It featured a two-layered hull, the external planking running lengthwise and the internal planking crosswise. A sheet of cotton treated with white lead was placed between the layers which were secured with copper tacks, there being no ribs or battens.[19]

All such early canoe builders and their innovations contributed to the cedar rib canoe that became known as the "Peterborough Canoe." However, the name itself is primarily associated with the more recent Peterborough Canoe Company. This company evolved from the initiative of John Stephenson, with the entrepreneurial skill of Col. Rogers, on the basis of their Ontario Canoe Company. When that factory burned down in 1892, Col. Rogers opened a new one on the site of the Adam Scott Mill, beside the Otonabee River at Water and King Streets in Peterborough. With four new investors, William Hill, E. B. Edwards, E. B. Loucks, and George Schofield, and a capital stock of $10,000, the company was reincorporated as the Peterborough Canoe Company.[20]

As an 1896 business directory advertisement indicates, the Peterborough Canoe Co. factory manufactured a wide range of canoes along with other products such as camping goods, furniture and office fittings. The company boasted about the high standard of its Peterborough canoes and emphasized that it used "only the best materials, the best workmanship, and the best finish". The growing sales and reputation of the canoes, plus the medals they received at international exhibitions attest to the high quality of the product.[21]

Peterborough Canoe Awards*

1881 — Fisheries Exhibition, London, England
1883 — Fisheries Exhibition, London, England
1885 — The World's Exhibition, Antwerp, Belgium
1886 — The Colonial and Indian Exhibition, London, England
1887 — The Colonial and Indian Exhibition, London, England
1891 — The Jamaica Exhibition
1893 — The Chicago Exhibition (Gold Awards), USA
1900 — The Paris Exhibition (Gold Awards), France
1901 — The Glasgow Exhibition, Scotland

Along with a half century of developing craftsmanship and technical expertise, the quality and success of the Peterborough Canoe can be attributed to the competitive nature of the canoe building business in this area. In 1893 another company, the Canadian Canoe Company, began building canoes in a factory at the corner of Brock and Water Streets in Peterborough. With the English Canoe Company and these two companies, there were about 60 people employed in canoe building in Peterborough in 1902 and some 90 people in 1908.[22] Accordingly, one might regard this as the heyday of canoe building in Peterborough.

In 1911, the Canadian Canoe Company moved to new premises at 216 Rink Street, near Little Lake, but suffered declining fortunes during the ensuing war years. In May 1919 workers at the plant, who made only the minimum wage of fifty cents an hour, went on strike for higher wages. The company refused to recognize the union or its members' demands.[23] It may have been in no position to do so: its profits in 1924, for example, were only $1,823. The company's survival was jeopardized still further when a factory fire on December 17, 1926 caused $25,664 damage.[24]

---

*Source: Rogers, 1967; *Cobourg Star*, 29 December, 1975; Peterborough Canoe Company Catalogue, no date.

Changes in the economy after World War I, labour unrest, declining supplies of suitable wood in the local area, and the growing popularity of outboard motor boats probably all contributed to the subsequent rearrangement and consolidation of the canoe companies in Peterborough.

In January 1918, the Peterborough Canoe Company factory was burned but immediately rebuilt on the same site and successfully managed in the interwar years by Col. Rogers' son, Claude H. Rogers, and a Mr. William A. Richardson. They acquired the financially troubled English Canoe Company in 1923. Then, the following year, the Peterborough Canoe Company merged with the Chestnut Canoe Company* of Oromocto, New Brunswick to form an operating company, Canadian Watercraft Limited.[25] The Company had issued capital stock of 4922 shares, split almost evenly between Peterborough and Fredericton shareholders and valued at $492,200. Finally, in 1927, the failing Canadian Canoe Company was sold to Canadian Watercraft Limited. The combined companies made a total profit, less losses, during the period 1923-1938 of $302,972, the Chestnut Company seemingly being the main contributor. Further reorganization occurred in 1938, as follows:

> to simplify the operation, inasmuch as the Canadian Canoe Company was a separate Capital organization, and as business with the public was done under the names of "Peterborough Canoe Company" and "Chestnut Canoe Company" respectively, and as the Charters of each of these Companies had been kept in force, it was decided to transfer the Assets back to each Company, so that there would be three distinct organizations or Capital structures, the shares of which would be held by Canadian Watercraft Limited. The result was that after the closing of the 1938 accounting period, Canadian Watercraft Limited became a holding Company, instead of an Operating Company.[26]

Until the 1950s the Canadian Canoe, Peterborough and Chestnut companies all maintained a satisfactory level of business. From 1938 to 1950 the Peterborough Canoe Company made an operating profit of $588,387 and the Chestnut Canoe Company one of $418,977. After the Second World War, however, the economic environment and market for recreational craft changed, new materials and techniques for canoe construction emerged and the Peterborough area canoe industries were forced to respond.

In 1952 the Peterborough Canoe Company had a net operating profit of $246,595; business was booming. The manager of the company, Jack Richardson, explained:

> The shorter work week, the boom in our economy, and the improved roads into Canadian hinterlands have made and will make boating popular and more a part of our way of life.[27]

He went on to say that the sale of canoes in 1953 was "a way above the total for any recent year" and "the demand for paddles is so great . . . [we] can't keep up

---

* The Chestnut Canoe Company was named after Mr. Harry G. Chestnut of Fredericton — not the wood!

with production," even though it averaged 12-15,000 paddles per year.[28]

Accordingly, the company finally decided to vacate the site used since 1891 and move to better premises. The old factory on Water Street contained only 3,000 square feet of floor space and was described as having an "antiquated, inefficient layout—a hodge podge of buildings expensive to heat and maintain".[29] The new site, away from the river, at Monaghan Road and Braidwood Avenue, comprised fourteen acres of land and already included the company's lumber yard, planing mill and warehouse. A new two-storey factory provided 4,500 square feet of space for a "large scale production line system."[30] While it is believed the anticipated cost of the move was $500,000, the final cost was about $1 million.[31] In 1956 when the new site became fully operational, the company employed 206 people and annually sold over 8,000 boats and canoes, worth $1.5 million, more than any similar company in Canada.[32]

Presumably, improved productivity and cost-saving were also intended when the Canadian Canoe Company operation was moved from its Rink Street site into the former Peterborough Canoe Company buildings on Water Street in 1958. However, in 1960, the Canadian Canoe Company ceased work as a manufacturing company, the Water Street site was abandoned and all its operations transferred to the Peterborough Canoe Company at its new site.[33]

Sadly, it was just as the company had completed its reorganization and rebuilding, and as the market for water craft was expanding, that a variety of problems led to its collapse. In 1961 the Peterborough Canoe Company, though not its sister Chestnut Canoe Company, filed a proposal under the Bankruptcy Act.[34] Faced with debts of $2 million, there was an immediate search for additional capital and new product lines, but the debts could not be eliminated and on October 24, 1962 the Company closed.

While not all the facts are available, a variety of explanations has been given for the sudden demise of such a long-established, apparently successful company with a world-renowned product.[35] First, it has been said that "the firm didn't move rapidly enough into fibreglass and aluminum construction, with its promise of easy maintenance to a comfort conscious public."[36] Actually the company started using fibreglass around 1956, and aluminum in 1957, though full production of fibreglass boats did not occur until 1961. Then the company's advertising manager, Fred Butler, announced:

> We have redesigned our water craft in order to obtain a complete departure from previous designs, and doing so, we have placed ourselves on a much better competitive level than ever before.[37]

Unfortunately, the combination of new designs and new materials in the hands of craftsmen used to wood, appears to have resulted in many inferior craft. In any case the switch to fibreglass canoes may have come too late, given the rapid expansion of competition in this field.

Problems may also have been experienced even with the traditional wooden "Peterborough Canoes." It is said that difficulties were encountered in finding high quality woods for both strips and ribs, especially in the local area and at reasonable cost. Apparently the substitution of swamp elm for the preferred rock elm resulted in ribs less resistant to rot.[38]

Labour problems, which occurred intermittently during the company's history, have been cited as a factor contributing to the failure. In particular, the unionization of workers around 1955, subsequent wage increases, and the elimination of piece work overtime may have placed additional stress on a company already faced with financial and productivity problems.[39]

The massive, and perhaps unanticipated, level of investment associated with the move to Monaghan Road and the expansion of new facilities may have been necessary, but were excessive and ill-timed. Indeed, the question of whether financial mismanagement, more than anything else, accounts for the closing of the company remains unanswered.

It is probably fair to say that all the above factors contributed sooner or later, to greater or lesser degree, to the failure of the company. The Peterborough Canoe Company, after a long and honourable history, exists no more. However, the tradition of producing canoes in the Peterborough area, both in the classic wooden style and with new designs and materials, is as strong as ever.[40]

The production of canoes in Lakefield, started by Tom Gordon, was continued by the Lakefield Canoe and Manufacturing Co. from 1913-1937. It persists today at the company of Peel Marine Ltd. and others. The tradition of producing canoes on Rice Lake, started by Herald and Hutchinson, was perpetuated after 1926 by the Pratts at the Rice Lake Boatworks and today by the Voyageur Canoe Company of Millbrook. In and around Peterborough, in the 1970s, there have been as many as nine businesses, from family operations to companies, producing canoes and maintaining Peterborough's canoe heritage.

While the importance of the "Peterborough Canoe" may be gleaned from the long history and repeated expansion of the canoe building industry in the Peterborough area, it will become more apparent from a summary of the markets served by the "Peterborough Canoes" and their diverse and historic uses at home and abroad.

Most initial use of "Peterborough Canoes" was for local subsistence and recreational purposes. However, use of local canoes in regattas and by tourists on the Kawartha Lakes, together with promotion efforts by the canoe companies, soon brought them to the attention of a market wider than just the recreationalists. In particular, "Peterborough Canoes" were used by government land and geological surveyors working in the West and North. For example, in 1887 and 1888 William Ogilvy, Dominion Surveyor, used them when he travelled the Yukon and Mackenzie Rivers.[41] In 1898, in one five-week period one hundred "Peterborough Canoes" were shipped to the Klondike.[42] Northern explorer George Douglas used a "Peterborough Canoe" to travel down the Coppermine River and on Great Slave Lake in 1911.[43] These canoes were often used by the North West Mounted Police and by the American and Canadian surveyors on the Alaska Boundary Survey.[44] In fact, a great many of the northern wilderness travellers featured in this volume accomplished their journeys in "Peterborough Canoes." These canoes became fundamental to the process by which the North in Canada retreated northward.

A major market that developed before the turn of the century was the United States. Shipping tabs of the Lakefield Canoe Company document canoes being shipped to Philadelphia in 1876 and Chicago in 1893.[45] A Peterborough Canoe Company catalogue indicates sales of canoes in Albany, Trenton and Westport, and the northeastern states appear to have been a major market. "Peterborough Canoes" were also shipped to Europe and other countries around the world. Gilbert Gordon recalled in 1965 that "some time after 1857 my father, through a contact with a sporting goods outlet in Picadilly, London operated by Ronald Ward, distributed canoes in England mainly to students of universities."[46] In 1896 the Lakefield Canoe Company is reported to have shipped some 600 canoes to England, while company tags for the period 1910-1914 recorded canoes going to London, Leicester, Oxford and Huntington. A Lakefield canoe was allegedly the first to be paddled across the English Channel.[47] Lakefield Company shipping tags record canoes going to Paris.

"Peterborough Canoes" also apparently saw service in Rhodesia and Tanganyika, on the Nile and Amazon, and in Hong Kong, Australia, India, New Zealand and Bermuda.[48] Not only were the canoes used around the world but they were also used by a variety of distinguished people from Theodore Roosevelt to royalty. In 1948 the City of Peterborough gave Princess (now Queen) Elizabeth a "Peterborough" cedar-rib canoe as a wedding gift. More recently, in 1977, the Town Council of Lakefield commissioned Walter Walker, a former Peterborough Canoe Company worker then with Peel Marine, to build a cedar-strip canoe for presentation to Prince Andrew while he attended Lakefield College School.

*   *   *

The early use of canoes and the origins of canoe building in the Peterborough area of Ontario, stems from the mid-nineteenth century pioneering period. A variety of local workshops sprang up in the 1850s in Lakefield, Ashburnham and Gore's Landing to provide light, reliable craft for local travel and recreational purposes. Given the area's numerous lakes and rivers, the availability of building materials, the growing demand for watercraft, and the arrival of ingenious craftsmen, it is hardly surprising that a thriving canoe building industry developed around Peterborough. However, its continued success must be attributed to innovation, improved construction techniques that led to production of the distinctively high quality "Peterborough Canoe," aggressive entrepreneurship, and the ability to establish a national and, later, export market.

As a result, the canoe industries of this area, notably the Peterborough Canoe Company, made a sustained and highly respectable contribution to Canada's canoe heritage. "Peterborough Canoes" were used extensively in the local area, in opening up our northern and western frontiers, and abroad. Their quality was reflected in the prizes they won, by their presentation to royalty and in the survival of many of them to the present day. Despite the sad demise of the Peterborough Canoe Company in the 1960s, numerous other firms, old and new, involved in producing both "Peterborough Canoes" and others, perpetuate Peterborough's canoe heritage.

ENDNOTES

1. R. Borg, (Ed) *Peterborough: Land of Shining Waters*, (Peterborough 1966).

2. C. P. Traill, *The Backwoods of Canada* (Toronto 1966; 1st pub. 1836).

3. Ibid, p. 10.

4. Ibid, p. 103.

5. S. Moodie, *Roughing it in the Bush* 1852; reprinted McClelland and Stewart, Toronto, 1962, p. 154.

6. J. S. Marsh, "The Historical Development of Resorts and Cottages in the Kawartha Lakes Area, Ontario", in: Marsh, J. S. (Ed) *Water-Based Recreation: Problems and Progress*, Occasional Paper 8, Department of Geography, Trent University, Peterborough, 1979, pp. 27-49.

7. C. Theberge and E. Theberge, *At the Edge of the Shield: A History of Smith Township, 1818-1980*, (Peterborough 1982), p. 143.

8. S. Strickland, *Twenty-Seven Years in Canada West* (Edmonton 1970; 1st pub. 1853), p. 123.

9. D. Cameron, "The Peterborough Canoe", paper read to the Peterborough Historical Society, March 18, 1975, on file Peterborough Centennial Museum and Archives.

10. Correspondence, Donald Cameron to John Marsh, undated, Peterborough.

11. Cameron, p. 7.

12. D. Nichols, "Peterborough's Canoe Industries", unpublished paper, Peterborough, 1978; M. S. Rogers, "The Peterborough Canoe", in R. Borg, *Peterborough: Land of Shining Waters* (Peterborough 1966), pp. 233-235.

13. Cameron, p. 10.

14. Ibid, pp. 10, 11.

15. Ibid, p. 11.

16. Quoted in Cameron, p. 12.

17. A. Sellers, "Report and Bibliography on the History of Canoeing and Canoe Building in the Peterborough Area", unpublished paper, Peterborough, 1981.

18. Cameron, p. 14.

19. Ibid.

20. Nichols, pp. 14, 234.

21. Ibid.

22. Nichols, p. 16.

23. Personal communication, Sheila Rutledge to Dave Nichols, March 15, 1978, Peterborough, cited in Nichols, p. 17.

24. Felix Brownscombe Papers, Centennial Museum and Archives, Peterborough.

25. Nichols, p. 17.

26. R. F. Tilden, "Selected Insights into the Peterborough Area Canoe Building Industry", unpublished paper, Peterborough, 1982, Appendix 'F'.

27. "Soothing Paddle Song", *Who's Who in Business*, April 28, 1956.

28. *Peterborough Examiner*, August 24, 1953 and February 13, 1954.

29. *Peterborough Examiner*, April 13, 1956.

30. *Peterborough Examiner*, February 16, 1956.

31. *Peterborough Examiner*, May 14, 1957.

32. "Soothing Paddle Song", *Who's Who in Business*, April 28, 1956.

33. Nichols, p. 20.

34. *Peterborough Examiner*, July 26, 1961.

35. Tilden, pp. 7-14.

36. *Kawartha Sun*, July 31, August 7, 1980.

37. *Peterborough Examiner*, March 30, 1961.

38. *Kawartha Sun*, op. cit.

39. Tilden, pp. 10-11.

40. Ibid.

41. Cameron, p. 15.

42. *Lakefield News*, October 28, 1898.

43. Douglas, G. *Lands Forlorn*, (New York 1914).

44. *Peterborough Examiner*, February 13, 1954.

45. Rutledge, S. "Otonabee Valley Canoe Builders", essay, March 31, 1978, on file: Centennial Museum and Archives, Peterborough.

46. Interview with Gilbert Gordon by his son Keith Gordon, January 25, 1965, tape recording on file, Centennial Museum and Archives, Peterborough.

47. Rutledge.

48. Sources of information on the use of Peterborough Canoes abroad are given in Tilden, p. 6.

Wilderness and Culture*

John Wadland

> The ultimate and the comprehensive meaning of Canadian history is to be found where there has been no Canadian history, in the North.[1]
>
> W. L. Morton

Two of Canada's most enduring symbols of cultural uniqueness—the canoe and the wilderness—are celebrated in this volume. For most of the people whose explorations and travels we follow through these pages, the wilderness was a cardinal fact of life, the canoe as essential to the passage of the day as the coming of the night. What we have is an indigenous craft, the landscape of its birth, and groupings of strangers engaged in an atavistic quest for something indescribable, but somehow understood. The duration of the quest is measured by strokes of the paddle, not by the ticking of clocks, but the conclusion of the journey—even though a destination may be reached—still awaits resolution.

* * *

Although modern Canadians tend to consider wilderness and culture antithetical notions, as consumers they unite in identifying both with their leisure time—with their recreation. Traditionally, culture has been perceived as the product of civilization; the growth of civilization has, in turn, been equated with the rise of the metropolis. The linear historical imagination to which we are heirs has also established and reinforced the assumption that the metropolis spawns and contains our realities. In this context, the wilderness is regarded as an ambiguous, detached, and ultimately romantic space to which we "escape" from the metropolitan reality—whether on skis, in canoes, or comfortably seated in the family car.

Yet the metropolis and the wilderness really embody different perceptions of order, the former anthropocentric, the latter ecological. Historically, Canadians have demonstrated a particular passion for order of the first kind. Our pastoral landscapes, subdivided geometrically "into chessboards of square-mile sections and concession line roads," mirror the grid-ironed city and betray, in the words of Northrop Frye, "the conquest of nature by an intelligence that does not love it."[2] Even the wilderness must be categorized and coralled within park boundaries to create what Wayland Drew has called another form of "managerial unit" with a specialized function.[3] The tentacles of the progressive, ordered

---

* A slightly different version of this article first appeared in *Park News*, Vol. 19, No. 2 (Summer 1982), pp. 12-13. The editors gratefully acknowledge the permission of *Park News* and the National and Provincial Parks Association of Canada to reprint the paper in this volume.

223

metropolitan culture reach everywhere, grasp everything.

Cultural questions in Canada are seldom (except by some artists) understood in organic, ecological terms. The land has seemed forever condemned both to receive and to perpetuate the compelling urban logic. At no time in our past have we wondered, even fleetingly, whether the wilderness contains rules—an order—to which we owe an allegiance. The very word "recreation," in some contexts, suggests that nature requires human intervention in order to achieve true meaning, that everything in nature automatically benefits from human alterations of it. Clearly one of the greatest deterrents to a serious criticism of this assumption has been the *amount* of wilderness (however defined) by which our metropolitan centres appear to be surrounded. Only very recently have we begun to take the most tentative steps toward an acceptance of the limitations implicit in a now visibly dwindling non-human nature.

The issue, then, becomes one of ascertaining whether culture can exist solely within extensions of the metropolitan order and as a parasite on wilderness, or whether wilderness, protesting its own diminishment by limiting our material culture, is demanding a voice which we ignore at our peril.

George F. Kennan once described totalitarianism as "a neurotic sense of tidiness." Several chilling controversies unearthed by the McDonald Commission[4] provided Canadians with ample evidence to question national tendencies in this direction—and certainly our fastidious manner of organizing space and time reflects and reinforces a profound sense of discomfort in the face of the unknown. Aspiring to make the unknown knowable, we attempt to render wilderness human, selectively picking off bits and pieces of the whole, reconstituting them as artifacts to serve preordained cultural values. Our culture, like the historical traditions of which it is both expression and culmination, creates and responds to its creations, almost invariably in metropolitan terms. The paradox, of course, is that the very immensity of land to which we are wedded, and which constitutes our geographical birthright, is at once alienated and alienating. We have never really learned the true meaning of adaptation to place, and despite our fascination with exploration, we have never found home.

The benchmarks by which we most often measure superior cultural achievement—grandiose architecture, Shakespearean theatre, classical ballet, the opera—are moulded by an aesthetic which mirrors what Brian Stock has labelled "The Great Tradition." This may have a marginal bearing on the lived experience of Canadians, but it is praised essentially for its "universality" and for its ability to win acceptance in the established cultural markets of the world. The spontaneously bred creativity of the "invisible culture" is demeaned and belittled by adjectives, like "primitive," "parochial," and "folkloric"—yet it is this dimension of our collective life which speaks most profoundly of our pluralism, of our regionalism, and ultimately of our quest for home.[5] The creativity of the true artist emerges from a felt experience of the known and the unknown. But although the capacity for artistry exists within us all, we have unwittingly permitted the alienating norms of the metropolitan reality to repress its expression.

Perceiving ourselves mere consumers of creation, receivers of communicated culture, we have become dependent upon its interpreters (notably its critics) who, in our own age, seem intent upon assessing its meaning in the context of "The Great Tradition"—a tradition which, in all other respects, has failed us miserably.

Before issuing its final report, the Applebaum-Hébert Cultural Policy Review Committee released a preliminary *Summary of Briefs and Hearings.*[6] Running through many of the submissions is the predictable theme of inadequate funding. Appeals for increased subsidization of the arts are directed at the public and private sectors. In common these apparently disparate funding sources, filtered through an exotic web of forward and backward linkages, have at their root the profits derived from the extraction of natural resources in the wilderness. Indeed, many of our most powerful and influential citizens come closest to wilderness while perusing daily stock quotations in the local newspaper. Columns of mining, pulp and paper and oil exploration companies, neatly itemized in numerical format, help to underline the fundamental absurdity of the wilderness/culture dichotomy. As David, Margaret Atwood's myopic macho-man in *Surfacing*, says (in a rare moment of insight): "this country is founded on the bodies of dead animals. Dead fish, dead seals and historically dead beavers, the beaver is to this country what the black man is to the United States."[7]

The continued consumption of commodities blast-furnaced from staples is, we tell ourselves, essential if the occupations, by and through which we produce the taxes and disposable income to sustain creativity, are to prevail. Yet in the process of manufacturing and consuming the material goods which constitute our artifactual heritage—and which, at least in theory, generate our ordered sense of well being and security—we are individually responsible for eroding wilderness. The silent smoke permeating our atmosphere, which is rained upon and which acidifies our northern lakes and rivers with far-reaching ecological consequences, is born of a deep-seated metropolitan alienation that treats culture as a bought, rather than as a lived thing. What is to become of this culture when extinct species, exhausted strip mines and clear-cut forests formally proclaim the non-renewability of wilderness?

Culture cannot be relegated to a class of industry without itself becoming an uncritical defender of industrialism. Viewed organically, culture threads the fabric of our existence. It demands a cyclical perception of life that guarantees the roles of the individual, society, *and* nature, all of which act upon, and are reacted upon, in a perpetually evolving, unpredictable manner.[8] Such an integrated culture will grow and mature through the ecological changes it effects (and by which it is effected) only if human reason can acknowledge and address its own limitation by nature. The *sine qua non* of what we have chosen to identify as Canadian culture is the wilderness. And on a symbolic level wilderness is the closest we shall ever come to absolute nature. In the end, the question of basic survival—whether of man or of all living things—is centered on culture, and therefore on nature. Our history, which has been preoccupied by the measurement of individual and societal concerns, must, along lines suggested by Fernard Braudel and the French *Annales* school,[9] expand its analytical framework to include wilderness/nature as a functioning participant in the cyclical drama of experience. To treat nature simply as the stage upon which the human play is enacted is to betray our ignorance of its ultimate power over us. "Nature will certainly triumph," observes Wayland Drew. "Whether it will triumph over us or in us and through us remains to be seen."[10]

ENDNOTES

1. W. L. Morton, "The 'North' in Canadian Historiography," *Transactions of the Royal Society of Canada*, Series IV, 8 (1970), p. 40.

2. Northrop Frye, *The Bush Garden: Essays on the Canadian Imagination* (Toronto 1971), p. 224.

3. Wayland Drew, "Killing Wilderness," *Ontario Naturalist*, 12 (September 1972), p. 23.

4. Canada. Commission of Inquiry Concerning Certain Activities of the Royal Canadian Mounted Police, *Reports*. (Ottawa 1979-1981)

5. Brian Stock, "English Canada: The Visible and Invisible Cultures," *Canadian Forum*, 52 (March 1973), pp. 29-33; "English Canada: Culture Versus Experience," *Canadian Forum*, 56 (April 1976), pp. 5-9.

6. Canada. Federal Cultural Policy Review Committee, *Summary of Briefs and Hearings*, (Ottawa: Ministry of Supply and Services, 1982). See also Francis Fox, *Culture and Communications: Key Elements of Canada's Economic Future*, (Ottawa 1983).

7. Margaret Atwood, *Surfacing*, (Toronto 1972), p. 40.

8. See Gregory Bateson, *Steps to an Ecology of Mind*, (New York 1972)

9. *Mediterranan World in the Age of Philip II*, Translated by Sian Reynolds (New York 1972) 2 volumes.

10. Wayland Drew, "Wilderness and Limitation," *Canadian Forum*, 52 (February 1973), p. 19. For a splendid fictional rendering of all the points raised in this essay, see Wayland Drew, *The Wabeno Feast*, (Toronto 1973).

Contributors

Editors

Bruce W. Hodgins—Professor of History, Trent University, Peterborough; Director of Wanapitei Wilderness Centre and past President of the Ontario Recreational Canoeing Association; author of several books and articles on the history of the Canadian North and on comparative federalism.

Margaret Hobbs—Ph.D. candidate at the Ontario Institute for Studies in Education; specialist in women's history; researcher and author for the *Historical Atlas of Canada* project (forthcoming).

Contributors

Jamie Benidickson—former Lecturer in the Department of History, Trent University, Peterborough; author of several articles on the North and on the history of canoeing.

Jean Murray Cole—author of *Exile in the Wilderness: The Life of Chief Factor Archibald McDonald, 1790–1853* (Seattle 1980); co-editor of *The Illustrated Historical Atlas of Peterborough County* (Peterborough 1975) and of *Kawartha Heritage* (Peterborough 1981).

C. E. S. Franks—Professor of Politics, Queen's University; author of *The Canoe and Whitewater* (Toronto 1977).

Shelagh D. Grant—author of several articles on northern and native administration and of a forthcoming book detailing the evolution of northern policy; tutor in Canadian Studies programme, Trent University, Peterborough.

Gwyneth Hoyle—Librarian, Peter Robinson College, Trent University, Peterborough.

William C. James—Professor of Religion, Queen's University; editor of *Needle to the North* (Ottawa 1982) and author of *A Furtrader's Photographs: A. A. Chesterfield in the District of Ungava, 1901–4* (Kingston and Montreal 1985).

John Jennings—Professor of History, Trent University, Peterborough; authority on the Mounties in the Northwest.

George J. Luste—Professor of Physics, University of Toronto; author; environmental activist, especially with the Sierra Club.

Craig Macdonald—Officer with the Ministry of Natural Resources, Huntsville; Cree-Ojibwa place-name linguist.

John Marsh—Professor of Geography, Trent University, Peterborough; co-editor of *Recreational Land Use: Perspectives on its Evolution in Canada* (Ottawa 1982).

John Wadland—Professor and Chairman of Canadian Studies Programme, Trent University, Peterborough; former editor of the *Journal of Canadian Studies*; author of *Ernest Thompson Seton: Man in Nature and the Progressive Era, 1880–1915* (New York 1978).

INDEX